海量阅读
海外名著系列
World Classics

U0528131

经典无删节版

图文美绘 双语典藏

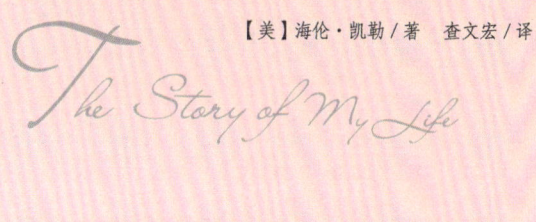

海伦·凯勒自传
我生活的故事

【美】海伦·凯勒/著　查文宏/译

The Story of My Life

江西人民出版社
Jiangxi People's Publishing House
全国百佳出版社

图书在版编目（CIP）数据

　　海伦·凯勒自传：我生活的故事/（美）凯勒著；
查文宏译. -- 南昌：江西人民出版社，2017.2
　　ISBN 978-7-210-07867-8

　　Ⅰ.①海… Ⅱ.①凯… ②查… Ⅲ.①凯勒，
H.（1880~1968）— 自传 Ⅳ.① K837.127=533

　　中国版本图书馆 CIP 数据核字（2015）第 233660 号

海伦·凯勒自传：我生活的故事（图文美绘　双语典藏）
The Story of My Life

（美）海伦·凯勒著；查文宏译

责任编辑：李月华
书籍设计：游　珑
出　　版：江西人民出版社
发　　行：各地新华书店
地　　址：江西省南昌市三经路 47 号附 1 号
编辑部电话：0791-86898143
发行部电话：0791-86898815
邮　　编：330006
网　　址：www.jxpph.com
E-mail：jxpph@tom.com　　web@jxpph.com
2017 年 2 月第 1 版　　2017 年 2 月第 1 次印刷
开　本：1/16　720mm×1000mm
印　张：16.25
字　数：250 千字
ISBN 978-7-210-07867-8
定　价：42.00 元
承印厂：深圳精彩印联合印刷公司
赣版权登字—01—2016—835
版权所有　侵权必究
赣人版图书凡属印刷、装订错误，请随时向承印厂调换

把脸向着阳光,就不会看到阴影。

——海伦·凯勒

目录 Contents

I	海伦·凯勒的生活和工作大事记
III	前言
3	第一章 通过阅读发现自我
8	第二章 遭遇不幸
15	第三章 童年片羽
19	第四章 希望之光
23	第五章 水的开悟
26	第六章 树的诱惑
30	第七章 『爱』的含义
36	第八章 知识的海洋
38	第九章 圣诞礼物
42	第十章 波士顿之旅
45	第十一章 拥抱大海
49	第十二章 金秋猎场

52	第十三章　学会说话
56	第十四章　《霜之王》事件
64	第十五章　芝加哥世界博览会
68	第十六章　学习拉丁语
70	第十七章　在纽约求学
73	第十八章　剑桥女子学院
79	第十九章　备考哈佛
84	第二十章　真实的大学
92	第二十一章　我的乌托邦
104	第二十二章　我的秘密花园
115	第二十三章　致我敬爱的朋友们
123	英文原著

海伦·凯勒的生活和工作大事记

1880年：6月27日，海伦·亚当斯·凯勒出生在亚拉巴马州的塔斯坎比亚镇。

1882年：19个月大的凯勒患病，导致她失聪并失明。

1887年：3月3日，安妮·曼斯菲尔德·沙利文成为凯勒的老师；4月5日，她的教学有了突破，教会凯勒拼写"water（水）"一词。

1890年：凯勒开始学习说话。

1891年：写了文章《霜之王》；并被指控为抄袭之作。

1896年：凯勒的父亲去世。

1900年：进入拉德克利夫学院学习。

1902年：《我生活的故事》开始在《妇女家庭杂志》上发表。

1903年：出版《我生活的故事》一书。

1904年：凯勒从拉德克利夫学院毕业，成为获得文学学士学位的第一位聋盲人。

1908年：出版《我所生活的世界》一书。

1909年：加入了马萨诸塞州社会党。

1913年：开始了一名职业演讲人的生涯；出版《冲出黑暗》。

1916年：与彼得·费根订婚；但母亲强迫凯勒解除婚约。

1920年：开始与安妮·沙利文一起旅行。

1921年：凯勒的母亲去世。

1924年：开始为美国盲人基金会工作。

1927年：出版《我的宗教》。

1929年：出版《中流：我后来的生活》。

1936年：安妮·沙利文去世。

1938年：出版《海伦·凯勒1936－1937年日志》。

1940年：出版《让我们拥有信仰》。

1943年：在部队医院探望伤兵。

1946年：为支持盲人的权益，开始周游世界。

1953年：反映凯勒生活的纪录片《不可征服的人》（后来又名《海伦·凯勒的故事》）公映，并获奥斯卡最佳纪录片奖。

1955年：出版《老师》一书，这是安妮·沙利的传记。

1957年：电视剧《奇迹的缔造者》播出；后被改编为百老汇剧目（1959年）和电影（1962年）。

1964年：荣获总统自由勋章，由林登·约翰逊总统向她授勋。

1968年：6月1日，她在康涅狄格州阿肯瑞脊的家中与世长辞，享年87岁。

前　言

通过阅读发现自我

　　海伦·凯勒曾说："只要我能被大家看作是有独立思想的常人，我并不反对严厉的批评。"凯勒年仅22岁时，就出版了《我生活的故事》。这本书不仅向读者展示了她是一位富有思想内涵的年轻女性，而且也揭示了她成长为一名活泼聪慧的女青年的历程。

　　我们大多数人都把海伦·凯勒看作是又聋又哑的小女孩，她因成功战胜厄运而举世闻名。也许我们都看过电影《成功的缔造者》，上面有一个众所皆知的场景：凯勒发现了"水"这个词的含义。也许我们曾听说——或是有人告诉我们——海伦·凯勒是一个笑话。但《我生活的故事》一书却昭示：海伦·凯勒既不是一场奇谈，也不是一块笑料，而是一个巨大的成就。从表面上看，在凯勒的余生中，似乎命中注定将被禁锢在黑暗和孤独中，但通过她老师安妮·沙利文卓有成效的指导，她却成了举世公认、倍受尊敬的人物。

　　凯勒对学习的毅力、对体验的激情和对上流社会的拒绝，使她被定义为一个鼓舞人心的象征，但人们又在某种程度上觉得她是高不可攀的。我们怎样才能像海伦·凯勒一样拥有强大的内心呢？那么，请读读她的故事吧，我们会看到她也是个凡人。当她随心所欲时，她会像我们一样大发脾气。而且，她会为人们的无知和愚昧而发怒；她也会为要写很多作业而抱怨。

总而言之，《我生活的故事》是一场发现之旅。是语言引导着海伦·凯勒去发现世界，而语言也是她努力探索世界和了解自我的手段。她发出了一个对人类而言，可能是最重要的疑问——我是谁？——而在回答这一问题时，她在某种程度上解释了我们究竟是谁。

我生活的故事

第 1 章

遭遇不幸

1880年6月，海伦·凯勒出生在美国亚拉巴马州的塔斯坎比亚小镇。凯勒家有一座绿荫覆盖的凉亭，鲜花盛开，芳香沁人，那是她儿时的乐园。当小凯勒6个月大时，她已能牙牙学语般地发出一些音节。可是，这些快乐的日子没能持续多久。在小凯勒19个月大时，突如其来的疾病使她失去了听力和视力，她只能逐渐习惯周遭的寂静和黑暗。

我怀着一种惶恐不安的心情，开始撰写自己的生活经历。可以说，一想到要揭开那像金色雾霭般环绕着我童年的面纱，我就有点迷信似地感到踌躇。撰写自传是一项艰巨任务。当我试图对自己最早的记忆进行归类时，我发现事实和想象似乎已穿越时空将过去和现在交织在了一起。妇女们都喜欢用自己的奇异幻想为童年的经历增添色彩。我生命伊始的一些记忆栩栩如生地浮现在脑海里，但"牢房一般的阴影将笼罩我的余生"[1]。此外，许多欢乐和悲伤也逐渐黯然失色，不再鲜明而尖锐；随着日后生活中那些令人激动的巨大变化，我已忘却了自己早期教育中的一些重要事件的细枝

---

[1] "牢房一般的阴影将笼罩我的余生"：参见英国诗人威廉·华兹华斯（1770－1850）的诗作《不朽的暗示》。

末节。因此，为了不使本书枯燥乏味，我试图将那些对我而言至关重要也最为有趣的事，用一系列的章节呈现给读者。

1880年6月27日，我出生在亚拉巴马州北部的塔斯坎比亚小镇。

我父亲的家族是卡斯帕·凯勒的后裔，他是瑞士人，曾定居在马里兰。在我的瑞士祖先中，有一个人曾是苏黎世聋人的首位教师，他还撰写了一本有关其教学科目的书。虽说国王的祖先可能是奴隶，而奴隶的祖先也可能会是国王，但冥冥之中，这真是一个奇特的巧合！想不到他竟会有我这样一位失聪且失明的后人。

我的祖父是卡斯帕·凯勒的儿子，他移居大西洋彼岸之后"正式占有"了亚拉巴马州一大片广阔的土地，并最终在此定居下来。家人告诉我，祖父每年都要从塔斯坎比亚骑马去一次费城，为种植园购买一些物资。我姑妈曾保存了许多祖父的家信，信里对他的旅行见闻有引人入胜的生动描述。

我祖母凯勒是拉法埃脱将军的副官亚历山大·穆尔的女儿，也是弗吉尼亚州早期殖民地的总督亚历山大·斯鲍茨伍德的孙女。此外，我祖母还是罗伯特·E.李[2]的二表妹。

我的父亲名叫亚瑟·H.凯勒，他曾是南部同盟军的一名上尉；我母亲凯特·亚当斯是他的第二任妻子，母亲比父亲的年龄小很多。母亲的爷爷本杰明·亚当斯娶了苏姗娜·E.古德休为妻，他们在马萨诸塞州的纽伯里生活了很多年。他们的儿子查尔斯·亚当斯就出生在马萨诸塞州的纽伯里波特市，后来他搬到了阿肯色州的海伦娜。当内战爆发时，他加入南军作战，并成为一名准将。他与露西·海伦·埃弗雷特结婚，而露西与爱德华·埃弗雷特和爱德华·埃弗雷特·黑尔博士同属于埃弗雷特家族。战争结束后，他们全家

---

[2] 罗伯特·E.李：李（1807—1870）是美国南北战争时南部同盟军的上将，后来成为南部同盟军的司令。

都搬到了田纳西州的孟菲斯居住。

在疾病夺去我的视觉和听觉之前，我一直生活在一座小房子里，这房子由一个大的方形房间和一个小房间组成，仆人睡小房间。这是南方人的风俗，在家宅的旁边加盖一座小房子，以备不时之需。这房子是我父亲在内战结束后建的，他与我母亲结婚后，就住在这儿。小房的房顶被藤本植物、攀缘的玫瑰和金银花盖得严严实实，从花园望去，那房子看上去就像是一座凉亭。小小的门廊隐没在由黄玫瑰和南方卵叶天门冬织成的屏风中。这里也是蜂鸟和蜜蜂们最流连忘返的地方。

家人居住的凯勒家宅，距我们小巧的玫瑰凉亭只有几步路远。由于房子、周边的树木及篱笆都被郁郁葱葱的常春藤所覆盖，所以这里也被称作"常春藤绿屋"，它那老式的花园是我童年的天堂。

在我的老师到来之前的日子里，我习惯于沿着方正而坚硬的黄杨木树篱，由嗅觉引导，去感知并寻找第一朵紫罗兰和百合花。每当我大发雷霆之后，我都会来到这里，寻求舒适的慰藉，把火辣辣的脸藏在凉爽的树叶和草丛中。能将自己隐匿在繁花似锦的花园中是多么令人欢悦啊！我欢快地从一处漫游到另一处，直到突然碰到一条美丽的藤蔓，我会根据其叶子和花来识别它，并且我知道，这就是那株覆盖着摇摇欲坠的"凉亭"、长在花园尽头的葡萄藤！这里还有席地蔓延的铁线莲、弯曲下垂的茉莉花和一种名叫蝴蝶百合的珍稀花朵，它那纤弱而芬芳的花瓣酷似蝴蝶的翅膀。但玫瑰花是所有花中最可爱的。我从来没有在北方的温室里发现过像我南方家中那般葳蕤攀缘、令人身心陶醉的玫瑰。它们常常在门廊上悬挂出一条长长的花链，令空中溢满馥郁的芳香，丝毫不带土腥气。每天清晨，经过露水的洗礼，玫瑰们是如此柔润、如此纯洁。此时，我总是情不自禁地想：它们是不是上帝乐园中的长春花？

我的生命伊始与许多其他小生命一样，是简单的。像任何家庭中的第一个孩子那样，"我来了，我

看过，我战胜了"[3]。为了给我起名字，长辈们讨论了许久。给家中第一个孩子取名是不能掉以轻心的，所以家人们对此事都很重视。我父亲建议的名字是米尔德丽德·坎贝尔，这是父亲极为崇敬的一位祖先的名字，父亲拒绝就这个名字做进一步的商讨。对此，我母亲则认为应该以她母亲的名字来为我命名，她母亲婚前的名字是海伦·埃弗雷特。可是，当大家欢欢喜喜地抱着我去教堂时，由于父亲对他自己给我起的那个名字并不中意，所以他在路上自然就抛却了那个名字。当牧师问他我的名字时，他只记起要以我外婆的名字来为我命名，于是他给我起名海伦·亚当斯。

　　家人告诉我，当我尚在襁褓之中，就显露出许多急躁和坚持己见的性格迹象。每当看到别人做什么事，我就一定要去模仿一下。在六个月大时，我就能牙牙学语般地发出"好的呀"（How d'ye）的音节，有一天，我十分清楚地说出了"替、替、替"（"茶"的英文发音），这引起了大家的注意。即便是在我生病之后，我仍能记起自己在几个月大时所学到的一个词，那就是"water（水）"。在忘记了所有其他的话语后，我仍能持续发出"water"这个词的音节。后来，当我学习拼写这个词时，我才停止发出"喔—喔（water 一词的前半部英文发音）"的声音。

　　家人们还讲了我在一岁时学走路的情景。那天，树叶在阳光下翩翩起舞，叶影投射在光滑的地板上，忽隐忽现。母亲刚把我从澡盆里抱出来放在她的膝盖上，我突然被摇曳生姿的光影所吸引，从母亲的膝上滑下来，跑向那光影。冲动过后，我摔倒在地，哭叫着扑向母亲，母亲赶紧把我抱起来。

　　这些快乐的日子并没有持续多久。只经历了一个伴随着知更鸟和模仿鸟歌唱的短暂春天，一个果实累累、玫瑰吐艳的夏天，以及一个姹紫嫣红的秋

---

[3] 这是朱利叶斯·恺撒在一场著名战争中击败本都国王法纳西斯后所说的名言。

天就匆匆而去，它们把礼物放在了那位热情奔放、兴高采烈的婴儿脚边。接着，在那可怕的2月，突如其来的疾病锁住了我的眼睛和耳朵，令我陷入了新生儿般无意识的状态。人们把这种病称作胃脑急性充血症④。医生认为我活不了了，但一天清晨，我的烧却突然退了，如同它到来时那样神秘。那天早晨，家人们都欣喜若狂，但没人甚至连医生都不知道我将再也看不见、听不见了。

　　我觉得在回忆这场疾病时，自己依然会有些糊里糊涂。当我被烦躁和疼痛惊醒时，我特别记得母亲那温柔的抚慰；我也记得当自己从翻来覆去的半睡眠状态中醒来时，内心充满了痛苦的挣扎和迷惘。我转动自己的双眼，感觉既干涩又火辣，于是我面向墙壁，避开那些我曾经热爱的光线，它们对我而言已是昏暗的一团，并日益黯淡。除了这些稍纵即逝的回忆，如果它们确实也算回忆的话，其他所有的一切都极不真切，宛如一场噩梦。我逐渐习惯了包围着我的寂静和黑暗，也忘却了曾经经历过的别样生活，直到她——我的老师来了——她使我得到了精神上的解放。但在我生命最初的19个月中，我曾对广阔无垠的绿野、阳光灿烂的天空，以及花草和树木有过惊鸿一瞥，这些印象是随后降临的黑暗所无法完全抹去的。只要我们曾经看见过，那么"这一天，以及这一天所展示的一切就都属于我们"。

④虽然有医生推测凯勒的病可能是猩红热或脑膜炎，但这仍是一个不解之谜。

第 2 章

童年片羽

小凯勒渐渐学会了用一些肢体语言来表达自己的想法。她活泼好动、顽皮淘气。厨师的女儿玛莎是凯勒儿时的玩伴，她们一起偷吃蛋糕、捡鸡蛋、乱剪头发、搞恶作剧，过着无忧无虑的日子。凯勒的父亲是报社编辑，他宽容慈爱，热情好客；母亲则仁爱善良，凯勒生活在浓浓的亲情之中。

我已记不得在我生病后最初的岁月里发生的那些事了。我只知道自己曾坐在母亲的膝上；或者在她四处走动做家务时，自己就紧紧拽着她的衣裙。我的双手可以感知每一个物体，也可以"观察"每一次移动。通过这种方式，我学着了解了许多事物。不久，我感到自己需要同别人进行交流，于是我开始做一些简单的动作。摇头表示"不"，点头表示"可以"；往里拉表示"进来"，向外推表示"出去"。如果我想要面包该怎么办呢？那么我会模仿切面包片和涂黄油的动作。如果我想让母亲晚餐时做冰激凌，我就会做出让冰箱运转和瑟瑟发抖的动作，来表示寒冷。此外，我母亲也成功地让我懂得了许多事情。当她想让我替她拿什么东西时，我总能心领神会，我会跑到楼上或者她指示的任何地方。实际上，在我生活的漫漫长夜里，是母亲用她的仁爱与智慧为我带来了光明和美好。

我懂得了许多与生活息息相关的事。当洗衣房送来干净衣物时，五岁的我会折叠好每一件衣物并把它们收好，并且我还能分辨出哪些是自己的。根据我母亲和姨妈的穿着打扮，我能判断她们什么时候会外出，并总是乞求她们带我一起去。我被大人们带着去参加聚会，当客人要离开时，我会向他们挥舞手臂。如今回想起来，其实当时我对一些姿势的表意是不大懂的。有一天，几位绅士来拜访我母亲，我感觉到了前门关闭的声音和其他一些预示着他们到来的声音。突然我灵机一动，在大家还来不及劝阻我时跑上了楼。我穿上了聚会时才穿的裙子，站到镜子前，模仿别人的梳妆打扮方式，把油软膏涂在头上，还往脸上扑了厚厚的粉。接着，我在头上别了一块面纱，让它遮住我的脸，层层褶折垂落到我肩上。我还绕着自己的纤腰系了一个庞大的裙撑，那裙撑在我身后摇荡，几乎要碰着我裙子的褶边了。然后，穿着这套盛装，就下楼去招待客人了。

我已记不得第一次意识到自己与别人不同是在何时，但在沙利文老师来到我身边之前，我就知道自己跟别人有差异。我注意到我的母亲和我的朋友在想表达时，都不像我那样使用手势，而是用嘴交谈。有时候，我站在两个正在谈话的人中间，试图去抚摸他们的嘴唇，但我却什么也没抓住，因此感到十分苦恼。我也会嚅动自己的嘴唇，狂乱地比画一些手势，结果这当然是徒劳的，无人能明白我的意图。这往往使我非常恼怒，有时我会任性地踢叫，直到把自己弄得精疲力竭才罢休。

当自己顽劣发狂时，我心中还是明白这样做是不对的。因为有一次，我曾使劲踢我的保姆埃拉，弄伤了她，发完脾气后，我有些愧疚。但我实在记不起当我得不到自己想要的东西时，因心存歉疚而没有撒泼耍赖的任何事例。

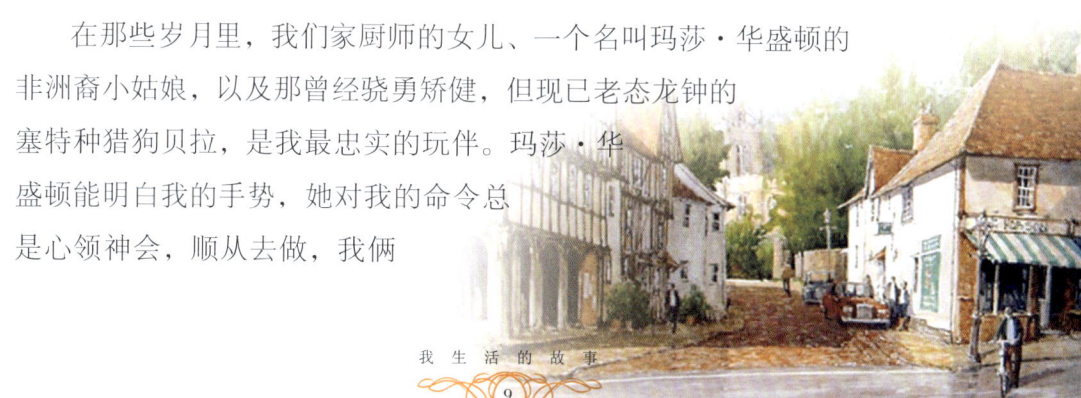

在那些岁月里，我们家厨师的女儿、一个名叫玛莎·华盛顿的非洲裔小姑娘，以及那曾经骁勇矫健，但现已老态龙钟的塞特种猎狗贝拉，是我最忠实的玩伴。玛莎·华盛顿能明白我的手势，她对我的命令总是心领神会，顺从去做，我俩

之间的沟通很少有什么困难。在她面前飞扬跋扈令我感到很高兴。她对我的专横总是逆来顺受,决不会冒险同我发生拳脚相加的冲突。我强健而活泼,做事不计后果。我明知自己太倔强,但仍为所欲为,即使发生激烈争斗也在所不惜。我们在厨房里度过了许多时光,揉生面团、帮着做冰激凌、磨咖啡、为抢蛋糕碗而争吵,或是给厨房台阶上成群的母鸡和火鸡喂食。大多数家禽都很温顺,它们会从我手里啄食,并让我抚摸它们。但有一天,一只高大的雄火鸡居然从我这里抢走一个番茄。也许是受勇敢的雄火鸡成功经验的启发,我们也偷偷拿了一个厨师刚撒上糖霜的蛋糕,然后躲到木柴堆里把这蛋糕吃得干干净净。但之后我却大病一场,我不知道那只火鸡有没有也遭受应得的报应。

珍珠鸡喜欢把她的窝藏在偏僻的地方,我最大的乐趣之一就是在草丛里寻找鸡蛋。当我想去找鸡蛋时,我无法直接对玛莎·华盛顿说这事,于是我会把双手叠加在一起,再把它们放在地上,表示草地上的圆圆的东西,而玛莎总能明白我的意思。运气好的话,我们会发现一个鸡窝,但我从来不会让玛莎把鸡蛋拿回家,我会通过有力的手势让她明白,如果让她拿的话,她会跌倒并把蛋摔坏。

储存玉米的棚子、饲养马儿的马厩和每天早晚给母牛挤奶的院子是我和玛莎无穷的快乐之源。挤奶工挤奶时,会让我把双手放在母牛身上。由于我好奇又好动,母牛们常常会用尾巴甩我。

准备圣诞节一向是我的一大乐事。当然,我并不知道圣诞节的来历,但我喜欢闻那飘荡在屋里的宜人食物醇香。大人们会给我和玛莎·华盛顿一些美味佳肴,让我俩安静下来。虽然我们碍手碍脚有点令人讨嫌,但这丝毫不会影响我们的快乐。大人们允许我们磨香料、挑选葡萄干或舔舔搅拌勺。当别人挂起长袜时，我也学着把自己的长袜挂起来。但我已记不起自己对相关仪式有多感兴趣了，我也从不会好奇地在天亮前就醒来查看我的礼物。

玛莎·华盛顿像我一样酷爱恶作剧。在7月的一个炎炎午后，两个孩子并肩坐在走廊的台阶上。一个孩子的肤色闪着乌木般的光泽，满头毛茸茸的头发被鞋带扎出一根根像开塞钻般突起的辫子；另一个则肌肤雪白，留着长长的金鬈发。一个孩子六岁，另一个只有两三岁。较小的孩子是个盲童——那就是我——另一个孩子是玛莎·华盛顿。我们正忙于剪纸娃娃，但我们很快就厌倦了这项娱乐，我们开始剪各自的鞋带，接着又剪完了我们够得着的所有金银花叶。然后，我开始把注意力转向玛莎那开塞钻般的辫子上，要剪她的辫子，起初她竭力反对，但随后就顺从了。她认为这个游戏要两人轮流剪才算公平，所以她也拿着剪子剪掉了我的一绺鬈发。幸亏我母亲及时干预，要不然她可能会把我的头发全部都剪光。

我家的狗贝拉是我的另一个玩伴，她老迈而懒散，宁愿在燃着的炉火旁打盹，也不愿意同我玩闹。我努力教她我的手势语言，但她却反应迟钝，心不在焉。有时，她会突然跳起，激动得全身颤抖，然后全身僵硬，做出狗儿发现小鸟时的示威动作。这时我会对她的举动一头雾水，但我明白她并没有照我的意图去做。这使我十分生气，所以，授课往往以我对贝拉单边的拳脚相加来结束。而贝拉只会站起来，懒洋洋地伸伸腰，轻蔑地哼一两声，然后就跑到壁炉的另一边再次躺下。于是，疲惫而失望的我，只能去找玛莎玩。

我记忆里镌刻着许多童年的往事，零碎、清晰而生动。它们使我对那段没有声音、漫无目标，但无拘无束的生活有了更深的感受。

一天，我不小心把水泼到了围裙上，于是，我摊着围裙站在客厅壁炉边那忽明忽暗的炭火旁烘烤。我觉得围裙干得太慢了，所以就更靠近火堆，不想围裙却触到了炙热的炭灰。火苗突然蹿上来，火焰包围了我。一瞬间，我

的衣服猛烈燃烧起来。我发出可怕的尖叫声,这引来了我的老保姆维妮,她赶紧救我,扔了条毯子盖住我,令我差点窒息,但她把火扑灭了。所幸我身上除了双手和头发被烧外,其他地方并未受伤。

大约在那个时候,我发现了钥匙的用途。一天早晨,我把母亲锁在了餐具室里。由于当时佣人们都没在屋子里,她被迫在里面待了三个多小时。母亲不停地重重敲门,虽然我能感觉到那些重击的猛烈震动声,可我却坐在走廊的台阶上高兴得哈哈大笑。这些顽劣而任性的恶作剧使我的父母意识到,必须让我尽快接受教育。后来,在我的老师沙利文小姐来到我身边后,我也很快就找到一个机会把她锁在她房间里。当时我爬上楼,手里拿着母亲叫我送给沙利文小姐的东西。但我刚把东西送给她,就跑出来猛地拉上了门,并锁住了它,然后把钥匙藏在了大厅的衣柜里。无论大人们如何劝导,我也不告诉他们钥匙在哪里。最后我父亲不得不找了把梯子,才帮助沙利文小姐从窗口爬下来——这让我无比兴奋。几个月后我才交出了钥匙。

在我大约五岁时,我们从那藤蔓覆盖的小房子搬到了一座新的大房子。家里有我的父亲、母亲、两个同父异母的哥哥,后来还有了小妹妹米尔德丽德。

我最早对父亲的清晰记忆是我穿过一座座巨大的报纸堆来到他身边,发现他正独自坐在那里,面前举着一张报纸。我对他在做什么感到迷惑不解,但我会模仿他的动作,甚至戴上他的眼镜,心想眼镜也许能帮我解开心中的谜团吧!但直到多年以后,我才了解其中的奥秘。我明白了那是些什么报纸,也知道了父亲是在编辑一份报纸①。

①海伦·凯勒的父亲编辑的报纸是《北亚拉巴马州的塔斯坎比亚报》。

我父亲是非常宽容慈爱、对家人极有责任心的人。除了狩猎季节，他很少离开我们。人们告诉我，他是一名优秀猎人和杰出射手。除家人之外，他最钟爱他的狗和猎枪。他热情好客得似乎都有些过头了，他很少有不带客人回家的时候。他特别为家里的那个大花园而感到骄傲。据说，他培育出了全镇最棒的西瓜和草莓。他常常把最先成熟的葡萄和精选出的草莓拿给我吃。我还记得他领着我在树木和藤蔓之间漫步，无比怜爱地抚摸着我，他的激情和快乐也潜移默化地感染了我。

他还是一个有名的会讲故事的人，在我掌握了语言之后，他常常会把那些生动的趣闻轶事，笨拙地拼写在我手上。每当我把这些故事及时"复述"出来时，那就是他最快乐的时刻。

1896年，我正在北方享受着夏日最后的美好时光时，却收到了父亲去世的消息。他病的时间不长，在经历了短暂而剧烈的痛苦后，他的一生就结束了。这是我第一次经历巨大的悲恸——也是我对死亡的第一次亲身体验。

我该怎样描写我的母亲呢？她与我是那么亲近，以致对她的任何语言描述都显得苍白无力。

在很长一段时间里，我都觉得我的小妹妹是一个入侵者。我知道自己已不再是母亲的唯一宝贝，这使我满怀嫉妒。妹妹随时都坐在母亲的膝盖上，而那是我曾经坐过的地方，她似乎把母亲的关爱和时间也全都夺走了。有一天，发生了一件事，更让我觉得痛上加辱。

那时我有一个自己最宠爱，但又最喜欢虐待的洋娃娃，后来我给她起名叫南希。呜呼！她其实只是我大发雷霆时或溺爱发作时的无助牺牲品，所以她的衣服也变得破旧不堪。我有会说话的洋娃娃、会哭的洋娃娃，以及会睁眼闭眼的洋娃娃，但是我最钟爱的却是破破烂烂的南希。她有一个摇篮，我经常会把她放在摇篮里，花一小时或更多的时间摇来摇去。我会用最精心的关爱，守护着洋娃娃和摇篮。但有一次，我却发现我的小妹妹静静地睡在摇篮里。我猜想，当时的我根本没有爱和亲情的概念，于是我立刻怒火冲天，冲过去推翻了摇篮，要不是我母亲在妹妹跌落时及时接住了她，那么也许妹妹会丧命的。因此，当我们行走在双重孤寂笼罩的山谷中②时，我们对善良的话语、行为和友情所能产生的温馨情感是毫无体验的。后来，当我重新恢复了人类的善良天性后，我和米尔德丽德也成长为心心相印的好姐妹。无论前方的路如何变幻莫测，我们俩都愿意一起手牵手地走下去。虽然她不懂我的手势语，而我也不明白她那稚气十足、咿咿呀呀的话语。

②按字面理解，指的是失聪和失明，但此处也引用了上帝的祈祷文："我虽然行过死荫的幽谷"（圣经旧约中的《诗篇》第二十三）。

第 3 章

希望之光

> 小凯勒日益渴求能自如表达自己的意愿,但她所会的手势已无法满足需求。父母带她去巴尔的摩市拜访一位著名的眼科专家。虽然专家对凯勒的眼睛也无能为力,但他建议凯勒的父亲去找贝尔博士,贝尔博士则建议父亲给波士顿帕金斯学校的校长写信。这样,沙利文小姐来到了凯勒的身旁。

那时,我日益渴求能表达自己的意愿。我所使用的那几个手势已越来越不能满足我的需求。每当我无法让别人明白自己的想法时,我总是会异常愤怒。我觉得有一只看不见的手攥住了我,我疯狂努力想逃脱出来。我抗争着——虽然这种抗争无济于事,但我心中已充满了强烈的叛逆精神。我会号啕大哭,直到精疲力竭。如果母亲刚好在我身旁,我便会扑进她的怀抱,伤心不已,然后连自己发脾气的原因也忘了。没过多久,我更加迫切地想掌握一些新的交流方式,以至于我每天甚至每小时都会勃然大怒一场。

我父母对我的举动深感悲伤,却又茫然不知所措。我们的住处离任何一所盲人或聋人学校都很远,而要指望有人能来像塔斯坎比亚这样偏僻的地方教一个又聋又盲的孩子,这似乎也不大可能。事实上,我的朋友和亲戚们有时还怀疑我能否接受教育。狄更斯的《美国札记》为我母亲带来了一缕希望

之光，她曾读过狄更斯笔下的劳拉·布里奇曼①的故事，并依稀记得她虽然又聋又盲，却也接受了教育。但母亲的这份记忆又伴随着痛苦的绝望，因为那位探索出教育聋人和盲人之路的豪博士②已经去世多年。他的教育方法很可能已随他一起失传。如果他们都不复存在了，那么一个住在阿拉巴马偏僻小镇的小女孩又如何能从中受益呢？

在我大约六岁时，我父亲听说巴尔的摩市有一位著名的眼科专家③，曾经成功治好了许多看似无望的病人。于是，我父母立即决定带我去巴尔的摩，看看能否对我的眼睛做一些治疗。

我清楚地记得那趟旅程十分愉快。我在火车上交了许多朋友。一位女士给了我一盒贝壳。我父亲在这些贝壳上打孔，让我用线把它们串在一起。这串贝壳项链令我在很长时间里都无比快乐和满足。列车员也很友善，当他在车厢里巡视，检查乘客的车票并剪票时，我常常紧抓他的大衣后摆。他会把剪票钳拿给我玩，那真是个令人高兴的玩具。我蜷缩在座位的一角自娱自乐了几个小时，在几片纸板上打出了有趣的小孔。

我姨妈用毛巾帮我做了一个大大的娃娃。这是一个非常滑稽可笑的丑娃娃，由于是即兴创作，这个娃娃没有鼻子、嘴、耳朵和眼睛——甚至即使是

---

①劳拉·布里奇曼：布里奇曼（1829—1889）是美国第一位受过教育的失聪并失明的人。英国作家查尔斯·狄更斯（1812—1870）在他1842年出版的《美国札记》中写了她的故事。

②豪博士即塞缪尔·格瑞德里·豪（1801—1876），劳拉·布里奇曼在帕金斯盲人学校就读时的老师。

③指约翰·朱利安·奇泽姆（1830—1903），他是一位专攻眼睛疾病和视力障碍的眼科专家。

一个孩子，也很难凭借想象组合出它的脸来。奇怪的是，我不关注娃娃的其他种种缺陷，却唯独对它没有眼睛印象深刻。我坚持向大家指出这一缺憾，令家人们有些无可奈何，因为似乎没有人能承担为娃娃提供眼睛的重任。突然，一个绝妙的主意闪现在我脑海里，问题有解决之道了。我翻下座椅，在座位底下搜寻，直到发现了姨妈的斗篷，那斗篷上装饰着大大的珠子。我揪下两颗珠子，并向姨妈示意我希望她能把珠子缝到娃娃脸上。姨妈探询地举起我的手放在了她的眼睛上面，我立即使劲地点头。于是，珠子被缝到了恰当的位置，我也喜不自禁。但我很快又对这娃娃失去了兴趣。在整个旅途中，我一点脾气都没发，因为有太多新奇的事让我的大脑和手指忙个不停。

当我们到达巴尔的摩后，受到了奇泽姆医生的友好接待，但他对我的眼睛也无能为力。可他说我能接受教育，还建议我父亲向华盛顿的亚历山大·格雷汉姆·贝尔博士④进行咨询，他可以提供关于失聪或失明儿童的学校和教师信息。我们按照医生的建议，立即前往华盛顿去拜访贝尔博士。

我父亲内心悲伤，疑虑重重。可我完全没有意识到他的痛苦，只是觉得能从一个地方到另一个地方真是令我快乐和激动。虽然我只是个孩子，但我马上就感受到了贝尔博士的亲和力与同情心，正是这些品德使他深受人们爱戴，他取得的卓越成就也使他赢得了世人的赞赏。他把我抱在膝上，当我摸到他的手表时，他特意让手表为我鸣响报时。他能理解我的手势，当我知道这点后，立刻就喜欢上了他。但我并未幻想这次会面能成为一扇门，引领我穿越黑暗走向光明，脱离孤独走向友谊，去拥有伙伴、知识与爱心。

豪博士曾在帕金斯学校为盲人们努力工作过，因此贝尔博士建议我父亲

---

④ 亚历山大·格雷汉姆·贝尔博士（1847－1922）既是电话的发明人，又是聋人教师。

我 生 活 的 故 事

给波士顿帕金斯学校的校长阿纳戈诺斯先生[5]写封信,问问他那里有没有适合教我的老师。我的父亲立即照做了。几星期后,阿纳戈诺斯先生便回了一封友好的信,他承诺说已经找到了一位老师,这令我们非常欣慰。当时是1886年夏,沙利文小姐直到第二年3月才来到我身边。

就这样,我走出了埃及,站到了西奈山前[6]。一位伟大的天神触摸着我的心灵,给我一双慧眼,让我"看见"了许多奇观。从那神圣的山峦中,我听到了一个声音:"知识是爱,是光明,也是梦想。"

[5] 在凯勒年少时,迈克尔·阿纳戈诺斯(1837—1906)是帕金斯盲人学校的校长。

[6] 参见摩西率古以色列人离开埃及的《旧约圣经·出埃及记》。

第 4 章

水 的 开 悟

沙利文小姐的到来是凯勒一生中最重要的事情。在老师的指导下，凯勒对手指拼写产生了兴趣，模仿着掌握了好多单词的拼写方法。当老师让凉爽的水流喷涌到凯勒的一只手上，又在她的另一只手上拼写出"water（水）"这个词时，凯勒终于茅塞顿开，明白了水是什么东西。从此，她明白了语言的奥秘，开始用新的视角来看待万物。

在我的记忆里，自己这一生中最重要的一天就是我的老师安妮·曼斯菲尔德·沙利文[1]来到我身边的这一天。每当我想到这一天能将两个有着巨大差异的生命连在一起时，我就觉得这真是太奇妙了。这天是 1887 年 3 月 3 日，再过三个月我就满七岁了。

在这一重大日子的午后，我默默地站在门廊里，心中满怀期待。我从母亲的手势和屋子里人们来回走动的气氛中，隐隐猜到家里将要发生不寻常的事。所以我走到门外，到台阶上等待着。午后的阳光穿透覆盖在门廊上的大片金银花，流泻到我仰起的脸上。我的手指几乎是无意识地流连于那些熟悉的叶子和

---

[1] 安妮·曼斯菲尔德·沙利文（1866—1936）是凯勒的终身同伴。她也曾是帕金斯学校的学生，在童年时代失明，后来通过手术恢复了视力。

花朵上，刚刚萌生出的花和叶正在迎接南方美好的春天。我不知道未来会带给我什么样的奇迹或惊诧。几星期来，愤怒和痛苦不断地折磨着我，激昂暴躁的抗争之后，我变得无精打采。

你是否曾置身于浓雾弥漫的大海上？你似乎陷入了一片白茫茫的可触摸的蒙昧之中，而那大船，正焦急紧张地用铅锤和测深线探寻着靠岸的航路。此时，你是否只能提心吊胆地等待那即将发生的一切？在我开始接受教育之前，就像是那艘船，所不同的是我连指南针和测深线也没有，更无从知晓港口是否就近在眼前。"光明！给我光明！"这是我发自内心的无言的呼喊，然而，正在这时，爱的光芒照耀在了我身上。

我感觉到了越来越近的脚步声。我伸出双手，就像迎接母亲那样。有个人握住了我的手，她用双臂把我紧紧拥入怀中，她就是来帮我揭示万物之谜的人。除此之外，更重要的是，她是来爱我的人。

我的老师到来后的第二天清晨，她把我领到她房间，给了我一个洋娃娃。这个洋娃娃是帕金斯学校的小盲童们送的，劳拉·布里奇曼给它穿了衣服，但这一切我是后来才知道的。我拿着娃娃玩了一会儿后，沙利文小姐慢慢在我手上拼写了"doll（洋娃娃）"这个词。我立即对这种手指游戏产生了兴趣，并试着去模仿。最终，当我成功地正确写出这几个字母时，我内心充满了童真的快乐和骄傲。我冲下楼去找母亲,举起自己的手,拼写出了"doll"的字母。其实，当时我并不知道我拼写的是一个单词，我甚至根本就不知道世间有单词的存在。我只是像猴子一样用手指进行模仿而已。在随后的日子里，我凭借这种浑然不解的方法学会拼写了很多词,其中有"pin（别针）,hat（帽子）,cup（小茶杯）"，还有"sit（坐），stand（站立），walk（行走）"等几个动词。直到老师跟我一起生活了好几个星期之后，我才知道世间万物都有一个名字。

一天，我正在跟新洋娃娃玩，沙利文小姐却把我的那个又大又破的旧娃娃放在我膝盖上，她拼写出"doll"，并试图让我明白，"doll"指的是这两个娃娃。在这之前，我们曾为单词"mug（杯子）"和"water（水）"展开过一场争论。沙利文小姐试图让我明白"杯子是杯子"，以及"水是水"，但我老是把两者混在一起。沙利文小姐毫无办法，她只好把这个话题搁置一边，等有机会时再重新教我。我对她反反复复的尝试感到极不耐烦，于是抓起新娃娃，猛地把它砸在地板上。当我感觉到脚边有摔坏的娃娃的碎片时，我十分痛快。暴躁地发完脾气后，我既不伤心，也不后悔。我已不再爱那个娃娃。因为在我生活的那个寂静漆黑的世界里，并没有强烈的感伤或柔情。当我觉察到老师把那些碎片扫到了壁炉的一旁时，我的不快也随之而去，对这一切感到心安理得。接着，老师拿来了我的帽子，我知道她要领我去外面沐浴那温暖的阳光了。这个想法——如果一种无言的感受也能被称作想法的话，立刻令我高兴得欢呼雀跃。

我们沿着小路向井亭走去，一路上呼吸着覆盖在井亭上的金银花那沁人心脾的芳香。有人正在抽水，于是老师把我的手放在喷口下。当凉爽的水流喷涌到我的一只手上时，她在我的另一只手上拼写出"water（水）"这个词，起先她的动作很慢，接着就变快了。我静静地站着，全神贯注地感受她手指的动作。突然，我感到一种朦胧的知觉——仿佛是对某些被遗忘的东西失而复得后的兴奋；不知怎么地，语言之谜就这样在我面前揭开了。于是，我知道了"水"的意思是从我手上流过的这清凉美妙的东西。这个生气勃勃的词唤醒了我的心灵，给我带来了光明、希望和欢乐，使我获得了解放！虽然我仍面临许多困难，但我坚信，所有的困难终将被一一克服。

离开井亭后，我如饥似渴地想学习。原来万事万物都有一个名字，而每个名字还会诞生一种新思想。当我们回到家时，我觉得自己碰到的每一个物体似乎都有了生命的悸动。这是因为我在尝试以刚刚获得的好奇而崭新的视角来"看"万物了。进门之后，我想起了那个被我摔坏的娃娃。于是，我摸索到壁炉旁，捡起了那些碎片，试着想把它们拼在一起，但这显然是徒劳无功的。此刻，我意识到自己做了错事，眼里涌起了泪水，第一次真正感受到了悔悟和伤心。

这天，我学到了许多新词。虽然我已记不全它们是哪些词了，但我知道，它们中间有这几个词——母亲、父亲、姐妹、老师——正是这些词为我营造了一个鲜花盛开的世界，"就像亚伦的魔杖，开出花朵"[2]。在这重要的一天即将结束的时候，我躺在自己的小床里，重温这一天的美好时光，觉得自己真是世上最幸福的孩子。我第一次开始渴望新的一天的来临。

[2] 参见《旧约全书·民数记》（第十七章），亚伦是摩西的哥哥，他的杖或权杖开花，预示他的部族将成为以色列人的领导者。

第 5 章

树的诱惑

> 沙利文小姐没有把凯勒关在房间里进行常规的死板教学,而是把大自然当作课堂,给她讲解动植物知识,让凯勒从万事万物中发现美,激发她的学习兴趣。通过亲身体验,凯勒也领教了大自然狂暴狰狞的一面。但自然的诱惑又怎能被拒绝呢?

我忆起在我的心灵被唤醒之后,随之发生在1887年夏的许多往事。我通过用自己的双手去探索,学会了我触摸到的每件东西的名字。我接触的东西越多,就越多地了解了它们的名称和用途,同时我也变得更加快乐和自信,对世上的其他事物也产生了亲近感。

当雏菊和金凤花盛开的时候,沙利文小姐牵着我的手穿过田野,田野里的人们正在准备播种。我们来到田纳西河岸边,坐在暖洋洋的草地上,在这里,我上了第一堂有关大自然之恩惠的课。我了解到太阳和雨水如何使大地上长出树木,令它们既赏心悦目,又能提供可口的食物;鸟儿们如何筑巢、如何在一片又一片的土地上生活并兴旺发达;松鼠、小鹿、狮子和其他动物又是如何寻找食物和居所的。随着知识的增长,我对自己所处的这个世界也越来越充满感情。在我学会数学运算或描绘地球的形状之前,沙利文小姐先教会了我如何在芬芳的森林、在每一片草叶、在我妹妹小手的曲线和漩涡里去发

现美。她将我最初的思想同大自然连在一起，使我感受到了"鸟儿、花儿和我是快乐的伙伴"①。

但在那时，我也通过亲身体验，明白了大自然并不会时时友好。一天，我和老师散步到了较远的地方。这天早上的天气很晴朗，但当我们走在回家的路上时，天气却变得湿热难耐起来。我们不得不在路边的树下休息了两三次。最后，我们停在了离家不远的一棵野樱桃树旁。树荫很凉快，而那树也易于攀爬。于是，在老师的帮助下，我爬上了树，并坐到了树杈上。树上真是太凉快了，沙利文小姐建议我们在这里吃午餐。我答应她自己会乖乖地坐在树上，由她回家取午餐。

突然，一种变化掠过树丛。太阳的温暖从空气中消失了，我知道天变黑了，因为阳光带给我的所有热量，都已消失在周围的环境里。一股奇怪的味道从地面上冒出，我知道这种气味。每当暴风雨来临之前，总有这种气味。一种不可名状的恐慌攫住了我的心。由于自己脱离了朋友和坚实的大地，我感到无比孤独。无边无际的未知世界包围着我，但我只能静静地期盼，全身都沉浸在冰冷的恐惧之中。我渴望老师的到来，我最想做的事就是从树上赶紧下来。

一阵不祥的寂静之后，树叶剧烈抖动起来，樱桃树也哆哆嗦嗦地摇晃起来。如果不是我拼尽全力抱紧树干，那么我肯定会被狂风刮下去的。树被刮得东倒西歪，那些折断的细枝纷纷打落在我身上。我有了一个突如其来的疯狂念头，那就是从树上跳下去，但我又被恐惧牢牢地钉在了树上。我蜷缩在树的枝丫间，枝条无情地抽打着我。我断断续续感到了不时传来的震动，仿佛某个重物跌落下来，而它的震动却又向上传到了我坐着的树枝上。我忧心如焚，紧张到了极点。正当我觉得自己要和树一起跌落时，我的老师抓住了

---

① 参见美国诗人詹姆斯·拉塞尔·洛威尔（1819—1891）的《致蒲公英》（To the Dandelion）。洛威尔是凯勒十分喜爱的一名诗人。

我的手，并帮我从树上爬下来。我依偎在老师身旁，欣喜得浑身颤抖，又一次感受到了脚下那坚实的大地。我学到了新的一课——大自然会"向她的孩子们发动公开战争，在最温柔的触摸之下，却潜藏着变幻莫测的魔爪"[2]。

有过这次惊险的经历之后，在很长一段时间里，我都不敢再爬树。一想起那次遭遇，我就恐惧不已。最终，是鲜花怒放的金合欢树用清雅的芳香吸引我战胜了恐惧。那是一个春天的早晨，我独自在凉亭里读书，突然闻到空气中有一股奇异的淡淡香气。于是，我起身向前走，并本能地伸开双手。此时，春天的气息仿佛也飘到了凉亭。"它是什么呢？"我问道。紧接着，我就分辨出这是金合欢花的气味。我知道那金合欢树就在栅栏附近，在小路的拐弯处，于是我摸索着来到花园尽头。是的，它就在那儿，在温暖的阳光下轻轻摇摆，那开满鲜花的枝条几乎都要垂落到草丛上了。难道世上还会有比它更清奇优雅的花朵吗？世间最细微的触碰，都会使它那精巧的花瓣收拢；它就像是一株被移植到尘世的天堂之树。我沐浴着缤纷的落英，走到了粗壮的树干前，迟疑地在那站了一分钟。接着，我把脚放在树枝间宽大的分叉处，奋力爬上了这棵树。我十分艰难地抱着树，因为这树的枝干巨大，树皮还磨破了我的手。但我油然而生一种奇特的感觉，觉得自己正在做一件极不寻常、妙不可言的事。所以我越爬越高，一鼓作气地爬到了别人很久前在树上搭的一个小小座位上。历经天长日久的洗礼，这个座位已与大树融为一体。我久久地坐在那里，觉得自己仿佛是绚丽云霞中的一个小精灵。此后，我在这棵天堂之树上度过了许多快乐时光，任遐思纷飞，憧憬着美好的未来。

---

[2] 参见苏格兰随笔作家和历险故事作家罗伯特·路易斯·史蒂文森（1850—1894）的散文《排笛》（Pan's Pipes）。

第 6 章

"爱"的含义

在利用自然教育启迪凯勒智慧的同时,沙利文小姐还用细腻的情感和善良的心性对凯勒进行道德教育,终于让她明白了抽象概念"爱"的含义,明白了爱与幸福是息息相关的。并且凯勒在沙利文小姐的循循善诱下还掌握了一些与人交谈互动的技巧。

现在,我有了开启各类语言的钥匙,我渴望学会使用它。对那些能听得见的孩子来说,学说话并不需要特别的努力;他们能原原本本、轻松而迅速地捕捉从别人嘴唇间飞出的话语;而对于一个失聪的小孩来说,要想弄懂这些话,却必须要经历缓慢,甚至是痛苦的过程。可是,无论这一过程如何艰难,其结果却是奇妙的。渐渐地,我们从学说物品的名字开始,逐渐向前稳步推进。从发出第一个结结巴巴的音节开始,我跨越了巨大的鸿沟,终于可以弄懂莎士比亚的诗行了。

最初,每当老师告诉我一件新事物时,我提不出几个问题。我的思维模糊,词汇贫乏,但是随着对事物认知的增加,并学习了越来越多的词汇后,我提问的领域也拓展了,我会反复探究同一主题,希望能进一步了解更多信息。有时,一个新词还会唤起那些铭刻在我脑海中的原始印象。

我记得一天早上,我第一次询问"爱"这个词的意思。那时我还不认识多少词。我在花园里发现了几棵刚刚绽放的紫罗兰，于是我采了花儿送给老师。老师想吻我，但当时，除了母亲，我不愿接受任何其他人的吻。沙利文小姐用手臂轻柔地拥着我，在我手上拼写出"我爱海伦"这句话。

"爱是什么？"我问。

她把我拉近她的身旁，一边说："它就在这儿"，一边指着我的心脏。这是我第一次意识到心脏的跳动。老师的话令我迷惑不解，因为那时我除了自己曾摸过的东西外，对其他的东西一概不能理解。

我闻着老师手中的紫罗兰，用单词加手势的方式接着问："爱是花朵的芳香吗？"

"不。"老师回答说。

于是我思考了一会儿，和煦的阳光照耀在我们身上。

"难道这不是爱吗？"我一边指着阳光发射出的方向，一边问："难道这不是爱吗？"

对我而言，世上似乎没有比太阳更美好的事物了，它的温暖使万物茁壮生长。但沙利文小姐仍摇摇头，这使我更加迷惑和失望了。我想，老师为什么不能把爱给我看看呢？这真奇怪呀。

大约一两天后，我练习用线串起大小不一的珠子。我先均匀地分组，然后再来串——两颗大的，配三个小的，如此而已。可我却总是出错，温柔的沙利文小姐非常耐心地再三帮我指出来，终于，我注意到了一个很明显的排序错误。刹那间，我突然可以把注意力集中在练习上了，我苦苦思索怎样才能排好这些珠子。沙利文小姐摸摸我的额头，鲜明而清晰地拼写出"Think（思考）"一词。

转瞬之间，我明白了这个词就是我脑海中进行的活动的名称，这是我第一次感知并理解抽象概念。

我静默了很长时间——我并没在想膝盖上的珠子，而是试图循着新的理

我 生 活 的 故 事

念，去发现"爱"的含义。这一整天，云层遮住了太阳，还下了一阵雨。可是突然间太阳又喷薄而出，令南方的万物熠熠生辉。

我再次询问老师："难道这不是爱吗？"

老师回答说："爱有些像太阳出来之前，那天空中的云朵。"然而，此时即使她用的是比这更简单的词汇，我也还是无从明白。老师继续解释道："你知道，你无法触摸云朵，但却能感知雨滴；在经受了一天的炎热后，花儿和干渴的土地如果能得到雨水的滋润，那该多么欢欣啊！同样，你也无法触摸到爱，但你能感受到它注入万物后所带来的美好。如果没有爱，你将不会幸福，也不会想玩耍。"

突然间，我明白了这美妙的真理——我觉得仿佛有无形的线，把我的心灵和他人的心灵连在了一起。

从我接受教育伊始，沙利文小姐跟我讲话的方式就与跟那些正常孩子的讲话方式一样，唯一不同的是，她在我手上拼写句子，而不是说出句子。当我找不到必要的词汇和成语来表达自己的思想时，她会提供给我；当我无法应付某段谈话时，她会给出建议，教我如何完成这段谈话。

这种学习过程持续了好几年。失聪的孩子不可能在一个月甚或两三年里就学会那些不计其数的日常最简单的成语和表达方式。听力正常的孩子可以通过不断重复和模仿来学习。他在家里听到的谈话会刺激他的大脑，启迪有关话题，由此引导他自然而然地表达出自己的思想。但失聪儿童却不可能有这种天生的思想交流。我的老师意识到了这些，她决心为我提供我所缺乏的那种刺激。于是，她尽可能对着我逐字逐句、再三重复她所听到的谈话，并向我示范应如何参与交谈。这真是一个漫长的过程，后来我终于敢冒险主动与人交谈了；但又经过了很长时间，我才学会如何在恰当的时间说恰当的话。

对失聪者或失明者来说，要掌握谈话的礼仪是非常困难的。而对于那些既失聪又失明的人来说，那更是雪上加霜、难上加难啊！他们无法分清声音的语调；若无人协助，他们将无法通过声调音阶的高低来强调重点词句；更有甚者，他们也无法观察说话者的面部表情，而表情往往是说话者内心想法的真实展露。

第 7 章

知识的海洋

  沙利文老师尊重孩子的天性，把教学融入玩耍之中。她用一些美丽故事和优雅诗句来讲解知识，带领凯勒在洒满阳光的森林里接触动植物，教她用鹅卵石筑堤、造岛、挖河，在游戏中学习地理。凯勒对数学不感兴趣，老师就用分组串珠的方法教她计数，用麦秆让她学会了加减法。还通过抚摸化石和海螺，养百合花和蝌蚪，引导凯勒从生活中轻松愉快地学习。凯勒完全进入了知识的海洋之中。

  在我的教育过程中，接下来的重要步骤是学习阅读。

  每当我学会拼写几个单词后，老师就给我一些硬纸卡片，上面用凸起的字母印着这些单词。我很快就理解了每个凸印的单词都代表一个物体、一种行为或者是一种特点。我还有一个拼写板，可以把单词放在里面排列成一些短句。但我在用卡片排出句子之前，习惯于先用实物来表现句子。我发现了那些卡片所代表的含义，比如"doll（洋娃娃）""is（是）""on（在……上）""bed（床）"这几个词，每一个词都有其自身对应的物体和形式。于是，我把洋娃娃放在床上，又把"is（是）""on（在……上）""bed（床）"这几个词都挪到洋娃娃身旁。这样既用单词造出了一个句子，同时又用相应的实物表现了句子的含义。

  一天，我按照沙利文小姐的教导，把"girl（女孩）"这个词别在围裙上，然后站在衣橱里。接着我在板架里排列出"is（是）""in（在……里）""wardrobe（衣柜）"这几个词。再没有什么比这种游戏更让我开心的了。我和老师每次一玩就是几小时，我们常常把屋里的每样东西都安排到我们的目标句子里。

认字卡片只是通往学习盲文书籍的一个步骤而已。我会翻开我的《初学者读本》，在里面寻找自己认识的单词；每当我找到它们时，我就会高兴得像是在捉迷藏游戏中获胜似的。我就这样开始了阅读书籍。以后，我还会谈谈自己是何时开始阅读那些相互关联的故事的。

长期以来，我从未正规地上过课。即使当我孜孜不倦地学习时，也只是像在玩耍，而不是上课。沙利文小姐在教给我知识时，总会用一些美丽的故事和优雅的诗句来加以说明。每当什么事使我兴奋或感兴趣时，她就会与我一起探讨，仿佛她也是个小女孩似的。那些让许多孩子一想起来就无比畏惧和痛苦的事，比如学习单调乏味的语法、高深莫测的算术，以及难以理解的词语解释等，今天在我看来，却全是最珍贵的回忆。

我无法解释为什么沙利文小姐会对我的快乐和愿望别具同情心，或许是因为她和盲人有着长期的感情联系吧。除了爱心，她还有高超的描述能力，她会飞快掠过那些无趣的细节；她从不拿难题折磨我，也不会絮絮叨叨地问我是否还记得前天的功课。她会循序渐进地为我介绍枯燥的科学术语，让每门科目都生动有趣，使我能毫不费力地记住她所教授的知识。

我们一般在户外读书学习，我们喜欢洒满阳光的森林，而不喜欢待在室内。我最早的课程都糅合着森林的气息——醇厚的松针树脂味，混合着野葡萄的清香。我们曾在一棵野生鹅掌楸的宽大树荫下席地而坐，在那里，我懂得了每件事都有其哲理，都能启迪心智。"万事万物令我领悟到了它们的魅力和功用。"[①]的确，那些嗡嗡哼鸣、喊喊喳喳、快活歌唱或纵情绽放的动植物，

[①] 参见詹姆斯·拉塞尔·洛威尔的诗作《阿德墨托斯国王的牧羊人》（The Shepherd of King Admetus）。

都是我的活教材——聒噪的青蛙、蝈蝈和蟋蟀趴在我手上，它们会忘却自己的困境，依然发出悠长的颤音；还有毛茸茸的小鸡、野花、鲜花盛开的山茱萸、草场上的紫罗兰和正在发芽的果树。我触摸过炸裂的棉荚，拨弄它们那柔软的纤维和绒毛般的种子；我感受过风穿过玉米秆时低沉的呜咽，长长的叶子发出的丝绸般的沙沙声，以及当我们在牧场抓住我的小马，给它套上嚼子时，它烦躁的呼哧声——啊，我的天哪！我至今还对它喷出的辛辣三叶草气味记忆犹新！

有时候，我黎明即起，悄悄溜进花园，草叶和花朵上都缀满重露。很少有人曾体会过用手轻轻按压玫瑰花的乐趣，或是欣赏过百合花在晨风中摇曳的风姿。偶尔我能在自己采摘的鲜花上捉到一只昆虫，在突如其来的恐惧面前，这只小生物也感知到了外界的压力，我能感觉到它的双翅相互摩擦所发出的微弱声音。

我最喜欢去的另一个地方是果园。7月初，果子成熟了，毛茸茸的大桃子会掉落在我手中；当欢快的风儿吹上树梢时，苹果会跌落在我脚下。啊！当我用围裙收集起这些水果，把脸颊贴在那留有太阳温暖的光滑苹果上，然后蹦蹦跳跳地回家时，我心里真是喜滋滋的！

我们最喜欢的活动是到"凯勒码头"散步，那是田纳西州河边一个古老的、摇摇欲坠的、装卸木材的码头，在内战时士兵们就是从那里登陆的。我们在那里度过了许多美好时光，并在游戏中学习地理。我用鹅卵石堆砌堤坝，做出岛屿和湖泊，又挖掘河床。我玩得不亦乐乎，做梦也想不到这是在上课。沙利文小姐向我描述那宽广的圆形地球，上面有熊熊燃烧的山脉、被掩埋的城市、移动的冰河以及其他许多稀奇古怪的东西。我听了以后，好奇心大增。她还用泥土做了凸起的地图，这样我就能触摸山脊和峡谷，并用手指去感知弯曲迂回的河道。虽然我喜欢这一切，但我却弄不懂地球的分区和两极，我在脑子里把它们混作一团。那些用作说明示例的带子和代表两极的橘树棍,做得非常逼真。时至今日,只要提到温度带,我就会联想起一连串盘绕的环状物。我相信,即使有人散布谣言说北极熊真的爬上了北极,我也会当真的。

算术似乎是我唯一不喜欢的学科。从一开始我就对数字科学不感兴趣。于是,沙利文小姐尝试着用分组串珠子的方法教我计数,又像幼儿园老师一样通过排列麦秆让我学会了加法和减法。但如果一次要排列五六组以上,我就会失去耐心。当我做完这些后,我就会一整天都心猿意马,无心学习,想赶紧出去找小伙伴玩。

通过同样轻松愉快的方式,我也学习了动物学和植物学知识。

曾有一位我记不得名字的绅士,送给我一套化石——有的化石上印着美丽的微小软体动物的壳;一小块砂岩上留着鸟爪印迹;而可爱的蕨类植物已化身成浅浮雕。这些化石是引领我开启上古世界宝库的钥匙。当沙利文小姐给我讲述那些名字奇特得难以正确发音的怪兽,践踏原始森林,撕下巨树的枝条当食物,却在一个未知年代,死在可怕的沼泽里时,我紧张得十指颤抖。在以后很长的一段时间里,这些古怪的生物总是纠缠着我的梦境。如今,我的生活又充满了阳光和玫瑰,还回荡着我的小马清脆而有节奏的蹄声。相比现今的欢乐,那段令人忧郁的记忆变成了留在心底的前尘往事。

还有一次,我得到一个美丽的海螺,对一名小孩子来说,这真是个令人无比欣喜的礼物。我了解到了一个微小的软体动物是如何建造这闪闪发光的螺壳,并把它作为自己的家的。在那静静的、没有一丝风的夜晚,海面上没有一朵浪花,鹦鹉螺乘坐他的"珍珠船"[②],航行在印度洋那碧蓝的海水里。此后,我还知道了许多有关大海的子民们的生活习性和趣事。比如,小小的

[②] 参见美国医生和诗人老奥利弗·温德尔·霍姆斯(1809—1894)的诗作《珍珠鹦鹉螺》(The Chambered Nautilus)。

我 生 活 的 故 事

珊瑚虫是如何在太平洋汹涌的波涛中建造出美丽的珊瑚岛的；有孔虫类又是如何把石灰质山体变成了礁石的。老师教我读了《珍珠鹦鹉螺》这首诗，并向我解释，软体动物外壳的形成过程象征着人的智慧的发展过程。鹦鹉螺之所以能有那创造奇迹的外壳，是源于它把从海水中吸收的物质变成了身体的一部分。同样，点点滴滴的知识经过不断的积累，也会变成思想的珍珠。

从植物的生长过程中，我也学到了新知识。我们买来一盆百合花，把它放在阳光明媚的窗台上。很快，那尖尖的绿色花苞就显露出即将开放的迹象，外围那些纤细得如手指般的叶子也慢慢张开了。我想，它们可能不太愿意展示自己珍藏着的宝贝吧。但既然已经开了头，绽放的过程就快速有序、有条不紊地进行了。总有一个花苞比其他花苞更大更美丽，这个穿着柔软丝质礼服的美女仿佛知道自己是天赋的百合花女王似的，于是，其他花苞就会给她披上最光耀璀璨的外衣。而当她那些胆怯的姐妹们也羞答答地摘下绿头巾时，整株百合花就变成了含笑点头、芳香扑鼻、美轮美奂的大花束。

家人曾在一个球形玻璃缸里养了 11 只蝌蚪，又把这鱼缸搁在长满植物的窗户旁。我记得自己迫不及待地想了解这些蝌蚪的奥秘。我会猛地把手插入鱼缸，让蝌蚪们四处活蹦乱跳，在我的手指间穿梭游动，这种感觉真是妙不可言。一天，一只野心勃勃的家伙跳出了鱼缸，跌落在地板上，当我发现他时，他已半死不活了，唯一的生命迹象就是他的尾巴还在轻轻扭动。但当他一回到水中，就冲向缸底，又欢快地游来游去了。他已完成了自己的奋力一跳，看到了广阔的世界，于是，他终于满足于待在大灯笼海棠树下那可爱的玻璃房里了。他终将会长成一只自豪的青蛙，去花园尽头那个飘满落叶的池塘里生活。然后，他也会唱着离奇有趣的爱情歌曲，奏响夏夜的乐章。

生活处处皆学问，我就是这样从生活中来学习的。最初，我只是一块充

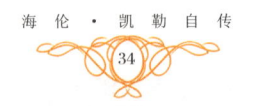

满未知数的毛石，是老师发掘并雕琢了我的潜质。当她到来之后，我周围的一切都沐浴在爱心和欢乐中，变得趣味无穷。她利用一切机会向我展示万物之美，她在思想上和行动上永不言弃，努力用实例引导我，使我的生活更甜蜜，使我的生命变得更有意义。

我之所以能接收到妙趣横生的早期教育，要归功于老师的卓越才智、深切同情心，以及她的仁爱和机敏。她总是抓住恰当的时机向我传授知识，使我能轻松愉快地接受教诲。她意识到，孩子的头脑就像是一条浅浅的小溪，泛着涟漪，欢快地跳跃过受教育过程中的那些拦路石。小溪会映出这里的一朵花，那里的一丛灌木，或是远处的一片白云。她试图顺从我的天性来引导我。她深知，一条小溪只有汇集了山间清流和地下暗泉，才能成长为一条深沉的大河，在它那宁静的河面上，才能够映射出巨浪般的山峰、明亮的树影和蔚蓝的天空，以及一朵小花的甜美笑容。

任何老师都能把一个孩子领进教室，但不是每一位老师都能让他热爱学习。无论这孩子是在忙碌还是在休息，只有当他感受到心灵的自由时，他才会愉快地学习。他必须体验过胜利的喜悦和失败的沮丧，才能下决心学习自己不喜欢的功课，并从那些枯燥的常规课本中，勇敢地探索出一条自己的路。

我的老师离我那么近，以至于我简直不敢想象与她分离的情景。我对美好事物的喜爱，有多少是天生的，又有多少是受了老师的影响，这是我永远也分辨不清的。我觉得她和我心心相印，是不可分离的，我的生活足迹上有着她的烙印。我的所有成绩都应归功于她——如果不是她用爱心唤醒了我，我是不可能拥有任何才能、灵感和欢乐的。

第 8 章

圣诞礼物

沙利文小姐已经成为凯勒家中的重要一员，她在这个大家庭里迎来的第一个圣诞节因而显得特别重要。年幼的凯勒尤其兴奋，她对节日的极大热情和对礼物的热衷欢喜其实都反映了她对沙利文小姐的喜爱与依恋。

对我们家来说，沙利文小姐在塔斯坎比亚迎来的第一个圣诞节可是件大事。家中的每个人都为我准备了惊喜，但最让我高兴的是我和沙利文小姐也为其他所有人都准备了惊喜。猜测礼物的秘密是我最热衷的娱乐。我的朋友们也尽其所能地勾起我的好奇心，他们会给我一些暗示，或者故意拼写半句话，然后假装说要到最后一刻才能揭晓。于是我和沙利文小姐就不断地玩这种猜谜游戏，我从游戏中学到的语言运用法，比在固定课堂上学到的还多得多。我们每晚都围坐在红通通的炉火边玩猜谜游戏。随着圣诞节脚步的日益临近，这种游戏也越来越使人兴奋。

在平安夜那天，塔斯坎比亚学校的孩子们准备了圣诞树，并邀请我去参观。教室中间立着一棵美丽的圣诞树，在柔和的灯光下熠熠闪烁，它的枝条上挂满了美妙而奇特的果子。那真是我无比快乐的时刻！我欣喜若狂地围着那棵树手舞足蹈，欢呼雀跃。当我得知每个孩子都有一份礼物时，我更高兴了。那些准备圣诞树的善良人们允许我给孩子们分发礼物。我乐此不疲地忙碌着，甚至没有停下来看看自己的礼物。当我忙完这些时，我的忍耐已到了极限，我迫不及待地盼望真正的圣诞节快点到来。我知道我的礼物并不是朋友们为逗我而暗示的那些东西，因为老师说给我的礼物要比那些东西好多了。可是，大家也劝我要满足于从圣诞树上得到的礼物，其他礼物且等明早再说。

那天晚上，当我把长袜挂好后，躺在床上久久不能入睡。我假装睡着了却又保持警惕，想看看圣诞老人会不会来做点什么。最后，我抱着一个崭新的洋娃娃和一只小白熊睡着了。第二天早上，我第一个起来叫醒了大家，并且祝他们"圣诞快乐！"令我惊喜不已的是，礼物不仅仅藏在袜子里，连桌上、所有的椅子上、门边和窗台上，都有无数令人欣喜的礼物。事实上，我总是碰着那些用薄绵纸包着的小巧圣诞礼物，搞得我跌跌撞撞，几乎都无法迈步了。当沙利文小姐送给我一只名叫蒂姆的金丝雀时，我简直乐不可支，心中溢满欢悦。

小蒂姆非常温顺，他会在我的手指上跳来跳去，吃我手中的樱桃蜜饯。沙利文小姐教我去全心全意地照顾我的新宠物。每天吃完早餐后，我就会给它洗澡，把它的笼子弄得干干净净、清香四溢，再给他的小杯子里添上新鲜的种子和井水，最后在它的秋千上挂一条纤细的繁缕枝。

一天早上，我去为他打洗澡水时，把鸟笼忘在了窗台上。等我回来开门时，感觉到一只大猫从我身边溜了出去。起初我并没意识到发生了什么事，但当我把手伸进笼子时，蒂姆那可爱的双翅却没有迎接我的触摸，它那小巧的尖爪子也没有抓住我的手指，我知道我将再也看不到我那啼声婉转的小歌手了。

第 9 章

波士顿之旅

在波士顿帕金斯盲人学校，凯勒认识了许多像她一样失去了天赋感官的孩子，但他们仍然快乐而知足。这是凯勒走出家庭迈向社会的重要一步，从此她不再孤单，同类之爱会进一步塑造这个天资聪颖的孩子。她的未来令人期待。

我生命中的另一件大事，是1888年5月的波士顿之行。那一切仿佛就发生在昨天，我仍记得旅行前的准备、跟老师和母亲一起出发最后抵达波士顿的整个过程。这次旅行与两年前我去巴尔的摩的旅行是多么的迥然不同啊！我已不再是那个兴奋好动，到处找乐，引得一车人注意的小丫头了，也不需要大家逗我开心了。我静静地坐在沙利文小姐旁边，津津有味地听她讲述她从车窗外看到的一切：美丽的田纳西河、宽广的棉花田、山脉和树林，以及车站上那群欢笑的黑人，他们向火车上的人们招手，把香喷喷的糖果和爆米花球传上火车车厢销售。而在我对面的位子上，则坐着我那个大大的破娃娃南希，她穿着一条新的方格花布裙，戴着一顶有褶皱的遮阳帽，用她那双玻璃珠子做的眼睛看着我。有时，当我听不大懂老师的描述时，我会想起南希的存在，把她抱进怀里。但通常情况下，我会让自己相信南希正在睡觉，所以我会变得很安静。

恐怕我再也没机会提起南希了，所以我想讲讲当我们到达波士顿后她的一段悲惨经历。她全身都是脏泥巴——那是我强迫她吃泥巴馅饼时粘到她身上的，虽然她从未表露过她对这种馅饼有什么特殊喜好。于是，帕金斯盲人学校洗熨衣物的女工悄悄地把她拿出去，给她洗了澡，这对破旧的南希来说简直是灭顶之灾啊！等我再见到她时，她已成了一堆没有形状的棉花了，若不是那两只怒目而视的玻璃眼珠，我简直无法认出她了。

最终，当火车到达波士顿车站时，一个美丽的童话故事仿佛变成了现实，童话故事里的"从前"就是现在，而那"遥远的地方"正是在这里啊！①

我们一到帕金斯盲人学校，我就和那里的小盲童们交上了朋友。当我发现他们也会手语字母时，我真是高兴得无以言表。能用我自己的语言同其他孩子交谈，这是多么令人欢欣鼓舞的事啊！在此之前，我一直像个外国人，得通过翻译才能同别人交流。而在这所劳拉·布里奇曼曾接受过教育的学校里，我就像在自己的国度里一样。过了好一会儿，我才习惯自己的新朋友都是盲人这一事实。我知道自己看不见，但我很难想象那些围在我身边、跟我尽情嬉戏、热情友好的孩子们也都是盲人。我还记得，当我注意到自己与他们交谈时，他们会把手放在我的手上，并且他们也是用手指来阅读书籍时，我感到多么惊奇和苦恼啊！虽然人们以前也给我讲过这些，虽然我也明白自己丧失了某些感官，可我还是隐约地想到，由于他们可以听得见，他们一定有某种"第二视觉"。我一点也没有心理准备，想不到自己会发现一个又一个的孩子也被夺去了珍贵的天赋感官。但他们是如此得快乐和知足，以至于我在与他们相伴的欢乐气氛中，忘掉了所有的忧愁烦恼。

和盲童们一起度过的那一天，令我感到自己虽然身处新环境，却完全

①许多童话故事的经典开头都是："从前，在一个遥远的地方……"

像在家里一样。随着时光飞逝，我热切渴望一次又一次的快乐体验。我把波士顿看作了宇宙的起点和终点，我想象不出还会有其他更广阔无垠的世界。

在波士顿期间，我们还参观了邦克山②，在那里，我上了平生的第一堂历史课。故事里的勇士们曾在我们站着的这块土地上战斗，这真令我激动不已。我一边爬纪念碑，一边数着台阶。当我越爬越高时，心里真想知道当年的士兵们是不是也曾爬上了这高高的台阶，然后向下面的敌人射击呢？

第二天，我们乘船去普利茅斯。这是我第一次航行在海洋上，也是我第一次乘汽船旅行。那船是多么威武雄壮、动力十足啊！但机器的隆隆作响，竟让我以为是天在打雷。由于担心下雨后我们就不能享用露天野餐了，我居然哭了起来。我对普利茅斯最感兴趣的东西是1620年移居美洲的英国清教徒们登陆时踏上的那块大岩石。我用手触摸着这块大石头，感觉自己对清教徒的到来、他们的艰苦奋斗和辉煌业绩有了更真切的体验。在清教徒博物馆，一位善良的绅士送给我一块小巧的普利茅斯岩石模型。我常常拿它把玩，用手指触摸它的曲线、中间的一条裂缝以及上面的浮雕数字"1620"。当时，我满脑子都是清教徒先民们开疆拓土的神奇故事。

在我幼稚的想象中，他们的开拓进取精神是多么的可歌可泣啊！我把他们理想化了，看成是敢于在陌生土地上寻找家园的最勇敢、最有气魄的人。我认为他们是在为自己，也在为同胞们追求自由。多年以后，当我了解到他们那令人羞愧的宗教迫害行为③后，我感到无比震惊和极度失望。但我们依然为他们对"美丽祖国"所奉献的勇气和力量感到自豪。

②美国独立战争中，于1775年6月17日在马萨诸塞州进行的第一场主战役的旧址。
③清教徒迫害宗教的少数教派，如贵格会教徒等。

我在波士顿交了许多朋友，其中有威廉·恩迪科特先生④和他的女儿。他们对我的友爱就像种子，萌生出许多美好的回忆。有一天，我们拜访了他们在贝弗利农场的美丽家园。我仍愉快地记得自己是如何穿过他们家的玫瑰园的；他们的狗狗——高大的利奥和小巧的长耳朵卷毛狗弗里茨是如何跑来迎接我的；那跑得最快的马儿尼姆罗德⑤，又是如何觊觎我手中的糖块，还让我抚摸它的。此外，我还记得那个海滩，在那里，我第一次在沙子中玩耍。那里的沙子坚硬而光滑，和布鲁斯特的那些松软而尖锐、混杂着大型海藻和贝壳的沙子是完全不同的。恩迪科特先生告诉我，那些大船是从波士顿开来的，它们将驰往欧洲。后来，我又多次见过他，他一直是我的好朋友。其实，每当我把波士顿称为"热心之城"时，我都会想起他。

④威廉·恩迪科特（1826—1914）先生是帕金斯学校的理事。
⑤这匹马是以《圣经》"在耶和华面前的英勇猎人"（《创世纪》10：9）中的尼姆罗德来命名的。

第 10 章

拥抱大海

> 儿时的凯勒曾将孩童的好奇与想象热情地付之大海,直到这个夏天终于有机会目睹它。大海的壮阔磅礴带给小凯勒强烈的冲击;温柔的海风,还有神秘的海洋生物世界令她痴迷流连,久久难以忘怀。

在帕金斯盲人学校关门放暑假之前,按照计划,我和老师,还有我们亲密的好友霍普金斯夫人①将一起去科德角②的布鲁斯特度假。我乐滋滋的,大脑里一边憧憬着未来欢乐的旅程,一边回想我所知道的有关大海的精彩故事。

那个夏天,我最栩栩如生的回忆就是大海。我一直住在遥远的内地,从未如此近距离地吹过带咸味的海风。但我曾读过一本厚厚的书,名叫《我们的世界》,书中对海洋的描写,使我心中充满了好奇,强烈渴望能够触摸那浩瀚的大海,感受一下它的咆哮。当我知道自己的愿望终于就要实现时,我那颗小心脏也激动得狂跳起来。

刚换好游泳衣,我就迫不及待地跳上温暖的沙滩,毫不畏惧地冲进凉爽

---

① 霍普金斯夫人,即索菲娅·霍普金斯,当沙利文在帕金斯学校学习时,她是该校女舍监。
② 科德角位于美国马萨诸塞州南部。

的水里。我感到了巨浪的升腾与下落。我在海水中轻快地游动,玩得兴高采烈,幸福得浑身战栗。突然,我的脚撞在了一块岩石上,随后一股奔腾的急流冲到我头上。于是,恐惧战胜了欢乐,我伸出双手,想抓住某个支撑物,但我抓到的只是海水和波浪抛在我脸上的海草。我所有疯狂的努力都是徒劳,浪花好像在跟我做游戏,它们在野蛮的恶作剧中把我抛来抛去。这真是太可怕了!舒适而坚实的大地已从我脚下溜走,那陌生的、全方位包围我的海水隔绝了一切——生命、空气、热情和爱心。谢天谢地,最后大海好像厌倦了它的新玩具,又把我抛回岸上。随后,我抓住了老师的双臂。哦,那绵长而温柔的拥抱是多么令人舒服啊!可当我从惊慌失措中恢复过来后,我却立即就问:"是谁把盐放在了水里?"

我刚从海水中的这次历险恢复过来,却又想如果我穿着泳衣,坐在大礁石上去感受层层波浪拍击岩石,朵朵浪花飞溅四周,那一定会其乐无穷。可是,当波浪拖着沉重的身躯扑向岸边时,我感觉到鹅卵石在嘎嘎作响,整个海滩似乎都将毁于它们的恐怖袭击,空气中也颤动着它们的脉搏。那些打在海岸上的碎浪花,还会出其不意地撤退,积聚力量后进行更凶猛的反扑。于是我紧紧地抓住礁石,感受着汹涌大海的冲击和咆哮,竟有些心醉神迷了。

我对海滩总是流连忘返,待再长的时间仍觉得意犹未尽。纯净、清新而自如的海风,散发出一股强烈的味道,就像是一种能让人冷静而克制的思想。贝壳、鹅卵石、海草以及附着在海草上的小生物都向我展示着无穷的魅力。一天,沙利文小姐引导我看了一个奇怪的家伙,那家伙正在浅水里舒舒服服地晒太阳,却被沙利文小姐给捉住了。原来那是一只巨大的马蹄蟹,这是我第一次见到这种动物。我摸着它想,它为什么要在背上驮着自己的房子呢?这真奇怪呀!忽然,我突发奇想,觉得它可以做一只讨人喜欢的宠物,于是我用双手抓着他的尾巴把它拎回了家。我对自己的行为沾沾自喜,因为这家伙确实很重,我费了九牛二虎之力,才把它拖了半英里路。我一直缠着沙利文小姐,直到她把马蹄蟹放在井旁一个很安全的水槽之后我才放心。但是第二天一早，我来到水槽边一看，马蹄蟹竟然无影无踪了！没人知道它去了哪里，也没人知道它是怎么逃跑的。当时我真是失望之极，愤愤不平。但我逐渐意识到强迫那可怜的、默默无言的生物离开它的生存环境是既不仁慈也不明智的。片刻之后，想到它也许已重归大海了，我又感到非常高兴。

第 11 章

金秋猎场

别样的金秋猎场生活带给所有人无尽的欢乐。凯勒用她敏锐的思维丈量着成年人的小把戏,当然更多的时候,她在经历自己的冒险,把种种惊讶化作知识与欢乐。

满载着绚丽的记忆,我在秋天回到了南方的家中。每当我忆起此次北方之行,总会沉浸在那一连串丰富多彩、妙趣横生的奇闻轶事中。一切似乎刚刚开始,一个崭新美好世界里的所有珍宝都躺在我脚下。在每一次惊讶中,我都可以领悟到知识和快乐。我全身心地投入每一件事,一刻也不得闲。我的生命充满了活力,就像那些成群结队的小昆虫,哪怕生命只有短暂的一天,也要尽全力来展现自我的存在。我遇到了许多人,他们通过在我手上拼写来与我交谈,他们对我的感情,也从同情升华到了思想上的意气相投。看啊!奇迹真的发生了!我的思想和其他人思想之间的荒芜之地也开出了像玫瑰一样的花朵。

我和家人一起在家族的避暑农舍度过了那个秋天,农舍坐落在离塔斯坎比亚大约14英里的一座山上。那里又被称为"弗恩采石场",因为其附近有一座久已废弃的石灰石采石场。三条快活的小溪流从此地流过,虽然岩石企图阻挡它们前进,这些源自山泉的溪流却左突右闪,欢腾跳跃,一往无前。空地上长满了蕨类植物,它们完全遮掩了石灰石矿床,也把小溪藏匿其中。

山上的其他地方都是茂密的树林。这里有高大的橡树，也有郁郁葱葱的常青树，其粗壮的树干宛如长满苔藓的柱子，枝条上则垂悬着常春藤和槲寄生的花束。柿子树的气味渗透了树林的每一个角落——那是一种迷离馥郁、令人神清气爽的芳香。野生的圆叶葡萄和斯卡珀农葡萄在树与树之间攀缘，形成了一座座天然凉亭，蝴蝶翩翩起舞，各种昆虫嗡嗡萦绕。黄昏时分，你可以把自己沉浸在这层峦叠嶂、绿意丰沛的氤氲中，闻闻那在一天结束之际，从泥土中散发出来的沁人香气，那真是心旷神怡啊！

我们的小屋只是个简陋的露营棚，漂亮地掩映在山顶的橡树和松树丛中。房子的中间是一个长长的露天过道，两旁排列着一些小房子，环绕房子的是一圈宽广的游廊。山风吹来，空气中溢满树木的芬芳和清香。我们的大多数时间都是在游廊上度过的——我们在那劳作、吃饭和游戏。房子后门有一棵高大的灰胡桃树，环绕着这棵树修建了一些石阶。我可以近距离地站在那些树前，触摸它们，感觉风儿摇动着树枝，以及树叶在阵阵秋风中旋转。

许多人都会到弗恩采石场游玩。晚上，男人们围坐在篝火旁打牌、聊天、做运动来消磨时光。他们述说自己猎杀禽类、鱼和四足动物的卓绝手艺——他们曾射中了多少只野鸭和火鸡、捉住了多少凶猛的鲑鳟鱼、如何用袋子逮住狡猾的狐狸、怎样设巧计击败最精明的负鼠，以及如何追上疾驰的驯鹿等。我想，在这些足智多谋的猎人面前，哪怕是狮子、老虎、狗熊及其他野生猛兽也不可能有立足之地的。夜深了，围坐一圈高谈阔论的人们散去时，高喊着互道晚安："明天再去打猎！"这些人就睡在我们屋外的过道里，我在屋里也可以感觉到狗儿们的呼吸声，以及睡在简易床上的猎人们沉沉的鼾声。

黎明之时，我被咖啡的醇香、枪支的撞击声以及人们沉重的脚步声所唤醒。猎人们大步流星地来回走动，预示着在这个季节里他们会好运连连。我还能感觉到马蹄的踩踏声，人们骑着这些马从镇上过来，把马儿拴在树下。在树下站了一整夜后，马儿们发出响亮的嘶鸣，极不耐烦地盼着早点出发。最终，猎人们骑上马，正如古老的歌谣里

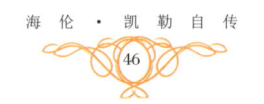

所唱的那样：套着缰绳的骏马嗒嗒奔驰，皮鞭啪啪响，猎犬往前冲，英勇的猎人出发了。"喘息声和召唤猎犬的呼喊声此起彼伏！"①

临近中午时分，我们开始为烧烤野餐做准备。火从地下深坑的底部燃起来，上面交叉架起粗大的树枝，树枝上悬挂的肉嗞嗞作响。黑人们蹲在火旁，用长长的枝条驱赶着苍蝇。虽然餐桌还没有摆好，但烤肉发出的阵阵浓香味儿，已使我垂涎欲滴了。

正当喧闹忙碌的准备工作达到高潮时，猎人们三三两两地归来了，他们满头大汗、疲惫不堪。马儿口吐白沫，精疲力竭的猎犬气喘吁吁、垂头丧气——唉！什么也没打着！每个人都宣称自己至少看见了一只鹿，那鹿已近在眼前，但即使是猎犬马上就要追上，猎枪已经精确地瞄准好，可当扳机啪啪扣响时，那鹿却无影无踪了。他们的运气就好像是那个小男孩，他总说自己离一只野兔很近了——其实他看见的只是兔子的踪迹。无论结果怎样，失望的情绪很快就被晚会的欢笑驱散了。大家围坐下来，根本不提野味的事。我们仍会好好地享受小牛肉和烤乳猪这类家庭美食。

有一个夏天，我把我的小马带到了弗恩采石场，我叫他"黑神驹"，因为我刚读过《黑神驹》（*Black Beauty*）②一书，里面有匹马就叫这个名字。我的小马"人如其名"，披着乌黑发亮的黑外套，额头上有星星般的白色花纹。我在"黑神驹"的背上度过了许多快乐时光。偶尔，在非常安全的情况下，我的老师会松开主缰绳，让小马自由漫步，小马也会停留在他喜爱的植物旁，吃一口青草，或啃一嘴那些长在狭窄小路旁的树叶。

---

①参见苏格兰作家沃尔特·司各特爵士（1771—1832）的诗作《湖边夫人》（The Lady of the Lake）。

②《黑神驹：一匹马的自传》（*Black Beauty，The Autobiography of a Horse*）（1877）是英国作家安娜·西韦尔（1820—1878）所著的一部很受欢迎的儿童书籍。

如果早上我不想骑马，我和老师就会在早餐后一起到树林中散步。我们往往会迷失在树与藤之间无路可走，只能循着牛马踏出的小径前行。我们会被灌木丛挡住去路，不得不绕道另辟蹊径。当我们回到农舍时，总是环抱着一大把月桂树枝、秋麒麟草、蕨类植物和光彩夺目的湿地花卉等南方特有的植物。

有时，我会和米尔德丽德及小表妹们去摘柿子。虽然我不吃柿子，但我喜欢闻它们的芳香，喜欢在树叶间和草丛里寻找柿子的感觉。我们也会去采拾坚果，我帮她们剥开那带刺的栗子，砸开山胡桃和核桃的外壳——那些核桃真是又大又香啊！

山脚下有一条铁路，孩子们可以看到火车风驰电掣般地飕飕驶过。有时，它会发出一声尖厉的长啸，于是我们就赶紧爬到台阶上。米尔德丽德会极其兴奋地告诉我，有一头牛或一匹马在铁轨上迷路了。在离这约1英里之外，有一座高架桥横跨在幽深的峡谷之上，这桥很难走，桥身上的铁路枕木间距很宽，枕木又非常狭窄，走在上面就仿佛在刀刃上行走一样。我从没有走过这座桥。直到有一天，我、米尔德丽德和沙利文小姐在树林中迷路了，转来转去走了几个小时也找不到回家的路。

突然，米尔德丽德用小手指着前方高喊："高架桥在那！"我们真是宁愿走其他任何路，也不想走这座桥，无奈当时天色已晚，夜幕即将降临，走高架桥是回家的唯一捷径。我不得不用脚趾去感知那些轨道，但我并不害怕，走得也很稳健，突然，从远处模模糊糊传来了"噗噗"的喷气声。

"我看见火车了！"米尔德丽德喊道。如果不是我们立即爬下去趴在支撑拉条上，那么火车很可能就撞上我们了。火车从我们头顶呼啸而过，我感到发动机的热气喷在了我脸上，而烟雾和灰尘也几乎令我们窒息。当火车隆隆疾驶而过时，高架桥摇摇晃晃，我觉得我们好像都要被掷入下面的深谷中了。我们用尽全力重新爬上了铁轨。直到夜色阑珊时，我们才回到家，却发现农舍里空无一人，原来全家人都出去找我们了。

第 12 章

冬日丽景

北方的冬季有冰封的湖泊和宽广的雪野。这茫茫的冰雪宝库带给小凯勒无限的惊奇与快乐,她置身其中,领略自然的奥秘。透过这一章的描述,可以发现沙利文小姐的自然教育已然将小凯勒雕琢成一名具有诗人气质的优雅姑娘。

自从我第一次去了波士顿之后,我几乎每个冬天都在北方度过。有一次,我游览了新英格兰地区的一个村子,那里冰封的湖泊和宽广的雪野令我印象深刻。在那儿,我有生以来第一次有机会跨入冰雪宝库,去领略其中的奥秘。

记忆中,当我发现似乎有一只神秘的手,剥去了树木和灌木的绿衣,它们只剩下零星几片枯萎的叶片时,我感到非常惊异。鸟儿飞走了,它们的空巢留在光秃秃的树枝上,堆满了积雪。冬天笼罩了小山和田野,大地在它那冷冰冰的触摸下似乎已麻木了。树木精灵们都撤到了树的根部,在黑暗中蜷作一团,沉沉睡去。所有的生命似乎都在消逝,即使有太阳,白天也依然是:

短暂而寒冷,

仿佛她的血脉已经老化而枯萎,

她颤巍巍地爬起来,

只是为了最后再看一眼心中的大地和海洋。①

枯萎憔悴的草丛和灌木变成了一座冰柱林。

随后而来的是一股强冷空气,这预示着暴风雪即将来临。我们冲到室外,去感受最先飘落的小雪花。柔软的雪花寂静无声、飘飘洒洒地从空中落下,连续好几个小时,旷野变得越来越平整,白茫茫一片。清早,人们几乎无法辨认出东西南北的景物。所有的道路都被隐藏起来了,看不见任何标志,只剩下一片被皑皑白雪覆盖的森林。

夜幕再次降临的时候,刮来了一股东北风,狂暴的雪花漫天纷飞。我们围坐在熊熊燃烧的炉火旁,讲着有趣的故事,嬉戏玩耍,完全忘了我们正处在一个偏僻荒凉的地方,与外界的联系渠道也被切断了。可是,夜里风势却越来越大,呼啸着在旷野上肆虐,我们在朦胧中被吓得瑟瑟发抖。椽子被吹得咯吱作响,屋子周围的树木枝条也嘎嘎作响,猛烈抽打着窗子,一切都在狂风的肆虐下苟延残喘。

暴风雪一直到第三天才停下。太阳冲破云层,照耀在广阔无垠、蜿蜒起伏、银装素裹的平原上。高高的土丘,被堆砌成金字塔状以及其他各种稀奇古怪的形状,令人难以置信地向四面八方散播开来。

人们在雪堆里铲出一条条狭窄的小路。我穿上外套,戴上兜帽走出去。寒风把我的脸颊刺得火烧火燎的痛。我们一会儿走小路,一会儿又艰难地越过小雪堆走到积雪中,最后终于成功到达了那位于大牧场旁的松树林。松树们一动不动地立着,像装饰着大理石饰带的洁白雕像,可是闻不到松针的味道了。阳光洒落在树木上,那些细枝条像钻石一样熠熠生辉,我们稍稍一碰,积雪就纷纷飘落。强光非常刺眼,甚至穿透了遮住我眼睛的那片黑暗。

随着时间的流逝,积雪慢慢消融。可是雪还没完全融化,另一场暴风雪

---

① 参见詹姆斯·拉塞尔·洛威尔的诗作《郎佛尔爵士的幻想》(The Vision of Sir Launfal)。

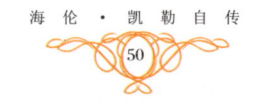

又降临了。因此整个冬天，我几乎没有感受过脚下的大地。暴风雪的间歇，笼罩在树木上的冰衣不时地融化，芦苇和灌木丛露出了身形，只有阳光下的冰湖展现着冬日的美景。

在冬季，我们最喜欢的娱乐是滑雪橇。有些地方，湖岸和湖面的落差很大，我们常常沿着那些陡峭的斜坡快速滑雪橇。坐上雪橇后，一个男孩会从后面使劲一推，我们就冲下去啦！穿过积雪，跃过小坑，向湖面猛冲。我们飞越那闪闪发光的湖面，射向湖对岸。太开心啦！这是多么让人痴迷的疯狂啊！在那令人激动的欢悦时刻，我们砸断了把我们束缚在大地上的锁链，恍若与风儿牵手，感觉飘飘欲仙。

第 13 章

学会说话

学会说话对凯勒而言无疑是一件有着非凡意义的事，但这是一项艰辛的工程。她需要克服常人难以想象的困难与挫折，更重要的是秉持耐心与毅力，以超常的信心与热情去不断模仿，反复练习。幸运的是，凯勒遇见了执教有方、经验丰富的萨拉·富勒校长还有天才教师沙利文小姐。在他们的帮助下，凯勒迎来了人生无比幸福的时刻。

1890 年春，我开始学说话。我一直都有一股强烈的冲动，希望自己能发出别人可听懂的声音。于是我常常一边发出一些声音，一边把一只手放在自己的喉咙上，另一只手则去感知嘴唇的移动。我很喜欢那些能发出声音的东西。我喜欢通过触摸感知猫的咕噜声和狗吠声。我也喜欢把手放在歌手的喉咙上，或正在弹奏的钢琴上。在我失明和失聪前，我学说话很快；可自从我生病后，由于听不见，我就停止了咿呀学语。我常常整天坐在母亲的膝上，并把双手放在她脸上，因为我觉得她嘴唇动来动去的很好玩。而我也学着蠕动自己的嘴唇，虽然我早已忘了说话是怎么回事。我的朋友说我的笑声和哭声都很自然。有时，我会发出许多声音和词素，但这并不是在练习与人交流，而是因为我必须锻炼自己的发音器官。至今我仍然记得学习"水（water）"这个词的过程，一开始，我总是发出"喔－喔（wa-wa）"的声音，这样的发音是令人难以理

解的。直到沙利文小姐来教我，在我学会用手指拼写这个词后，我便放弃了用发音进行交流的方式。

很久以前，我就知道周围的人使用的交流方式与我的方式是不同的。甚至在我知道失聪儿童也能学会说话之前，我就意识到自己所拥有的交流方式无法满足需要。一个完全依靠手语字母交流的人，总会有一种受限制和太局促的感觉。这种感觉令我无比懊恼，我觉得应想办法来弥补这种缺憾。这一想法就像迎风飞翔的小鸟一样总在我头脑里冒出来，于是我坚持使用嘴唇发出声音。有些朋友试图劝我放弃，唯恐这会导致我品尝失望的痛苦，但我依然坚持不懈。后来，我偶然听说了朗希尔德·卡达的故事，她的故事激励着我最终突破了不会说话的巨大障碍。

1890 年，刚从挪威和瑞典访问归来的拉姆森夫人[1]来看我，她曾做过劳拉·布里奇曼的老师。她告诉我，朗希尔德·卡达是挪威的一名失聪失明女孩，已经学会了说话。不等拉姆森夫人给我讲完那个女孩的成功故事，我心中就燃起了希望之火。我下决心要学会说话。之后，我简直静不下心来，直到我的老师带我去见了霍瑞斯曼学校[2]的校长萨拉·富勒小姐，请她给我指导和帮助。这位诙谐有趣、和蔼可亲的女士愿意亲自教导我，于是我们从 1890 年 3 月 26 日那天正式开始学习。

富勒小姐的教学方法是：她在发出一个音时，把我的手轻轻放在她脸上，让我感知她舌头和嘴唇的位置。我干劲十足地模仿每一个动作，在一小时内就学会了六个字母的发音，即 M、P、A、S、T、I 这六个字母。富勒小姐一共给我上了 11 堂课。当我说出第一个连贯的句子"天气很暖和"时，我永远也不会忘记自己是多么欣喜若狂！的确，我说出的只是断断续续、结结巴巴的一些音节，但这却是人类的语言。我的灵魂挣脱了束缚，感受到了新的

[1]拉姆森夫人即玛丽·斯威夫特·拉姆森，是帕金斯学校的一名教师。
[2]霍瑞斯曼学校是波士顿的一所聋人学校。

我 生 活 的 故 事

力量，它将通过这些断断续续的语音符号，去坚定信心，探索知识。

　　任何一个失聪的孩子，只要他曾认真试着去说出那些他从未听过的话语——去走出那没有爱的音符、没有鸟的歌声，也没有能消除孤寂的音乐的寂静监狱——那么他就不会忘记，当他发出第一个词时，那传遍全身的欣喜战栗和无限欢愉。我兴致勃勃地跟我的玩具、石头、树木、鸟儿和不会说话的动物们讲话，只有有过相同体验的人才会欣赏我的热情。当米尔德丽德听见我的召唤向我奔来，当狗狗们听从我的指令时，我是多么快乐呀！只有学过说话的失聪人才能体会到这种快乐。对我而言，能够说出那些像长了翅膀一样的语言，又不需要别人的翻译，那真是上苍赐给我的无上恩惠。在我说话时，快乐的思绪也随着我的语言流淌，但如果想通过手指来传达这种快乐，那肯定是徒劳无功的。

　　但是，不要以为在这么短暂的时间里我就真的学会说话了。其实我只学到了一些讲话的基本要素，并且只有富勒小姐和沙利文小姐能够听懂我的话。对其他大多数人来说，恐怕我讲的 100 个词中，他们未必能听懂其中的 1 个。也不能说在我学会了那些基本要素后，就能靠自己去独立摸索其余的技能。要不是沙利文小姐的卓越天赋、不懈的坚持和奉献，我是不可能取得这么大的进步，也不可能学会自如说话的。从一开始，我就夜以继日地苦练，终于，我最亲密的朋友能够听懂我说的话了。然后，沙利文小姐给我持续不断的帮助，努力使我的发音清晰准确。我们运用了上千种方法，练习所有的音节组合。时至今日，她每天都还在提醒我注意一些我发错了音的单词。

　　只有失聪儿童的老师才能明白这意味着什么，也只有他们才能体会到我要克服的是多么巨大的艰辛。我不得不用触觉来捕捉喉咙的震动、嘴唇的运动和脸部的表情，但触觉常常会出错。每当碰到这种情况时，我就强迫自己重复相关的单词和句子，有时要练几小时，直到我感觉自己发出的音是正常的才行。我的工作就是练习、练习、再练习。我常常感到灰心丧气、疲惫不堪，但转念一想，我很快就能回家向我挚爱的亲人们展示自己的成绩了，我多么希

望他们能对我的成绩感到高兴啊！正是这个念头激励着我不断奋进。

"我的小妹妹将能听懂我的话"，这是我战胜一切困难的力量源泉。我常常孜孜不倦地重复："我现在不是哑的了。"当我憧憬着与母亲交谈的喜悦，以及根据她的嘴唇读出她的反应时，我就不再意志消沉了。我惊喜地发现说话要比用手指拼写交流容易得多，于是我就想抛弃那用作交流媒介的手语字母。但沙利文小姐和一些朋友仍然用手语字母与我交流，因为同读唇相比，手语字母更方便、也更快捷。

在此，为了解除大家的疑惑，我想说明一下我们使用手语字母的过程。一名想跟我说话或读书给我听的人，会用手拼写出聋人们常用的单手手语字母。我把手轻轻地放在说话者的手上，我的动作会轻到不妨碍对方的任何行动。手对位置的变化很敏感，如同长了眼睛一样。当你们为我阅读时，我辨别词语的速度并不会比你看的速度慢。不断的练习能使手指非常灵活。我的一些朋友拼写起来相当快——就仿佛高手在用打字机写作一样。当然，这种拼写方式只是一种不得已而为之的行为。

当我学会说话后，我真是归心似箭。最终，那无比幸福的时刻来到了，我踏上了归家之路。我不时地和沙利文小姐说话，这不仅仅是为了交流，更是为了利用这最后的时间来提升自己。不知不觉中，火车停在了塔斯坎比亚站，全家人都在站台上迎接我们。母亲默默无言地拥抱我，兴奋得全身颤抖；小米尔德丽德抓住我的手亲吻，高兴得手舞足蹈；父亲则用长长的沉默来表达他的骄傲和慈爱。即使现在我回想起这一切时，依然会热泪盈眶。这仿佛是《以赛亚书》中的预言在我身上得到了应验："你面前的山脉和丘陵放声歌唱，旷野的树木鼓掌欢呼！"③

---

③参见《圣经·以赛亚书》（55∶12）。

第 14 章

《霜之王》事件

凯勒写的故事《霜之王》，由于在思想上和语言上都与坎比小姐的《冰霜精灵》非常相似，所以人们怀疑她是有意抄袭以博取众誉。凯勒在本章中袒露了整个事件的本末，不回避真相，不忌讳过往。其实每个人初学写作，往往会吸收和模仿自己喜爱的文字，再把它们付诸文章中。伟大的作家，都是经过若干年的积累和历练，才能自如地遣词造句。

1892年冬天，我童年的明媚天空被一朵乌云搅得暗无天日。欢乐离我而去，在很长一段时间里，我生活在怀疑、焦虑和恐惧之中，对书籍也失去了兴趣。甚至时至今日，一想起那些可怕的日子，我依然不寒而栗。事情的起因是我写了一篇名叫《霜之王》的小故事，并寄给帕金斯盲人学校的阿纳戈诺斯先生，结果却种下了祸根。为了拨开此事的迷雾，还我老师和我本人以公道，我强迫自己详尽写下有关真相。

我是在学会说话后的那个秋天在家里写下这篇故事的。那年秋天，我们住在弗恩采石场，睡觉的时间比平时晚得多。当时，沙利文小姐向我描述了深秋树叶的五彩斑斓，她的描述似乎唤醒了我记忆中的某个故事，这个故事应该是别人曾读过给我的，而我在不知不觉中就记住了。于是我想，我也要编写一个故事。我趁一些念头从自己脑海里溜走之前，热情高涨地坐着写下了一个故事。我文思泉涌，感受到了写作的快乐。生动的词汇和形象轻快地从我指尖跳出，我一边思考一个接一个的句子，一边把它们写在我的盲文记录板上。当然，如果词汇和形象是毫不费力地闪现在我脑海里，那么这也应是个确凿的证据，说明它们并不是我思维的产物，而是依附在我脑海里的一些零星记忆。那时，我如饥似渴地吸收所有读过的东西，从不去想著作权的问题。即使现在，我也不能完全划清自己的观点和我读过的那些书之间的界限。我猜想，这也许是因为我对事物的许多印象都是以别人的眼睛和耳朵为媒介而得到的吧！

当故事写完后，我把它念给老师听。现在我还清楚地记得，自己从那些优美段落里得到的欢愉，以及被老师打断纠正某个词的发音时所感到的气恼。晚饭后，我又读给聚在一起的家人们听，大家都对我竟然能写得这么好而深感惊讶，甚至有人问我是不是从某本书里读过这个故事。

这个问题使我大吃一惊，因为我绞尽脑汁也想不起曾有人给我读过这个故事。于是，我响亮地说："哦！不，这是我写的故事，是我为阿纳戈诺斯先生写的故事。"

接着，我誊写了这篇故事，并按照人们的建议，将标题"秋天的树叶"改为"霜之王"。我要把它寄给阿纳戈诺斯先生，以庆祝他的生日。我洋洋得意地拿着这个小故事亲自去了邮局。我丝毫没有想到，我将为这份生日礼物付出惨重的代价。

阿纳戈诺斯先生看了《霜之王》之后非常高兴，并把它刊登在了帕金斯盲人学校的一份刊物里。我登上了快乐顶峰，但很快又跌入谷底。我刚回到波士顿不久，就有人发现《霜之王》与玛格丽特·T.坎比小姐写的一篇名叫《冰霜精灵》的故事非常类似，早在我出生前就有这篇故事了，它被收录在一本名叫《小鸟和他的朋友们》的书中。这两个故事在思想上和语言上都非常

相似，令人不得不相信我曾读过坎比小姐的故事，也就是说，我的作品是抄袭来的。起初我很难理解这一切，但当我真正明白这事之后，我感到既惊讶又悲伤。没有哪个孩子曾痛饮过比这更剧烈的悲痛。我颜面扫地，那些我深爱的人们也对我产生了怀疑。而这一切究竟是怎么发生的呢？我绞尽脑汁去回想自己在写《霜之王》前究竟读过哪些与冰霜有关的文章，想得精疲力竭，也回忆不起什么。终于我想起有关杰克·费罗斯特（费罗斯特是"霜"的意思）的一些参考资料，以及一首儿童诗《霜的奇想》，但我绝对没有在自己的文章中用过这些资料。

起初，虽然阿纳戈诺斯先生也深为此事困扰，但他似乎还相信我。他一向对我友善而慈爱，然而没过多久，事态却恶化了。在我得知那坏消息后没几天，就是华盛顿的诞辰纪念日，为了让阿纳戈诺斯先生高兴，我依然强颜欢笑，尽全力认认真真地参加了相关庆祝活动。

在由失明女生们表演的类似假面戏剧[1]的演出中，我饰演女神色列斯[2]。我清楚地记得，自己身上围着优雅漂亮的衣饰，头戴一个用鲜艳的秋叶做成的花环，脚上和手上装饰着水果和谷物。但在假面舞会那五彩缤纷的欢悦之中，我却被病态的压抑感弄得心情沉重。

在庆典开始的前一晚，学校的一位老师曾问了我有关《霜之王》的一个问题。我告诉她，沙利文小姐曾跟我谈起过杰克·费罗斯特，以及他那些精湛的作品。但我的某些话却使她误认为我承认了自己确实记得坎比小姐的故事《冰霜精灵》。虽然我一再重申她明显是理解错了，但她还是把这一结论报告给了阿纳戈诺斯先生。

于是，一向对我和蔼可亲的阿纳戈诺斯先生认为我欺骗了他，他对那些认为我清白的辩护充耳不闻。他相信或至少是怀疑，沙利文小姐和我故意偷

---

[1]一种精心设计集戏剧、音乐和舞蹈表演为一体的综艺节目。
[2]色列斯是罗马的农业女神。

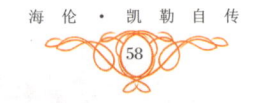

窃了别人的思想精华,再用这些思想成果去欺骗他,以博得他的赞美。我被带到一个由学校老师和官员组成的调查法庭上接受质询,沙利文小姐被要求暂时回避。我被翻来覆去地问讯,这令我感到他们似乎是在强迫我承认有人给我读过坎比小姐的《冰霜精灵》。虽然我无法用文字把一切感受表述出来,但我觉得他们提的每一个问题都暴露出他们的满腹狐疑,我也觉察到那位慈爱的朋友正在以责备的目光看着我。我血脉贲张,心怦怦直跳,除了能说出几个单音节词外,几乎无言以对。即使我意识到这只是一个可怕的误解,却仍然无法释放内心的痛苦。最后,当我被允许离开这间屋子时,我感到一片茫然。虽然沙利文老师和朋友们都说我是一个勇敢的小姑娘,大家为我感到骄傲,但我根本没注意到他们的安慰。

当晚,我躺在床上哭泣,我希望世上不要再有其他孩子像我这样痛哭流涕。我浑身很冷,我想象着在明早来临之前我将死去,这个想法使我略感安慰。我想,假如我年龄再大些时才碰到这样悲伤的事,那么我一定会精神崩溃、难以复原的。在这段忧伤的日子里,多谢遗忘天使带走了大部分的不幸和痛苦,让我重新振作起来。

沙利文小姐从未听说过《冰霜精灵》,也从未听说过发表这篇文章的那本书。在亚历山大·格雷汉姆·贝尔博士的协助下,她仔细调查了这件事。最后发现,1888年,索菲娅·C.霍普金斯夫人有过一本坎比小姐的《小鸟和他的朋友们》的复印件,而这年夏天,我们正好和她一起在布鲁斯特度假。霍普金斯夫人已经找不到那份复印件了,但她告诉我,当时沙利文小姐休假外出,她为了让我开心,常常给我读五花八门的书籍。虽然她比我还更记不清是否念过《冰霜精灵》,但她确信她给我读过《小鸟和他的朋友们》。她解释之所以找不到这本书的原因是:在她卖掉房子之前,曾处理了许多青少年读物,诸如老课本和童话故事之类,《小鸟和他的朋友们》很可能就在被处理的书籍之列。

那时,这些故事并没有给我留下什么印象,

但是对于我这个没什么娱乐活动可消遣的孩子而言，仅仅拼写那些奇特的生词就足以令我心花怒放了。虽然我一点也回想不起自己曾读过那个故事，但我却情不自禁地想起自己孜孜不倦地背诵生词的情景。在老师休假归来后，我马上让她给我讲解那些生词。因此，有一件事是确凿无疑的，那就是书中的句子已永远地镌刻在我脑海里了，虽然在很长时间里没有人、特别是我本人也不知道这一点。

沙利文小姐回来后，我没跟她提起过《冰霜精灵》，也许是因为她一回来就开始给我读《小少爷方特罗伊》[3]，使我无暇顾及其他事。但事实是的确有人曾给我念过坎比小姐的那篇故事。随着时间流逝，我忘了这件事。当故事情节自然而然地浮现在我脑海里时，我根本就不曾怀疑它是别人的智慧结晶。

在我深陷痛苦之时，我收到了许多表示友善和同情的慰问，他们都来自我最亲爱的朋友。其中有一人，我对她的关怀至今仍念念不忘。

那就是坎比小姐，她亲自写信向我表达关爱，信中说："将来有一天，你一定会写出源自你自己头脑的精彩故事，这将使许多人备感欣慰，也会使许多人获得鼓舞。"但她的预言还未曾实现，我再也不想舞文弄墨了，哪怕是仅仅作为一种游戏和娱乐。实际上，从那以后，我总害怕自己写出的东西不是源于自己的思想，并为此深受折磨。在很长一段时间里，每当我写信时，甚至在给妈妈写信时，都会被突如其来的恐惧所攫住。我会反复拼读那些句子，以确保我不曾从哪本书中读过它们。若不是沙利文小姐坚持不懈地鼓励我，我想自己也许会彻底放弃写作。

事实上，那时我不但读了《冰霜精灵》，我还发现自己写的一些信中运

---

[3]出版于1887年的一部非常畅销的小说，作者是出生于英国的美国作家弗朗西斯·霍奇森·伯内特（1849—1924），书中讲的是一个美国小男孩成为英国伯爵的巨大财富继承人的故事。

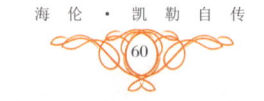

用了坎比小姐的观点。如在1891年9月29日给阿纳戈诺斯先生的信中，有一些遣词造句和观点与那本书真的有相似之处。当时我正在写《霜之王》，从这封信和其他许多信中的短语可以看出，我的思想深受那篇故事的影响。在文中，我代表自己的老师，向我本人描述那金色的秋叶："是的，它们美不胜收，在夏季飞逝之后，带给我们五彩斑斓的慰藉。"——这是直接源自坎比小姐故事里的观点。

  我习惯于消化吸收那些自己喜爱的文字，然后再把它们运用到我早期的信件和最初试写的作文中。我曾在一篇作文中，写到了希腊和意大利的古老城市，我借用了一些栩栩如生、多姿多彩的描写，但那些描写的出处我却忘记了。我知道阿纳戈诺斯先生对于文物古迹情有独钟，对希腊和意大利的美好风物更是热情有加。因此我就从自己读过的书中，收集相关的诗歌和历史知识，从而给他带来快乐。阿纳戈诺斯先生在谈到我那篇有关城市的作文时说："本质上充满了富有诗意的想象。"但我不明白他为什么会认为一个11岁的失聪且失明的孩子能够创造出这样的作品。当然，我也不认为由于自己写的不是源于自己思想的东西，我的文章就毫无趣味了。毕竟，这篇文章表明了我已能用生动流畅的语言，来表达我对那些诗意盎然的美好思想的理解。

  那些早期的作文都是思想上的体操运动。我像所有没有经验的年轻人那样学习，通过吸收和模仿，把观点付诸文字。凡是书中令我感兴趣的东西，我都会有意或无意地存在记忆里。正如史蒂文森[④]所述，年轻作者会本能地去模仿自己最钦慕的作品，然后再把这些作品转换为多姿多彩、令人惊叹的文学形式。哪怕是伟人，也要经过若干年这样的历练，才能对那些汩汩涌现在大脑中的千千万万个词汇信手拈来，运用自如。

[④] 罗伯特·路易斯·史蒂文森（1850－1894），苏格兰小说家和随笔作家。

恐怕我至今仍未完成这个过程。我确实常常不能区分我自己的思想和我从书上读到的思想，而我读到的东西往往会成为我思想的组成部分。但是，几乎在我写的所有文章里，都创造了某些东西，它们类似于我初学缝纫时，所补缀出的杂七杂八的百衲衣。这件百衲衣由各种零碎的布头组成——虽有几小块华丽的丝绸和天鹅绒，但更多的则是手感粗糙的粗布。同样的，我的文章也是由我自己的一些未经加工的天然思想所组成，但其中也蕴涵着我读过的一些作者的璀璨思想和成熟理念。对我来说，似乎写作的最大困难就是当自己本能的思绪还处于杂乱无章的状态时，如何用受过教育的大脑去组织语言，来表达我混乱的思绪、不成熟的情感和观念。尝试写文章与努力去解开九连环等中国智力玩具非常相似。我们脑子里勾勒出一幅图式，希望把它用语言表达出来，但这语言又与那幅图式不匹配，或者文字根本不适用于这个范畴。可我们还是不断尝试，因为我们知道有人成功了，而我们也不愿做失败者。

史蒂文森曾说："除非是有先天禀赋，否则没有人能仅靠后天努力就成为有独创性的人。"虽然或许我没有这种天赋，但我仍希望有朝一日，我的文章能日臻完善，不再带有那些人造的、假发般的成分。也只有到那时，可能我自己的思想和经历才会在文章中显现。所以，我满怀信念和希望，百折不挠地坚持着，努力不让《霜之王》的苦涩记忆阻挡我前进的步伐。

由此看来，这段悲伤的经历可能也给我带来了益处，它促使我去思考有关写作的一些问题。我唯一的遗憾是，它导致我失去了一位最可敬的朋友，阿纳戈诺斯先生。

当我在《妇女家庭杂志》上发表了《我生活的故事》后，阿纳戈诺斯先生给梅西先生写了一封信，他在信中写道：在处理《霜之王》事件时，他相信我是清白无辜的。他说，我被带入的那个调查法庭由八个人组成：其中四人是盲人，另外四人是有视力的人。当时，共有四人认为我知晓有人曾给我念过坎比小姐的那篇故事，但其他人则持不同观点。阿纳戈诺斯先生声明，

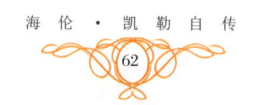

他和那些相信并认同我的人观点一致，并投了他的票。

　　但是，不论这事是如何定夺的，也不论阿纳戈诺斯先生投票时是站在哪一边的，一切都已过去。以前，在那间被用作法庭的屋子里，阿纳戈诺斯先生常常把我抱在他膝上，给了我许多关爱，还和我一起嬉戏玩闹。可是那天，当我走进那间屋子时，我发觉里面的人似乎在怀疑我，我感到那里弥漫着某种敌意和威胁恐吓的气氛，而随后发生的事也证明了我的那种感觉。整整两年间，阿纳戈诺斯先生似乎已相信我和沙利文小姐是无辜的。然而，我也不知是什么原因，他又用确凿的证据撤回了对我有利的判决。我不知道此次调查的详细情况，我也从不知道那些不为我说话的"法庭"成员的姓名。当时我太激动了，以至于没有关注其他事；我也太害怕了，以至于不敢问任何问题。事实上，我几乎也想不起当时自己说过的话，或者别人跟我说了些什么。

　　我之所以要详细记述《霜之王》事件，一是因为它在我的生活和教育中占有重要地位；二是为了消除误解。我必须把所有事实原原本本地展示出来，我不想为自己辩护，也不想责怪任何人。

第 15 章

芝加哥世界博览会

《霜之王》事件的苦涩记忆影响深远。但凯勒并未因此一蹶不振,她的心理和思想被锻炼得更加成熟。对于世界、人类及生活,她依然满怀新奇之心。但她也从一名只对童话故事和玩具感兴趣的小孩子,成长为能从平凡世界中感悟出真善美的人。

《霜之王》事件发生之后,我和家人一起在阿拉巴马度过了那年的夏季和冬季。那些与家人团聚的时光,总是很愉快。万事万物都经历了抽枝发芽、竞相怒放的过程。归家的欢乐让我把《霜之王》事件忘到了九霄云外。

当地面上铺满了红彤彤、金灿灿的秋叶时,花园尽头凉亭上那硕果累累、散发着麝香味的葡萄,也在阳光的照耀下变成了金黄褐色。此时离我写《霜之王》刚好一年,我开始酝酿着用笔勾勒我的生活。

我对写东西依然十分谨慎。我总是担心写出的东西可能并不完全来源于自己的思想,这一念头时时折磨着我。除了我的老师以外,其他人都不知道我有这种恐惧心理。我异常敏感,绝不愿再提《霜之王》。常常在谈话时,某种灵感闪过我的脑海,我就会轻柔地拼写给老师:"我不能肯定这是否是我的原创。"有时,我正写到一段话的中间,却突然暗自思忖:"你写的这些东西可能早已被别人写过啦!"接着,一阵戏谑般的恐惧攫住了我的手,这一天我就无心再写下去了。即使是现在，我有时也会同样感到不安和焦虑。沙利文小姐千方百计地安慰和帮助我，但那次可怕的经历却给我的心灵造成了长久的伤害，我渐渐明白这伤害有多么深重。为了让我重新扬起自信的风帆，老师鼓励我给《青年之友》写一篇短小精悍的生活自传。那时我只有12岁，现在回头看看，自己创作这篇小故事时也经历了一番内心挣扎，也许我已预感到这次努力会给我带来好运，否则我肯定不能坚持写完的。

在老师的敦促下，我小心翼翼、战战兢兢，但却义无反顾地动笔了。老师知道，只要我坚持不懈地写下去，我就又能找回精神上的立足点，展现自我的才能。在《霜之王》事件发生以前，我过的是小孩子那无忧无虑的生活；但现在我变得内敛了，并注意到了一些无形的东西。磨难使我的思维更加清晰，也更透彻地领悟了生活的本质。慢慢地，我走出了那段经历的阴影。

1893年，我经历的几件大事包括在克利夫兰总统的就职典礼期间的华盛顿之旅，参观了尼亚加拉瀑布和世界博览会①。在这种情况下，我的学业不时地被打断，常常要搁置好几个星期，所以我也就不可能对自己的整个进程做连贯的描述。

我们是在1893年3月去尼亚加拉的。当站在飞流直下的美国大瀑布②的悬崖边上，感受着空气的震动和地面的颤抖时，真是难以用语言描述自己的激动心情。

我竟可以感受到尼亚加拉大瀑布的壮观和美丽，这点对许多人来说似乎都是不可思议的。他们反复追问我："这美景和声音对你有什么意义呢？你看不到惊涛拍岸，也听不到巨浪咆哮，它们对你有什么意义呢？"其实，我最明显的感觉是，它们能代表一切。就如同我能领悟和解释"爱""信仰"

---

①指的是1893年的哥伦布纪念博览会，又名芝加哥世界博览会，是一个巨型展览，展出了娱乐项目、艺术品、科技成果和商业发明。
②尼亚加拉瀑布，位于美国和加拿大边境。

或"善良"一样，我也完全能领悟和解释美景和声音对我的意义。

　　1893年夏，我、沙利文小姐以及亚历山大·格雷汉姆·贝尔博士一起参观了世界博览会。每当我回忆起那几天，心里就充满了最纯净的快乐。我那千千万万个童贞的幻想，都在那几天变成了美妙的现实。我似乎天天都在周游世界，我见识了世界各地林林总总的奇观——伟大的发明、工业的结晶、精湛的技艺，以及多姿多彩的人类生活，都一一在我的指尖之下滑过。

　　我喜欢参观大道乐园，它就像是《一千零一夜》这本书一样，琳琅满目地陈列着各种新奇而有趣的事物：有我的书籍里描述过的摆着湿婆神③和象神的奇异印度街市；还有浓缩在开罗城模型里的金字塔之乡、清真寺和长长的驼队；远处是威尼斯的环礁湖，每晚华灯初上、喷泉闪闪发光之时，我们就泛舟湖上。我还登上了一艘维京海盗船，它与那些小巧的手工艺品相距不远。以前在波士顿，我曾登上过一艘军舰，所以，我对这只海盗船倍感兴趣，想看看船上水手曾经历的生活。总而言之，我想了解水手是如何航行、如何以大无畏的精神镇定自若，迎战风暴的；我还想追逐那些水手"我们属于大海！"的呼喊，凭借智慧与力量在大海中搏击，自强自立，自给自足，而不希望像今天的水手那样，被湮没在愚蠢的机械文明中。由此看来——"男人只应做属于男人的事。"④

　　离这船不远处，是一艘"圣玛丽亚号"船⑤的模型，我仔细参观了这艘船。船长向我展示了哥伦布的驾驶室和放着一个沙漏的甲板。这个小小的沙漏令我印象深刻，它使我不由地想起：当陷入绝望的水手们正密谋反对哥伦布时，这位英勇无畏的航海家看着沙子一粒接一粒地往下坠落，他一定也感到疲惫不堪吧？

　　世界博览会主席希金博特姆先生友好地允许我抚摸展品。我就如同当年

---

③湿婆神是印度教中兼具毁灭与再生双重性格的神。
④此句出自生于苏格兰的英国作家托马斯·卡莱尔（1795—1881）所著的《法国革命》。
⑤1492年，哥伦布航行到新大陆时所使用的三艘船中的一艘。

皮泽洛[6]在秘鲁掳掠珍宝那样，急切而贪婪地用手指去领悟博览会的精华。西部的白城建筑群就像是一个触手可及的万花筒，里面的每件展品都令我心醉神迷，尤其是那些法国的青铜艺术品，如此惟妙惟肖，以至于我想它们应该是艺术家捕捉了天使的形象后，又以尘世的形式塑造出来的。

在好望角[7]展区，我了解了许多钻石开采的知识。只要有可能，我就去摸那些正开动着的机器，以便对钻石怎样称重、切割和抛光有更清晰的理解。我在洗出的矿物里搜寻，亲自找到了一块钻石——人们告诉我它是在美国发现的唯一一块真正的钻石。

贝尔博士陪同我们四处参观，用他那令人愉快的方式向我描述那些趣味无穷的展品。在电子大厦里，我们参观了电话机、对讲机、留声机及其他一些发明。贝尔博士使我了解了信息是如何超越时空限制，通过双层模拟电线传递的，这如同普罗米修斯[8]从天上盗取火种一样神奇。我们还参观了人类学展厅，我对古代墨西哥的遗迹以及那些常被当作某个时代唯一记录的粗糙石器颇感兴趣，这是大自然的孩子们在未创造出文字以前留下的简易纪念品（这是我在用手触摸它们时的感想），似乎只有它们能流传千古，而那些国王和圣人们的功劳簿却早已灰飞烟灭。但在埃及的木乃伊面前我却缩回了手，不敢触摸。通过这些遗物，我对人类的进程有了进一步的了解，这远比我曾听到或读到的知识要广博得多。

所有这些经历，大大丰富了我的词汇量，使我掌握了许多专用名词术语。在博览会上度过的三个星期，令我的思想产生了极大的飞跃，从一名只对童话故事和玩具感兴趣的小孩子，成长为能从平凡世界中感悟出真善美的人。

[6]法兰西斯克·皮泽洛（约1470－1541），一名西班牙的殖民者和秘鲁的征服者。
[7]非洲大陆的最南端，现在是南非的一部分。
[8]在古希腊神话中，普罗米修斯从众神处窃走了天火并交给人类。为此，他受到了处罚，被用锁链缚在一块岩石上，每天都有一只饿鹰来啄食他的肝脏。

我 生 活 的 故 事

第 16 章

学习拉丁语

在凯勒的世界里,学习不仅是一项任务,它也是娱乐和消遣,更是通向外部世界的唯一一扇大门。综观凯勒的一生,她对语言学习的热情始终不减。法语、拉丁语这些外语的一一掌握,不仅令她的阅读面得以拓展,更令她掌握了种种新的表达工具,使得她的"思想穿越精神的天空"。

1893年10月以前,我用一种多少有些散乱无章的方式自学了许多科目。我阅读了希腊、罗马和美国的历史。我有一本盲文版法语语法书,而且我对法语已略知一二,所以我常常用偶然碰到的新词,在脑海里做一些短小的练习,以此来自娱自乐,但我不太理会那些语法规则和技术性问题。当我发现那本语法书还讲解了所有的字母和音节的发音时,我甚至尝试在无人帮助的情况下去掌握法语发音。当然,这是一项我力所不能及的重任,但这种学习至少使我在下雨天不会无所事事。随后,我所掌握的法语知识足够令我可以津津有味地阅读拉·封丹的《寓言诗》、莫里哀的《屈打成医》和拉辛的戏剧《阿达莉》[①]的片断。

我也拿出相当多的时间来提高说话能力。我对着沙利文小姐大声朗读,

[①] 若望·德·拉·封丹(1621—1695),在《伊索寓言》的基础上,创作了很受欢迎的寓言;《屈打成医》是法国喜剧作家莫里哀(1622—1673)所著的戏剧;《阿达莉》是法国剧作家让·拉辛(1639—1699)所著的戏剧。

背诵我最喜欢的诗歌片断，而她则纠正我的发音，帮助我划分句子，并教我让语调抑扬顿挫。这些都已保留在我的记忆之中。但是，直到1893年10月，当我从参观世博会的疲倦和激动中恢复过来之后，我才开始在固定时间内学习一些特殊课程。

那时，我和沙利文老师正在宾夕法尼亚州的休尔顿市，探访威廉·韦德先生②一家。他们的邻居艾恩斯先生是一位优秀的拉丁语学者，我被安排跟他学习。我记得他是一位生性乐观、亲切和蔼且博学多闻的人，他主要教我拉丁语语法，但他也常常帮助我解决算术难题，可我总觉得算术是令人讨厌且枯燥无味的一门学科。艾恩斯先生还陪我一起阅读丁尼生的《悼念集》③。虽然以前我也读过很多书，但从未怀着批判性的态度去读书。这是我第一次学着去了解一位作者，认识他的风格，就像通过握手来辨认朋友一样。

最初，我极不愿意学拉丁语语法。我认为当词意十分明确时，还浪费时间去分析我遇到的每一个词——名词、所有格、单数、阴性等等，这似乎非常荒唐可笑。为了描述我的宠物猫，我倒可以用此法来一试——目：脊椎动物；门：四足动物；纲：哺乳动物；属：猫属；种：猫；个体：虎斑猫。但随着我逐渐深入这门学科，我对它的兴趣也日益浓厚，拉丁语的优美令我心醉神迷。我常常读一些拉丁语的文章段落来自娱自乐，同时，挑选一些我认识的词语，努力去理解其中含义。我从未停止过享受这种消遣。

我认为最美好的事，莫过于能用一种刚熟悉的语言去表现稍纵即逝的形象和感情——这仿佛是用变幻莫测的想象力去塑造思想，为其增添绚丽的色彩，而那些思想又穿越精神的天空。上课时，沙利文小姐会坐在我旁边，在我手上拼写出艾恩斯先生所说的一切，并帮我查一些新词。当我返回亚拉巴马州的家中时，我就开始读恺撒的《高卢战记》了。

②一位帮助盲人和聋人的慈善家。
③阿尔弗雷德·丁尼生男爵（1809－1892）是维多利亚时代英国最著名的诗人，在凯勒生活的时代，他非常受欢迎。

第 17 章

在纽约求学

凯勒的聪颖好学为她带来了全新的学习机会。莱特—休梅森聋人学校的教学更加专业、系统，在这里，她很快又掌握了一门新的语言——德语。这种惊人的学习能力和成长速度令常人也难望其项背。

1894 年夏天，我参加了"美国聋人语言教学促进协会"在肖托夸举办的文化讲习班。根据安排，我应该前往纽约市的莱特—休梅森聋人学校就读。1894 年 10 月，沙利文小姐陪同我到了那里。之所以专门为我选择这所学校，是因为它在发音训练和读唇训练方面有着极强的优势。我将在这所学校学习两年，除了上述训练外，我还将学习算术、自然地理、法语和德语等课程。

我的德语老师瑞米小姐会用手语。在我掌握了一些德语词汇后，我们就利用一切机会用德语交谈，几个月后，我几乎就能弄懂她说的任何事了。不到一年，我就能趣味盎然地阅读《威廉·泰尔》[①]了。的确，我认为自己在学德语方面的进步比学其他科目都要大。而且我觉得法语比德语更难。教我法语的奥利维尔夫人是位不懂手语的法国女士，她只能以口授来教我。但我

[①] 德国作家弗里德里希·冯·席勒（1759—1805）创作的戏剧。

很难读懂她的唇语,所以我的法语进步得比德语慢得多。尽管如此,我还是再次重读了《屈打成医》。虽然这本书也很有趣,但我却不像喜欢《威廉·泰尔》那样喜欢它。

我在读唇和说话能力方面的进步,并没有像我和老师曾希望和期待的那样快。我有要像其他人一样说话的雄心壮志,我的老师也坚信我能实现这一志向。但是,尽管我们坚持不懈地刻苦训练,却没有达到预期的目标。我想这也许是因为我们的目标定得太高了,难免会产生失望。我仍旧把算术看作是一个充满陷阱的系统。我在"猜想"的危险边缘荡来荡去,还要避免给自己以及别人惹一身深奥推理的麻烦。每当我没有乱猜时,我就会直接跳到结论,这样只会错上加错。此外,我感官上的缺陷更加剧了我理解的困难。

虽然有时这些令人失望的事会使我深感沮丧,但我对其他功课,尤其是自然地理却有着浓厚的兴趣,能孜孜不倦地认真学习,并觉得探索自然的奥秘是一件令人快乐的事。比如,风如何就像《圣经·旧约》描述的那样自天堂的四个角落吹遍四方;水蒸气是怎样从陆地的尽头向上升腾的;河流是如何绕过岩石迂回前进的;山脉如何被从底部震塌;以及人类又是如何战胜那许多比自己强大的力量的。在纽约学习的那两年我过得非常快乐,每当忆起那段时光,总有许多的乐趣令我回味无穷。

我特别记得,每天我们都要一起去中央公园散步,这座公园是纽约城里唯一与我趣味相投的地方。在这座大公园里,我从未遗漏掉半点快乐。我喜欢对每一次的公园漫步进行描述,因为这里的美无处不在,我在纽约度过的九个月里,时时都能感受到中央公园那日新月异的盛景丽境。

春天,我们进行了多次短途旅行,游览了风格迥异的有趣地方。我们在哈德逊河上泛舟,在布赖恩特②曾经吟唱的芳草依依的河岸上漫步。我喜欢那些质朴荒凉、宏伟庄严的河边断崖。此外，我们还参观了西点军校、作家华盛顿·欧文的故乡塔瑞镇等地，在欧文的故乡，我们还在"睡谷"③里走了一遭。

莱特—休梅森聋人学校的老师们总是千方百计地让学生们发挥优势，尽可能让他们接收到有听力的孩子所享有的教育。对于年幼的学生，老师们会充分利用他们的兴趣爱好和记忆力强的能力，引导他们走出生活环境所带来的束缚。

但在我离开纽约前，我那些欢乐的日子却被巨大的悲哀所吞没。这是我有生以来，除了父亲去世外，所感受到的最大痛苦。波士顿的约翰·P.斯伯丁先生④于1896年2月去世了。只有那些最了解和敬爱他的人，才能懂得他的友谊对我意味着什么。他用令人如沐春风、润物细无声的方式，把快乐带给了身边的每一个人，他对我和沙利文小姐总是和蔼可亲、热情周到。每当我们感受到他的慈爱，知道他非常关心我们的生活时，尽管前路充满了重重险阻，我们也不会垂头丧气。他的逝世，给我们的生活带来了永远无法弥补的损失。

---

②威廉·卡伦·布赖恩特（1794—1878），美国诗人和编辑。

③《睡谷的传说》是美国作家华盛顿·欧文（1783—1859）撰写的一篇通俗故事，他还著有《瑞普·凡·温克尔》。

④波士顿的一位慈善家，他曾资助过凯勒。

第 18 章

剑桥女子学院

以常人难以想象的勇气和毅力去克服即使是常人也难逾越的重重障碍,达到常人亦难以企及的目标和高度,这是凯勒的经历中最撼动人心的所在。上大学是很多少年的梦想,而凯勒在小时候就树立了"一定要上哈佛大学"的坚定理想。在这一章中我们将读到凯勒为实现理想是如何迈进的。

1896年10月,我进入剑桥青年女子学院学习,为进入哈佛大学拉德克利夫学院做准备。

当我还是个小女孩时,曾去韦尔斯利学院参观,在那里,我发表了宣言:"将来有一天我也要上大学——并且我一定要上哈佛大学!"这令我的朋友们无比惊讶。当我被问道为什么不上韦尔斯利学院时,我回答说:"因为这所学院只招女生。"之后,上大学的想法就在我心里生了根,并且进而变成一个诚挚的愿望。这个愿望激励着我不顾许多真诚而明智的朋友们的竭力反对,去与那些能看得见,也听得见的姑娘们一起竞争,以赢得一纸学位。在我离开纽约时,这个愿望已变成了一个坚不可摧的目标,因此我下定决心去剑桥学习。这是能促使我迈进哈佛校门、实现幼年宣言的最便捷的一条路。

在剑桥学院,沙利文小姐被安排同我一起上课,为我翻译课程内容。

当然，我的教师们没有任何教授非正常学生的经验，而我与他们交流的唯一方法就是读他们的嘴唇。我第一年学习的科目有英国历史、英国文学、德语、拉丁语、算术、拉丁语写作和一些临时课程。当时，我还没有计划要选择学习某些课程，以便为上大学做准备。但就英语这科来说，由于沙利文小姐的教导，我对此早已训练有素。所以我的老师们很快就明白，对于这一科我并不需要特别的辅导，只需对学校指定的课本做一些重点学习即可。此外，我的法语基础很好，还曾专门学习了六个月的拉丁语，而德语则是我最熟悉的科目。

尽管我有这些优势，但仍有重重障碍阻挠着我前进。沙利文小姐不可能把所有指定的书籍都拼写在我手上。虽然我在伦敦和费城的朋友们愿意加班加点地为我赶制盲文课本，但他们还是很难及时将课本印成盲文供我使用。因此，有一段时间，我不得不将拉丁语课文用盲文抄写下来，这样我才能和其他姑娘们一起同步完成背诵。我的老师们很快就熟悉了我那不太标准的发音，他们能及时解答我的问题并纠正我的错误。虽然我在课堂上无法记笔记或做练习，但我回家后，会用打字机写完所有的作文并完成翻译作业。

沙利文小姐每天都和我一起去上课，她会无比耐心地把所有老师的授课内容拼写在我手上。在我学习时，她还要帮我查生词，反复为我读笔记和那些还没有盲文版的书籍。这项工作之单调乏味是令人难以想象的。我的德语老师格罗特夫人和学校负责人吉尔曼先生[1]是全校仅有的两位能用手语给我上课的老师。没有人能切实体会到亲爱的格罗特夫人的拼写是多么缓慢和不熟练。尽管如此，她仍怀着一颗善良的心，专门一周两次勤勉地为我拼写她的授课内容，从而让沙利文小姐稍事休息。虽然大家对我们都很友好，并随时准备帮助我们，但只有沙利文小姐的"一只手"才能把这份单调乏味的苦差变成令我高兴愉快的乐事。

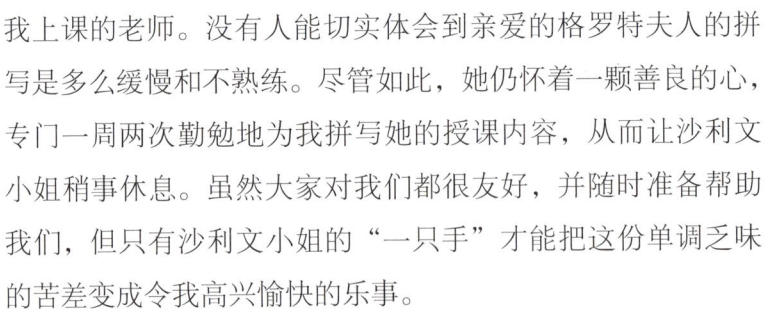

[1] 亚瑟·吉尔曼（1837—1909），是剑桥学院的创始人和校长。

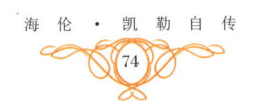

海伦·凯勒自传

这一年，我学完了算术，复习了拉丁语语法，还读完了三章恺撒的《高卢战记》。另外，一半靠自己的手指，一半靠沙利文小姐的帮助，我还阅读了一些德文著作，如席勒的《钟之歌》和《潜水者》、海涅的《哈尔茨山游记》、弗莱塔克的《腓特烈大帝统治时代散记》、里尔的《美的诅咒》、莱辛的《明娜·冯·巴恩赫姆传》以及歌德的《诗和真》。这些德文书籍里包含的席勒优美的抒情诗、腓特烈大帝取得丰功伟绩的历史，以及歌德的生活记事等都使我兴致盎然。读完了《哈尔茨山游记》后，我仍觉得意犹未尽，这本书里妙语连珠，对蔓藤覆盖的山峦进行了引人入胜的描述：溪流在阳光下潺潺流淌，一路欢歌；在传说和传奇文学中提到的偏僻荒野，有着久已消失、风华正茂的"灰衣姐妹"——只有那些把大自然看作是有"一种感情、一种爱恋和一种嗜好"[2]的人，才能够写出如此生动的描绘。

吉尔曼先生曾在这年抽时间辅导我学习英国文学。我们一起阅读了《皆大欢喜》、伯克的《论与美洲殖民地和解演讲》和麦考利的《塞缪尔·约翰逊传记》[3]。吉尔曼先生有着渊博的历史和文学知识，他的讲解惟妙惟肖，使我能在轻松愉快的氛围中学习，学习效果远比只是在课堂上机械地阅读带有短语注释的笔记要好得多。

伯克的演讲集是我所读过的政治书籍中最具有教育意义的。我的心随着那个动荡的时代而跌宕起伏。书中围绕着中心人物，活灵活现地在我面前展现了两个相互竞争国家的世间百态。令我百思不得其解的是，当伯克那高超

---

[2]参见威廉·华兹华斯的诗作《廷特恩修道院》。
[3]为英国作家和历史学家托马斯·巴宾顿·麦考利（1800－1859）所著。塞缪尔·约翰逊（1709－1784）是一位有名的作家和文学评论家，也被认为是第一部英语字典的编写者。

的演讲汇集成气势磅礴、滔滔不绝的雄辩时，乔治国王和他的大臣们怎么可能对他那"我们美国的胜利和他们英国的耻辱"的预警置若罔闻呢？然后，我开始研读那些令人忧伤的细节，里面讲述了这位伟大的政治家与他的党派和人民代表的关系。我想，像这样一粒宝贵而聪慧的真理种子，竟然落在了无知而腐朽的稗子之中，这是多么的奇怪啊！

麦考利的《塞缪尔·约翰逊传记》则因另一种风格而生动有趣。我的心牵挂着那位孤独的人，他在格拉布街（以前英国穷苦文人集居的街道）吞咽着困苦饼[4]。然而，即使在身体和心灵备受摧残和折磨的情况下，他仍能给那些穷苦不堪、受人歧视的人们送上温馨的话语，并伸出援助的双手。我为他的成功而欢欣鼓舞，却对他的缺陷视若无睹。我想弄明白的不是他有没有缺陷，而是这种缺陷为什么没能摧毁他的意志，并使他的形象黯然失色呢？麦考利妙笔生花，他能把寻常事物描绘得生动而清新，这真令人赞叹！他的断言偶尔也会令我感到厌倦，但他为探求真理而孜孜以求的精神，使我看待事物的态度变得更加理性了。这与我在聆听了"大不列颠的德摩斯梯尼"[5]的演说后所产生的崇敬之情是截然不同的。

在剑桥学校，我平生第一次感受到了那些与我同龄的、能看见和听见的姑娘们的友情。我与几个同学住在与学校相连的一幢舒适的房子里，豪厄尔斯先生[6]曾在这里住过，在此可以充分享受家居生活的乐趣。我参与了同学们的许多游戏活动，甚至在雪中捉迷藏、搞恶作剧；我和她们一起远足；我们会讨论功课，并大声朗读我们感兴趣的作品。有几个女孩甚至还学会了同

---

[4] 指以色列人逃离埃及后不得不准备的未经发酵的面包（《圣经·旧约·申命记》16：3）。

[5] 德摩斯梯尼（公元前384—322）为古希腊的雄辩家。

[6] 指美国作家威廉·迪安·豪厄尔斯（1837—1920）。

我"讲话",这样沙利文小姐就不必为我再重复她们的谈话了。

那一年,我母亲和小妹妹陪我一起度过了圣诞节,吉尔曼先生友好地提议让米尔德丽德也来这所学校学习。所以米尔德丽德和我一起在剑桥度过了快乐的六个月时光,期间我们几乎形影不离。我们在学习上互相帮助,一起休闲娱乐。每当我回忆起这段时光,总是乐滋滋的。

1897年6月29日至7月3日,我参加了拉德克利夫学院的预备考试。我报考的科目有初级和高级德语、法语、拉丁语、英语、希腊语和罗马历史,总共考了九小时。我通过了所有的考试,而且德语和英语成绩都是"优"。

在此,我介绍一下自己参加考试的方式也无伤大雅吧。考生们被要求进行总共十六个小时的测试——包括十二个小时的初级考试和四个小时的高级考试。做完这些试卷一般需要五个小时。试卷于早上九点钟从哈佛大学发出,由一位专门信使送到拉德克利夫。每位报考者都有一个登记的考号,而不是用姓名来登记。我是233号,由于我必须使用打字机,所以我的身份是无法隐瞒的。

校方考虑周全,我被单独安排在一个房间考试,以免我的打字机发出的噪音影响其他姑娘。吉尔曼先生亲自用手语为我读了所有的试卷。为了不受干扰,房间门口还设置了一名门卫。

第一天,我参加了德语考试。吉尔曼先生坐在我旁边,他先把试卷从头到尾通读一遍,然后再逐字逐句地读;同时,我也跟着大声重复,以表明我完全理解了他。试卷很难,我一边用打字机打出答案,一边也感到有些焦虑不安。吉尔曼先生把我的答案拼写给我,如果我觉得有必要,还可以做一些修改,由他帮我把修改插入答案中。在这里,我想说的是,此后,在我参加的所有考试中,再也没有这样的优惠待遇了。在拉德克利夫学院,开考后,没有人会为我读考卷。除非我提前做完答卷,否则我也没机会修改错误。如果还有多余的时间,那么监考老师允许我利用这几分钟,根据自己的记忆来修改错误,并在我的试卷底部做修改备注。假如说我的预试成绩要比终试好得多的话,那是因为两个原因:一是终试时没人为我读我的答案;二是预试

时我报考的一些科目在我进入剑桥学校前就比较熟悉。还好,在那一年年初,我已经通过了英语、历史、法语和德语的考试,吉尔曼先生给我用的就是以前的哈佛正规试卷。

最后,吉尔曼先生把我的答卷和一份证明一起交给监考员,证明这是我——第233号报考人独立完成的答卷。

其他几科的预备考试也都是以这种方式进行的,不过后面的几科都没有第一科那么难。我记得在发拉丁语试卷给大家的那天,西林教授进来告诉我,我已圆满通过了德语考试。这一消息令我倍受鼓舞,于是,我怀着轻松的心情,凭着坚定的双手,加速抵达了这场严峻考验的终点。

第 19 章

备考哈佛

自小,沙利文小姐为凯勒的个人教育提供了大量的帮助和扶持,凯勒已经完全依赖这种扶持。但在通往大学之路上,显然她必须减弱这种依赖,掌握应对变化的技术工具,这是非常痛苦而艰难的,但她闯过了一个又一个难关。凯勒如愿按时参加了哈佛拉德克利夫学院的入学终试,她一一攻克了考试中的困难,实现了上大学的梦想。

当我在吉尔曼先生的学校开始第二年的学业时,我满怀希望,对成功充满了信心。但是在最初的几周里,我却遇到了意想不到的难题。吉尔曼先生同意我在这一年主修数学。我还要学物理、代数、几何、天文学、希腊语和拉丁语。不幸的是,我需要的许多书都没有盲文版,因而在学习一些学科时,我缺乏必要的学具,这耽误了我及时跟进课程。我上的都是大课,老师们不可能为我做专门辅导。沙利文小姐不得不把所有的课本读给我听,还要为我翻译老师们的授课内容。十一年来,她那双神奇的手似乎第一次无法胜任这项繁重的工作了。

在课堂上,我必须做代数和几何笔记,解物理题,起初我无法做到,直到我们购买了一台盲文打字机,这些问题才迎刃而解。通过这台打字机,我可以记下我的解题步骤和过程。我无法用眼睛看到那些画在黑板上的几何图

形，所以我弄清这些图形的唯一手段，就是在靠垫上用直的金属丝或带尖头的弧形金属丝拼出各种图形。正如基思先生在他的报告中所说，我不得不把这些图形上的文字、各种假设和结论、证明的推理过程等统统装入我的大脑。总而言之，每一门学科都有其障碍。有时，我会失去所有勇气，并发泄情绪。特别是到后来，当我觉得困难重重时，竟会向沙利文小姐发脾气，而在我所有的朋友中，她是唯一在这里陪伴我的人，她能够"将弯曲的东西拉直，让崎岖之地变成坦途"①。至今想来，我仍羞愧不已。

但是，慢慢地，我的困难开始消失了。当我拿到盲文版书籍和一些学具后，我又恢复了信心，重新投入学习当中。代数和几何仍在继续挑战我的努力，它们是我难以理解的两门功课。正如前面所述，我没有学数学的天分，无法完全弄清不同的点面关系。几何图形尤其令我苦恼不已，因为我无法看见不同图形相互之间的关系，即使在垫子上反复摆弄也难以领悟。直到基思先生来教我之后，我才踏进了几何学的门槛。

正当我开始克服这些困难时，随后发生的事却改变了一切。

就在那些盲文书到来之前，吉尔曼先生劝说沙利文小姐不能让我过度用功。接着，他不顾我诚恳的抗议，减少了我背诵的次数。一开始，我们曾达成协议，如果有必要，我可以用五年的时间为上大学做准备。但是在第一年年末，我以优异的考试成绩向沙利文小姐、哈勃小姐（吉尔曼先生聘用的院长）和另一位老师证明：再用两年多的时间，我也可以不必过度努力，就完成入学准备。起初，吉尔曼先生同意这一观点，但当我对某些功课有些疑惑不解时，他就坚持认为我是用功过度了，我应该在他的学校里再多学习三年时间。但我不喜欢他的计划，因为我希望和班里的其他同学一起进入大学深造。

11月17日早晨，我感觉身体不舒服，就没去上课。虽然沙利文小姐知

---

① 参见《圣经·以赛亚书》（40：4）。

道我的小病并不严重,但是吉尔曼先生听到这消息后,却断言我是被累垮的,并对我的学习进度做出了调整,这将使我不可能与班上的其他同学一起参加期末考试了。最后,吉尔曼先生和沙利文小姐的分歧导致了我母亲让我和米尔德丽德从剑桥学校退学。

耽搁了一段时间后,家人安排来自剑桥的默顿·S.基思先生做我的家庭教师,让我继续学习。我、沙利文小姐,以及我们的朋友们张伯伦[2]一家一起住在离波士顿25英里远的伦瑟姆,在那度过了这年冬天的剩余时光。

1898年2月至7月,基思先生每周来伦瑟姆两次,教我代数、几何、希腊语和拉丁语。沙利文小姐则翻译他的授课内容。

1898年10月,我们返回了波士顿。连续八个月,基思先生每周给我上五节课,每节大约一小时。每次上课,他都给我讲解上一节课我没弄懂的地方,布置新作业,再把我当周用打字机完成的希腊语练习带回家,认真进行批改,等下次上课时又发还给我。

我正是以这种方式,毫不间断地为上大学做准备。我发现,比起在课堂上接受教导,自学要更容易、也更有乐趣。自学时不需要赶时间,也不会对知识点稀里糊涂。我的家庭教师会留出足够的时间,为我讲解不懂的地方。所以,我学得更快了,学习效果也比在学校时好得多。在所有的科目中,我仍认为理解数学难题是最令我头痛的。要是代数和几何能有语言和文学的一半容易就好了!但即使是数学这样的课程,基思先生也能讲得妙趣横生。他

②约瑟夫·埃德加·张伯伦,文学评论家,凯勒的朋友。

成功地将复杂问题分解至我能够理解的最小片段。他令我思维活跃，求知欲旺盛。他训练我缜密推理，冷静而合乎逻辑地寻求结论，而不是天马行空、不着边际地胡乱揣测。他总是温和而宽容，尽管我像榆木疙瘩一样难开窍，我的愚钝甚至会令约伯（《圣经》中的约伯是极有耐心的人）也失去耐心，但他却一直对我抱有信心。

1899年6月29日至30日，我参加了拉德克利夫学院的入学终试。第一天考初级希腊语和高级拉丁语，第二天考几何、代数和高级希腊语。

学院管理层不允许沙利文小姐为我读试卷，所以，学校就聘请帕金斯盲人学院教师尤金·C.维宁先生，用美式布莱叶盲文为我抄写试卷。维宁先生对我而言就是个陌生人，除了通过用盲文书写，他并不同我交流。此外，监考人也是位陌生人，他也不打算同我做任何交流。

盲文足以胜任语言表达，但如果要用盲文表示几何和代数，那就困难重重了。尤其是代数，我在这科上浪费了许多宝贵时间，仍是糊里糊涂，这真使我感到灰心丧气。事实上，我对自己国家通用的所有字母盲文都很熟悉——英式、美式，以及纽约点式；但这三种系统中，对几何和代数的各种符号及标记的表示方法是截然不同的，而我在代数课中，只使用过英式盲文[3]。

在考试前两天，维宁先生给我寄来了一份用盲文抄写的、哈佛以前的代数试卷。当我发现这份试卷用的是美式表达法时，我感到十分焦急。于是，我立即坐下来写信给维宁先生，请他给我解释那些符号的意思。维宁先生在回信中，给我寄了另一份试卷和一张数学符号表，于是我开始着手学习这些表达法。在代数考试的前一天晚上，我还在拼命地分辨那些异常复杂的标注。但还是无法分辨出圆括号、大括号和根号的组合式。基思先生和我都烦忧不

---

[3] 在凯勒的青年时代，美国和英国都有许多种给盲人使用的凸字系统，彼此相互竞争。直到1932年，才有了统一的盲文标准。

安，并对次日的考试有了不祥的预感。好在我们提前一段时间到达学院，维宁先生给我详细解释了美式符号的用法。

在几何考试中，我遇到的主要问题是：过去我一直习惯于阅读一行行印制的命题，或是让人把命题拼写在我手上；但考试时最莫名其妙的是，虽然命题就在我面前，我还是对那些盲文一头雾水，无法把读到的内容清晰地在大脑里组合出来。在考代数时，我感到更加艰难。那些我刚刚学过的符号，本以为我已弄懂它们了，现在却令我茫然不知所措。更糟糕的是，我无法看见自己用打字机打出的答案。以往我总是用盲文做题，或进行心算。基思先生过于注重培养我用心算解题，而没有训练我如何书写试卷。因此，我答题时缓慢而费力，不得不反复阅读答题示例，才能勉强搞清答题要求。其实，直到现在我也不敢说我能正确读懂所有的符号。我发现随机应变实属不易。

但我是不会责怪任何人的。拉德克利夫学院的行政委员会并没有意识到他们为我设置的考试是多么艰难！他们也不会理解我必须要克服怎样的特殊困难才能完成考试！也许他们是无意间在我的道路上设置了障碍，但令我备感欣慰的是我知道自己必将完全攻克这些障碍。

第 20 章

真实的大学

> 大学并非凯勒想象中的浪漫学苑。学生们机械听讲，匆忙做笔记，无暇感悟讲授者的风格，也无暇思考更深层次的问题。与别人相比，凯勒要花费更多时间预习功课、阅读文章，这令她非常急躁。但繁重枯燥的学业修炼了她包容与忍耐的心性，即使她对大学里填鸭式的授课方式，特别是要求学生对文学作品加以牵强附会的分析评论保留自己的态度。

为上大学所进行的奋斗结束了，只要我愿意，我随时都可以进入拉德克利夫了。但在我入学之前，人们认为我最好再跟基思先生学习一年。所以，直到1900年秋天，我才终于实现了上大学的梦想。

我仍记得第一天进入拉德克利夫的情景。对我而言，那是充满趣味的一天，也是多年来我梦寐以求的一天。在我心里升腾着一股强大的力量，它比朋友们的劝说更有效，甚至比我内心的祈求更强烈，它促使我竭尽全力去达到那些耳目健全的人们所能达到的目标。我深知这条路上困难重重，但我渴望克服这些困难。我将睿智的罗马人所说的话牢记于心："虽然被驱逐出罗马，却依旧活在罗马城下。"我不过是被阻挡在了宽阔的知识大道之外，被迫另辟蹊径，越过田野去走人迹罕至的小路——如此而已！我知道大学里有许多这样的小路，在路上，我能用双手触摸到那些像我一样思考、奋斗和热爱生活的姑娘们。

我满腔热忱地开始了大学生活。在我面前，开启了一个光明而美好的新世界；我准备去探求一切未知的奥秘。我想与其他人一样，自由地遨游在这智慧的仙境里。这里的人们、景物、风格、欢乐和悲伤也应是现实世界的真正写照。这里的讲堂应该洋溢着伟人和智者的精神，我把教授们都视作智慧的化身。当然，即使后来我在这里认识到一些有别于此的事实，我也不打算告诉任何人。

但我很快就发现大学并非我想象中的浪漫学苑。那些令年幼无知的我欢欣鼓舞的许多梦想，其美丽的光环却慢慢褪去，"在平淡的日光中黯淡"①。渐渐地，我开始发现上大学也有一些不好的方面。

首先，我感到了时间的紧迫，而时间不够用一直是我最深的感触。以前，我有时间去深思熟虑，慎重表达自己的思想。我们会在夜晚围坐一起，倾听从心灵深处发出的美妙旋律。当然，只有在悠闲自在的时刻，当你喜爱的某位诗人用诗句深深触动了你那静如止水的灵魂，拨动了你那甜美的心弦时，你才能听到这旋律。但在大学里，我却没有时间去冥想，并梳理自己的思想。上大学的目的似乎就是学习，而不是去思考。当你迈入学习的大门后，你就必须把最珍贵的乐趣——独处、书籍和幻想——连同那呼啸的松树林一起留在门外。也许我应该这样想，我现在是为了将来的欢悦而储蓄珍宝，以此来进行自我安慰。但我却是个目光短浅的人，我宁愿要现时的欢悦，也不愿未雨绸缪，去为将来囤积财富。

第一年，我学习的课程有法语、德语、历史、英文写作和英国文学。在法语课上，我阅读了高乃依、莫里哀、拉辛、阿尔弗雷德·德·缪塞和沙尔·奥古斯丁·圣伯夫等人的作品；在德语读物方面，我阅读了歌德和席勒的德语

---

① 参见威廉·华兹华斯的诗作《不朽的暗示》。

著作。我还快速复习了从罗马帝国灭亡到 18 世纪这整个阶段的历史。在英国文学方面，我尝试去学习评论弥尔顿的诗歌和他的著作《论出版自由》。

　　常常有人问我是如何克服在大学学习中所遇到的特殊困难的。的确，在课堂上我确实很孤独。教授的声音很微弱，他仿佛是通过电话来授课。虽然授课内容会以最快的速度拼写在我手上，但为了努力跟上课堂进度，我简直就没有时间去品味老师们的独特魅力。词汇争先恐后地涌入我的手掌，速度快得简直就像是猎犬们在追逐一只它们难以捕获的野兔。但我也不觉得自己的境况比那些能记笔记的姑娘们糟糕多少。我认为如果一个人的大脑已被机械听讲和匆忙在纸上凌乱地做记录所占据，那么她就不大可能去留意应该考虑的主题或去感悟演讲者的风格。我无法在课堂上做笔记，因为我的双手要忙碌地"听课"。所以我回家后，通常会草草记下我所能忆起的内容。我用我的打字机做练习，写每日论文、评论文章，完成课时测验、期中考试和期末考试，这样，教授们就易于发现我的不足之处了。当我开始学习拉丁语音韵学时，我设计出一套符号系统，可以表示不同的韵节和音量（指元音或音节的长短），我还向教授解释了这套系统。

　　我用的是哈蒙德牌打字机。我曾试用过很多打字机，后来终于发现哈蒙德牌打字机最适合我对工作的特殊要求。这种打字机能装上可移动的梭盘，每台可配备若干梭盘，每种梭盘都配有一套不同的字符。你可以根据要打的内容，转换成希腊语、法语或者数学符号。如果没有这种打字机，我简直怀疑自己能否上完大学。

　　在各门功课所指定的课本中，印出盲文版的寥寥无几，所以我不得不请人把那些无盲文版的课文内容拼写在手上。因此，我比别的姑娘们要花费更多的时间来预习功课。用手语阅读耗时更长，而且我还会碰到一些别人不曾有过的困惑。日复一日，我必须专心致志地学习那些琐碎的知识点，这使我感到十分焦躁；一想到自己要花好几个小时才能读完几个章节，别的姑娘有时间尽情地欢笑、歌唱和跳舞,而我却没有,我往往就会忍无可忍。但我很快又恢复了平静,对自己心中的不满也感到可笑。毕竟,每一个渴望获得真才实学的人都必须独自攀登"困难之峰",既然没有捷径通往顶峰,那我只能曲折前进,探寻自己的道路。多少次,我退步了、跌倒了,但我仍会爬起来,向着那无形的障碍奔跑。我每大发一次脾气,就能更好地学会控制自己的情绪。我艰难跋涉,一个小小的收获就使我倍受鼓舞。我满怀期望地攀登,越爬越高,视野也越来越广阔。每一次奋争都是一场胜利。再多一分努力,我就能触及那熠熠生辉的云朵、湛蓝的天空,以及希望的顶峰。而且,在奋斗的道路上,我并不总是孤身一人。威廉·韦德先生和宾夕法尼亚盲人教育学院的负责人 E.E. 艾伦先生为我提供了很多急需的盲文书籍。他们很难想象,他们的周到体贴对我是多么大的帮助和鼓励啊!

去年是我在拉德克利夫学院的第二年,我学习了英文写作、《圣经》文学、美国和欧洲的政体、《贺拉斯颂诗》和拉丁语喜剧。

写作课是最生动、最令人愉快的一门课。课堂上总是妙趣横生,洋溢着轻松活泼、诙谐幽默的气氛。授课教师是查尔斯·汤森德·科普兰先生[2]。以前,我从未见识过像他这样的老师,能带学生品鉴文学作品鲜美的原汁原味和其中蕴涵的力量。在短短的一小时里,没有多余的解释和说明,你可以尽情欣赏前辈大师们所创造出的永恒之美。你会为他们那深邃的思想而着迷;你会全心全意地享受《旧约全书》里那温柔的谴责,以至于忘了雅赫维和艾洛辛上帝[3]的存在;当你回家时,会感觉你已"瞥见精神和形式如此完美地和谐共存;真理和美德从古老的岁月之茎结出了新果"。

---

[2] 查尔斯·汤森德·科普兰先生(1860-1952),曾担任记者和评论员,是哈佛大学非常受学生欢迎的写作课教师。

[3] 雅赫维和艾洛辛是希伯来语对上帝的称呼。

这一年是我最开心的一年,因为所学的都是我很感兴趣的课程,比如经济学、英国伊丽莎白女王时代的文学、由乔治·L.基特里奇教授主讲的莎士比亚,以及由乔赛亚·罗伊斯教授主讲的哲学史。一旦步入哲学的殿堂,就会领略远古时代的传统,并理解那些在不久前似乎还被视为异端邪说的其他思维模式。

大学并不是我想象中的那个百花齐放的"雅典城"④。在这里,你不可能跟那些伟人和先贤进行面对面的交流;你甚至不会感觉到他们栩栩如生的抚摸。他们确实存在于此,但他们似乎已成了木乃伊。大学课堂的学习,要求我们从学问之墙的裂痕中费力地把先贤们抽出来,对他们进行解剖和仔细分析,仿佛唯有如此,我们才能肯定他是弥尔顿或是以赛亚,而不是一个巧妙的仿制品。在我看来,许多学者似乎都忘了,我们之所以会欣赏那些伟大的文学作品,是因为这些作品与我们意气相投,产生了共鸣,而不是因为我们的理解力。更糟的是,老师们煞费苦心地讲解,却没有在学生的记忆中留下多少痕迹。学生的大脑遗弃了这些讲解,如同熟透的果子从枝头坠落一般。如果我们不懂得欣赏沐浴着上天甘露的鲜花,那我们如何可能去弄懂一朵花的根、茎及其他知识呢?又如何能知道它的生长过程呢?一遍又一遍,我焦急地问:"为什么我要关注那些解释和假说呢?"它们像瞎鸟一样在我的思想里到处乱飞,徒劳地扇着无力的翅膀。我的意思不是说我反对透彻理解名著,其实我反对的只是那些冗长的解释和让人困惑的评论,从中我们只能懂得一件事:有多少人就会有多少种观点。但是,当基特里奇教授这样的大学者来诠释莎士比亚的语录时,那确实是"恰如给盲人带来了新的视力"⑤。他仿佛把诗人莎士比亚带到了我们面前。

④雅典是古希腊的首都,曾被视作哲学思想的中心。
⑤参见耶稣治疗盲人[《圣经·路加福音》(7:21)]。

有时我真的渴望自己要学的东西能减少一半，因为如果大脑过度疲劳，就无暇欣赏那些最有价值的思想珍宝。我觉得，如果在一天之内必须阅读四五本不同语言且涉及不同科目的书籍，又要不忽略任何细节，那是不可能的。当一个人一边匆忙而紧张地读书，一边满脑子想着书面测试和考试时，那么他的大脑就会被那些五花八门、没多少用处的小玩意拖住。当时，我的脑子里就塞满了这些杂七杂八的东西，以至于我简直无法理清思路。每当我进入自己的思想王国时，感觉就好像是一头众所周知的公牛闯入了瓷器店。成千上万条零碎的知识点像冰雹一样砸在我头上，我拼命想躲开它们，但论文妖精和大学里的各种妖魔鬼怪却对我穷追不舍，以至于我甚至希望自己能打碎那些我曾经崇拜的偶像——哦！请饶恕我居然有这么邪恶的念头吧！

　　形形色色的考试是大学生涯中最可怕的妖怪。虽然我已多次面对考试，并且我总能打翻它们，令它们一败涂地，但它们却会再次反扑，用惨白的面孔恐吓我。我觉得自己简直就像胆小的鲍勃·埃克斯[6]，勇气正从我的指尖偷偷溜走。在那些严峻考验降临的前一天，你是这样度过的：拼命往脑子里塞神秘的公式和难以消化的年代——都是些味同嚼蜡的食物，你简直恨不得自己能和书本、学问一起葬身于深不可测的大海。

　　最终，可怕的时刻来临了。如果你准备充分，能够让你的思维在恰当时间聚精会神地助你一臂之力，那么你真是个倍受上苍垂青的幸运儿。但常常也有这样的情况，你的集合号居然无人响应。而最令人困惑和恼怒的是，当你正要使用自己超强的记忆力和敏锐的辨别力时，这些能力竟然展翅飞走了。你煞费苦心积累的那些知识，在这紧要关头却倒不出来，导致你只能吞咽失

---

[6] 鲍勃·埃克斯是出生于爱尔兰的英国作家理查德·布林斯莱·谢立丹（1751—1816）所著剧本《情敌》（1775）中的一个角色。

败的苦果。

"简要论述哈斯[7]及其功绩。"哈斯？他是谁？他做过什么？这个名字看起来异常熟悉呀！于是你绞尽脑汁，在那个装着历史知识的"小皮包"里上上下下仔细搜索，就好像从塞满破布的袋子里搜出一小块丝绸似的。你可以肯定哈斯就在你大脑里，似乎已触手可及——前几天，你在查找宗教改革运动的开端时还见过它。但它现在在哪里呢？于是，你翻出所有零七碎八的知识点——革命、分裂宗派、大屠杀、各种政权体制等等；但"哈斯"是谁呢？你会惊奇地发现，所有你已掌握的内容都没有出现在试卷上。绝望之中，你抓起"小皮包"，把里面的东西倒了个底朝天，啊！在一个角落里有你要找的人，他正安详地独自沉思，浑然不觉自己曾给你带来过灾祸。

就在这时，监考官却通知你时间已到。于是，你满怀厌恶之情，把那一大堆垃圾踢到了角落，然后回家；你的脑子里充满了一个革命性的计划：那就是应该废除教授们不事先征求被提问者同意就提问的神圣权利。

我突然想到在本章的最后两三页里，我已经隐约提到了几个人物——他们一定会转过身来嘲笑我。哈，这正是他们的风格——在我面前趾高气扬，用混合了种种隐喻的言辞冷嘲热讽；他们都指向那头在瓷器店里遭受冰雹袭击的公牛，以及那惨白可怕的考试妖怪，会嘲笑说我是一朵不可理喻的奇葩！让他们嘲笑去吧。因为这些词句和比喻活灵活现地描绘出了我所处的竞争气氛和那些将被颠覆的观念，所以我将对这些嘲笑不予理睬，而且，经过深思熟虑之后，我还要郑重其事地说，我对大学的看法已完全改变了。

我在拉德克利夫学院的时光来日方长，这些日子曾被罩上浪漫的光环，现在却褪去了；但在从浪漫到现实的转变中，我也学到了许多东西。如果没有亲身体验，我是不会懂得这一切的。其中最宝贵的一条就是关于耐心的学

[7] 约翰·哈斯或简·哈斯（1372—1415），德国宗教改革家。

问。它教会我们要把受教育的过程看作是在乡间悠闲地漫步,我们的头脑要兼收并蓄,对各种观念敞开大门。这样,深邃的思想就会扬起无声的波澜,让知识潜移默化地滋润我们的心灵。"知识就是力量"⑧,不仅如此,知识更是幸福,因为如果有了知识——博大精深的知识——就能区分对错,分辨卑贱和高尚。当你了解了那些标志着人类进步的思想和行为,你就会感受到多少个世纪以来人类伟大心脏的搏动;如果一个人感觉不到这些奋发有为的搏动,那么他就一定会对美好和谐的生活置若罔闻。

⑧英国思想家弗朗西斯·培根(1561-1626)的名言。

第 21 章

我的乌托邦

书籍对常人来说是获取知识的工具,而对于凯勒来说,是了解外部世界的最重要的通道。通过阅读,她得以在知识的海洋里徜徉,独立思考并获得辨识力和认知力,更重要的是阅读令她忘却了身体的局限,逼仄的生命得以释放,精神世界得以升华。在精神的乌托邦里,她跟所有人一样自由而酣畅。

至此,我已简要记叙了自己的生活经历,可是我还没有展示自己对书籍的热爱程度。我爱书,这不仅仅是因为书籍会给阅读它的人们带来快乐和智慧,而且它还能使人们通过自己的眼睛和耳朵来获取知识。事实上,在我受教育的过程中,书籍的作用要远远大于其他求知手段,所以,我要回过头来讲讲我最初开始阅读的时光。

1887年5月,我第一次开始阅读连贯的故事,当时我七岁。从那时起,我就用自己那饥渴的指尖,去全神贯注地翻阅所能接触到的一切盲文书籍的页面。正如我前面所述,在我的早期教育阶段,并没有进行正规学习,因此,我读书也并未遵循什么规律。

一开始,我只有几本盲文书——几册启蒙读物、一套儿童故事集,以及一本关于地球的书——《我们的世界》。我天真地以为这些就是世上所有的书籍了，因此我一遍又一遍地读它们，直到书上的字被严重磨损而无法辨认。有时，沙利文小姐会给我读书，就是把一些她认为我能听懂的小故事和诗歌拼写在我手上，但是我更愿意自己去读，而不喜欢让别人读给我，我喜欢一遍又一遍地读那些有趣的故事。

直到我第一次访问波士顿时，我才正儿八经地开始阅读。当时，我被允许每天在学校图书馆里度过一段时光，可以在一个个书架间漫游，随意取下那些我用指尖发现的书，认真地读。当然，也许10个词中我只认识1个，或每一页里我只认识两三个词。但我对那些词汇十分着迷，反而不在意书的内容。在那段时期，我的记忆力很强，虽然我对许多词汇和句子的意思并不理解，但我却完整地记住了它们。后来，当我开始学习说话和写字时，这些词汇和句子就会自然而然地闪现出来，以至于我的朋友们都很惊讶我竟然有这么丰富的词汇量。我曾读了许多书籍的片段（在那些早期时光，我从来没有完整地通读过任何书籍），还囫囵吞枣地读过大量诗歌。直到我发现《小少爷方特罗伊》——这是我真正读懂的第一本书——我的阅读生涯才算正式开始。

一天，老师发现我在图书馆的一个角落里，正聚精会神地阅读《红字》。那时我约莫八岁。我记得她问我是否喜欢小珠儿①，并且还跟我解释了一些生词。然后她告诉我她有一本很有趣的书，讲的是一位小男孩的故事。她敢保证，相比《红字》而言，我一定会更喜欢那本故事书。故事书的名字叫《小少爷方特罗伊》，她还答应在随后的夏天读给我听。但我们直到8月才开始读，起初的那几个星期我们在海边度过，各种新奇和激动人心的事情令我应接不

---

① 《红字》是美国作家纳撒尼尔·霍桑（1804—1864）所著的一部小说，1850年出版。珠儿是小说的主人公赫丝特·普林的非婚生女儿。

暇，以至于我把那本故事书也忘到了九霄云外。接着，老师又去波士顿看望朋友，与我分开了一段时间。

当老师回来后，我们所做的第一件事差不多就是读《小少爷方特罗伊》。这是本引人入胜的儿童故事书。我现在还清楚地记得我们读第一章的时间和地点。那是8月一个暖暖的下午，我们并肩坐在离家不远的一个吊床上，吊床在两棵苍翠的松树间轻轻摇摆。为了尽可能有一整个下午来读故事书，午饭后，我们匆匆洗刷完餐具就出门了。当我们快步穿过高高的杂草奔向吊床时，受惊的蚱蜢在我们身边乱飞乱撞，有一些甚至跳到了我们身上。我记得老师坚持要把蚱蜢全部拿掉后才坐下看书；但在我看来，这简直就是浪费时间。自老师休假后，吊床就一直没用过，所以上面落满了松针。温暖的阳光照耀着松树，空气中弥漫着淡淡的松香味，同时还夹杂着一股强烈的大海气息。在开始读书前，沙利文小姐给我解释了一些她认为我可能不理解的背景，然后，她边读边向我解释一些生词。起初，我碰到许多不懂的词，导致阅读常常被打断；但当我完全沉浸在情节之中后，我就迫不及待地想了解故事的进展，而不愿意再去关注那些生词了。对于沙利文小姐认为很有必要的那些解释，当时我也听得有些不耐烦。后来，当她的手指累得无法再为我拼写时，我第一次产生出一种强烈的被剥夺了心爱之物的沮丧感。于是，我把书拿在手上，试图去感知那些字母，那种渴望之情，我永远也不会忘记。

后来，在我的热切请求之下，阿纳戈诺斯先生把这本书印出了盲文版，于是我一遍又一遍地读，几乎能把里面的内容都背下来了。在整个童年时代，《小少爷方特罗伊》一直是我爱不释手的好伙伴，给我留下了温馨甜蜜的美好回忆。我之所以要提及这些似乎有点冗长乏味的细节，是因为我早期的阅读记忆是模糊而混沌的，但这本书却给我留下了鲜明的印象。

从阅读《小少爷方特罗伊》起，我对书籍产生了真正的兴趣。在此之后的两年里，我在家中以及在游览波士顿时读了许多书。我已经记不清这些书的具体名字和我的阅

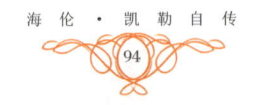

读顺序了，不过我记得有《希腊英雄》，拉·封丹的《寓言诗》，霍桑的《神奇的故事》《圣经故事》，兰姆的《莎士比亚戏剧故事集》，狄更斯的《写给孩子们看的英国历史》《一千零一夜》《来自瑞士的罗宾逊一家》《天路历程》《鲁滨孙漂流记》《小妇人》和《海蒂》。《海蒂》是个美丽的故事，后来我还读了它的德文版。我是在学习和玩耍的间隙读这些书的，读得津津有味。我既不研究也不分析它们——我不知道它们写得好不好，我也从未思考过写作风格和作者背景。书籍把它们蕴涵的珍宝摆在我脚下，我只需要接受它们，就像接受阳光和朋友们的友爱一样。我喜欢《小妇人》②，因为它让我觉得自己跟那些视听正常的男孩和女孩们有了亲近感。由于我生活中有种种不便，所以我不得不从书籍中去探寻外部世界的信息。

我极不喜欢《天路历程》，好像当时我都没有读完这本书。对于《寓言诗》也是如此。我最初读的拉·封丹的《寓言诗》是英文翻译版，我对这本书只是走马观花地浏览了一下。后来我又读了这本书的法文版，然后发现，除了书中那些生动逼真的描述，以及精妙绝伦的语言外，我对这本书别无好感。我也不知道为什么会这样，但让动物像人类一样谈话或做事的寓言故事从来对我都没有多少吸引力。我的头脑里只留下一些荒唐可笑的动物模仿秀，却并未领悟出其中的深刻寓意。

接着，再谈谈拉·封丹，他几乎不能引领我们到更高的精神层次，他所能达到的最高境界就是理智和自恋。在他所有的寓言中，都贯穿着人类的道德准则完全来源于自恋的思想，即如果自恋能被理智引导并控制，那么幸福就会随之而来。但在我看来，自恋却是万恶之源。当然，也许我是错的，因

---

② 美国作家露意莎·梅·奥尔柯特（1832—1888）的著名作品，1868年出版，描述的是一个有着4个女儿的快乐而勤勉的新英格兰家庭的故事。

为拉·封丹有大量机会去观察人类，而我却没这种可能。其实我并不反对那些愤世嫉俗的讽刺寓言，我只是不喜欢由猴子和狐狸来教导做人的至理名言。

但我喜欢《丛林奇谭》和《我所知道的野生动物》③，我对这两本书中的动物产生了真正的兴趣，因为它们是真实的动物而非荒唐可笑的人的化身。我对它们的爱与恨产生了共鸣，我为它们的趣事而欢笑，为它们的不幸而啜泣。即使这两本书中蕴涵着什么哲理，也巧妙得让我们不会直接就能感知到。

我天生就喜欢遐想古代的风物。古希腊对我有着神秘的魔力。在我的幻想里，异教徒的众神们仍在世间漫步，与人们面对面地交谈；而在我心中，已悄悄地为我最崇拜的神建起了圣殿。我熟知并热爱所有部族的女神、英雄和半神半人们——不，不是所有的，对于残忍而贪婪的美狄亚和伊阿宋④，他们的丑陋行径是不可饶恕的。我一直很奇怪为什么上帝会允许他们做那么多坏事，直到最后才对他们的邪恶行为进行惩罚呢？至今这仍是个未解之谜。我常常想知道为什么——

当罪孽狞笑着潜行在他的时光殿堂时，

上帝却装聋作哑。⑤

《伊利亚特》⑥使希腊成了我心中的乐园。我阅读原著之前，就已熟知特洛伊的故事。因而在我跨越了语法的樊篱之后，我就能毫不费力地去理解那些

---

③《丛林奇谭》是英国作家鲁德亚德·吉卜林（1865－1936）的作品；《我所知道的野生动物》是英国生的加拿大作家欧内斯特·汤普森·西顿（1860－1946）的作品。

④在希腊神话中，伊阿宋在美狄亚的帮助下曾取得金羊毛，但伊阿宋后来却背叛了美狄亚。

⑤引自美国诗人西德尼·兰尼尔（1842－1881）的诗作《承认》。

⑥描写特洛伊战争的古希腊英雄史诗，相传是公元前9至8世纪，由盲诗人荷马加工整理而成。

希腊语词汇，并发掘史诗中的宝藏。

伟大的诗篇，无论其是用希腊文还是英文写就的，只要你能产生心灵的共鸣，就无须多余的解释。一些好事之徒用牵强附会的分析评论使诗人们的鸿篇巨著变得面目全非，他们要是也能懂得这最简单的道理该多好啊！

事实上，要理解和欣赏一篇隽永的诗作，并不需要精确地解释每个词的含义，也不需要说出该词在句子中的语法状态和重要作用。我知道那些学识渊博的教授们从《伊利亚特》中发现了许多我从未见识过的瑰宝。但我并不是个贪婪的人，我不在意别人比我更聪慧。但即便教授们拥有博大精深的知识，他们也如我一样，无法酣畅淋漓地赏尽这恢宏壮丽的史诗。而当我读了《伊利亚特》中最精彩的段落之后，我就感到自己的心灵已从那狭窄局促的生活环境中升华出来。我忘却了身体上的缺陷——我的世界徐徐上升，那广阔无垠的浩瀚天空都属于我啦！

我不太欣赏《埃涅阿斯纪》⑦，但它的真实依然令人动容。我尽量不借助注释或字典，只是尽可能地读下去，我还喜欢把自己特别感兴趣的章节翻译出来。有时，维吉尔的描述精彩生动，但是他笔下的神和人却在激情、冲突、怜悯和爱恋之中游移，就如同那些戴着伊丽莎白时代面具的优雅人物。而《伊利亚特》中的众神与人类却能"跳三跳，纵情歌唱"。维吉尔像月光下的一尊大理石太阳神雕像，沉静而迷人；而荷马则是灿烂阳光中的一位秀发飘逸的英俊青年，朝气蓬勃。

乘着书的翅膀飞翔，是多么得惬意啊！但从《希腊英雄传》到《伊利亚特》的旅程却并非一蹴而就，其间也不总是风和日丽。有时别人可能已经绕地球好几圈了，而我却还疲倦地跋涉在语法和字典的曲折迷宫中，或者坠入了名曰考试的可怕陷阱里，而考试其实是学校和学院为了挫伤那些探寻知识的学

---

⑦罗马诗人维吉尔（公元前70—公元前19）所著史诗，讲述希腊神话中的英雄埃涅阿斯及其后代建立罗马城的故事。

我 生 活 的 故 事

子们的积极性而设置的。我相信天道酬勤,这种"天路历程"⑧的结局理应是公平的。但对我而言,尽管在道路百转千回之时,偶尔也会碰到惊喜,可这一历程却似乎没有尽头。

我刚开始读《圣经》时,自己完全不能理解它,现在看来这似乎很不可思议,我的心灵竟然有一段时间对《圣经》里的奇妙和弦置若罔闻。我清楚地记得在一个下着雨的周日清晨,我百无聊赖,就央求表姐给我读《圣经》里的一个故事。虽然她认为我可能无法理解这个故事,但还是把约瑟和兄弟们的故事拼写在我手上。不知什么缘故,这个故事没能引起我的兴趣。那不同寻常的语言和重复的叙述手法使这个发生在遥远的迦南地的故事显得极不真实。还没讲到约瑟的哥哥们拿着五彩衣去父亲雅各的帐篷,准备用邪恶的谎言欺骗父亲时,我就睡着了,迷失在了瞌睡乡。我无法解释为什么自己会觉得希腊人的故事魅力无穷,而《圣经》里的那些故事却索然无味。这也许是因为我在波士顿结识了几个希腊人,他们对自己祖国历史传说的热爱确实令我感动;而我从未遇到过任何希伯来人或埃及人,所以认为他们只不过是异邦人,关于他们的故事很可能都是编造的吧。奇怪的是,我怎么从不认为希腊人那源于父系的姓名"稀奇古怪"呢?

但我又该如何述说自己在《圣经》中发现的辉煌呢?多年来,我通过阅读《圣经》,使自己的视野不断拓展,得到许多快乐和启迪。《圣经》已成为我最喜爱的书。然而,《圣经》中也有很多观点与我叛逆的本性相悖。因此,我是带着愧疚强迫自己把这本书从头到尾通读了一遍。我觉得自己从书中获得的历史知识和原始资料并不能冲抵那些令人不快的细节所产生的负面影响。我与豪厄尔斯先生有着同样的看法,应清除过去的文学作品中那些丑陋和粗俗的糟粕。当然,我也反对任何人去篡改或歪曲这些名著。

⑧参见英国作家约翰·班杨(1628—1688)所著的宗教讽喻小说《天路历程》(1678),其中讲述了基督教徒的艰难旅程。

在《以斯帖记》中，以斯帖的质朴和率直给人留下极其深刻的印象。难道还有比以斯帖勇敢地站在她那邪恶的国王面前更激动人心的场景吗？她知道自己的性命就掌握在国王手中；如果惹怒了国王，没人能保护她。但是，她仍然克服了女性的恐惧，怀着对族人崇高的爱，走近国王，心里只有一个念头："如果我死了，仅仅是死我一人而已；但是如果我能活着，我的族人也将活下去。"

路得的故事也是如此——它是多么富有东方韵味啊！然而这些淳朴的乡下（犹太）人又是多么难以融入波斯人的首都！路得是如此忠心耿耿、仁慈善良，当她和收割者们一起站在随风起伏的玉米地里时，我们都会情不自禁地喜欢上她。在那艰难的岁月里，她美丽无私的精神熠熠生辉，宛如在黑夜里闪闪发光的星星。像路得那样的爱，那种能够战胜相互冲突的宗教信条和根深蒂固的种族偏见的爱，在世间已难以找到。

《圣经》带给我的最深切的感受并且抚慰我心灵的就是"所见之物均属过眼云烟；不可见之物实乃永恒"。[9]

记忆中，自从我有能力阅读书籍之后，我对莎士比亚的作品就一往情深。我无法确切说出自己是何时开始读兰姆的《莎士比亚戏剧故事集》的，但是我知道自己最初是怀着一个孩子的理解力和好奇心来读它们的。《麦克白》似乎给我留下了更深的印象。我只读过一次，就足以把故事情节永远地烙在脑海中。有很长一段时间，甚至在梦境里，我都会被鬼魂和女巫所追赶。我能看见，绝对能看见，匕首和麦克白夫人小巧而白皙的手——那该死的污迹[10]，

---

[9] 参见《圣经·哥林多后书》（4∶18）。

[10] 参见莎士比亚的戏剧《麦克白》的第5幕，场景1。那该死的污迹是指血迹和罪恶——在怂恿丈夫杀害国王邓肯之后，麦克白夫人无法洗掉手上那想象出来的血迹。

我的感受简直跟那黯然销魂的王后看到的一样真实。

在读完《麦克白》之后不久，我又读了《李尔王》。我永不会忘记当我读到葛罗斯特被剜去双目[11]时的恐怖感觉。我无比悲愤，手指也无法移动，呆呆地坐了很长时间，太阳穴血脉贲张，突突直跳，心中积满了一个小孩子所有的愤恨。

我一定是在同一时段认识了夏洛克和撒旦的，所以长久以来，在我脑海中，这两个人物总是连在一起。我记得我为他们感到遗憾。我隐约觉得，即使他们有心向善，他们也不可能成为好人，因为似乎没人愿意帮助他们，或者给他们一个公平的机会。直到现在，我也无法发自内心地去彻底谴责他们。有时，我觉得像夏洛克们、犹大们，甚至魔鬼，其实都是一个巨型"善之轮"上被损坏的辐条——届时都将被修复得完好如初。

说来真是奇怪，我第一次读莎士比亚就留下了那么多不愉快的记忆。而那些欢快、文雅和富于幻想的戏剧——是我现在最喜欢的戏剧——在当初似乎并没有给我留下什么印象，也许是因为它们反映的只是小孩子习以为常的无忧无虑的快乐生活吧。但是"没有什么能比孩子的记忆更变幻莫测的了。什么是应该牢记的？什么又是该失去的？"

此后，我又多次阅读莎士比亚的戏剧，并对其中的一些场景熟稔于心，但我却说不出自己最喜欢其中的哪一部。我对这些戏剧的喜好随自己的心情而变化不定。在我看来，短小精悍的诗歌和十四行诗蕴涵着跟戏剧一样清新而美妙的韵味。但是，虽然我对莎士比亚喜爱有加，但要从他的字里行间读出评论家和注释者们所给出的那些解释，那往往也是令人生厌的事。我过去曾努力去记别人的解释，但却被这些解释搞得灰心丧气、烦恼不堪。所以，

---

[11]参见莎士比亚戏剧《李尔王》的第3幕，场景7。由于葛罗斯特帮助李尔王从次女里根那里逃脱出来，里根就和丈夫康华尔剜去了葛罗斯特的双眼。

我跟自己签订了一份"秘密协定",再也不去记那些东西了。直到在基特里奇教授的指导下,我才撕毁了莎士比亚戏剧学习中的这项"协定"。我知道,莎士比亚的作品博大精深,我并不完全了解世界范围内的莎剧研究。我很高兴看到面纱逐渐被人层层揭开,一个思想和美的新王国呈现在我们面前。

除诗歌外,我最喜欢读的是历史书。我如饥似渴地阅读自己所能得到的每一本历史著作。从朴素的书页目录、大事年表到格林所著的客观公正、生动别致的《英国人民史》;从弗里曼的《欧洲史》到埃默顿的《中世纪》。第一本使我真正意识到历史价值的书是斯文顿的《世界历史》,它是我十三岁时收到的生日礼物。虽然我认为这本书已经落伍了,但是我仍把它视若珍宝,好好保管。这本书使我了解到,不同的人种如何分散到世界各地,并建立起庞大的城市;那几个杰出的统治者和世间伟人,是如何把万物置于脚下的,又如何以一句决定性的话语就能为成百上千的人开启和关闭幸福之门的;我还了解了各个民族是如何在艺术和知识的海洋里开拓创新,乘风破浪,驶向欣欣向荣的新世纪的;文明如何在遭受颓废时代的浩劫后,像凤凰城(菲尼克斯市)一样,在那些北方贵族后裔的喧嚣中,在印第安人的遗址上重新诞生;伟人和先贤们又是如何通过自由、宽容的精神和聪明才智开辟出拯救全世界的道路的。

在我的大学读物中,我比较熟悉的是法国和德国文学。德国人无论在生活中还是文学作品中,总是认为力量比美丽更重要,应坚守真理而不是惯例。他们做任何事,都有一股激情四溢、虎虎生威的气势。他们之所以要发言,并不是为了让别人印象深刻,而是如果他们不为自己灵魂深处燃烧着的思想寻找到一个出口,那么他们就会感到憋屈得无法承受。

接着我又发现,德国文学作品是一座我喜爱的博大精深的宝库,但我发现其中最耀眼的光芒就是对女性自我牺牲的仁爱精神所蕴含的巨大力量的赞颂。可以说所有德国文学作品中都渗透着这一思想,尤其以歌德的《浮士德》中表现得最为神秘:

万物皆短暂，

只是一虚影。

曾为不可及，

如今硕果成。

不可名状者，

在此皆达成。

女性之灵魂，

引吾向前进！

  在我读过其作品的法国作家中，我最喜爱的是莫里哀和拉辛。巴尔扎克和梅里美的作品内涵丰富，就像一股强劲的海风向你袭来，令人的精神为之一振。但阿尔弗莱德·德·缪塞是不可能做到这点的！我崇拜维克多·雨果⑫——我欣赏他的天分、他的卓越和他的浪漫主义情怀，虽然他并不是我最喜爱的文学大师。雨果、歌德和席勒，以及所有伟大民族中的伟大诗人，都是永恒价值的诠释者；我的灵魂只要恭敬虔诚地追随他们，就能进入一个真、善、美和谐统一的境界。

  我如此浓墨重彩地描述自己所钟爱的书籍，乃至提到了自己最喜爱的一部分作者，由此你可能会贸然推断出我的阅读面很窄，我选择书籍的方式也是武断的，这可是一个错误的印象。其实，我因多种原因而喜欢许多作家——我喜欢卡莱尔是因为他的豪放和对虚伪的不屑一顾；华兹华斯倡导人与自然的和谐统一；我在胡德奇特惊人的作品中发现了一种高雅的乐趣；而赫里克的诗句中，则散发着奇特的、可感知的如同百合和玫瑰的芳香；我喜欢惠蒂埃，因为他热情奔放、公正无私。而且因为我认识他，所以我在阅读其诗歌时，会怀着对我们友谊的温馨记忆，从而感受到双倍的快乐。我喜欢马克·吐温——谁会不喜欢他呢？即使是诸神，也会钟爱他，并赋予其各种智慧。为

---

⑫ 维克多·雨果：法国作家（1802—1885），著有《悲惨世界》和《巴黎圣母院》（又译《钟楼驼侠》）。

了不使他变成一个悲观主义者，诸神又在他的大脑中架起一条爱与信仰的彩虹。我喜欢司各特，因为其作品清新、充满张力、率真而公正。此外，我喜欢所有像洛威尔一样有思想的作家，他们的思想就像浸满欢乐和友善的喷泉，在乐观主义的阳光下汩汩冒泡，偶尔零星飞溅起一些愤怒的水花，还播撒着满怀同情和怜悯的和解喷雾。

总而言之，文学是我的乌托邦理想国，在这个乐园里，我不会被剥夺任何权利。没有任何感官上的障碍能阻挡我与那些和蔼可亲、彬彬有礼的书友们的交流。它们落落大方地与我交谈，没有丝毫的尴尬或局促。同它们的"大仁和大爱"[13]相比，我所了解以及学到的那点东西是多么微乎其微和不值一提啊。

---

[13]参见西德尼·兰尼尔的《约翰·霍普金斯大学颂》。

第 22 章

我的秘密花园

除了精神的乌托邦,凯勒还缔造了无数生活的秘密花园。纵使她的生活带有无法弥补的缺陷,她也不允许自己被与世隔绝的孤单感所征服,更要与冷酷无情的命运之手抗争,她像森林里追逐阳光的藤蔓,用生命的枝蔓努力触摸世间的美好。

从上一章对于书籍的描述中,我相信我的读者们并不会得出这样的结论:阅读是我唯一的快乐。事实上,我有多种多样的兴趣爱好和娱乐方式。

在我撰写自己的故事时,曾不止一次地提到我喜欢在乡间从事户外运动。当我还是个小姑娘时,我就学会了划船和游泳。而当我在马萨诸塞州的伦瑟姆度夏期间,我几乎是生活在船上。当朋友们来拜访我时,我们最大的乐事就是一起出去划船。当然,我不能很好地掌握行船方向。当我划船时,总有人要坐在船尾为我掌着方向舵,但有时不靠舵手我也能划。而循着水草、百合花和岸边灌木丛的气味来寻找方向是一件十分有趣的事。我使用的船桨配有皮带,可以把船桨固定在桨架的位置上。我可以通过水的阻力来感知船桨是否保持着均匀平衡。同样地,我也能辨别出船是否在逆流行驶。我喜欢惬意地享受风浪,让坚固的小船顺应着自己的意愿和体力,轻轻地飘荡在波光粼粼、起伏不定的水面,感受着那平稳或汹涌的波浪,这是多么令人心旷神怡的事啊！

　　我也喜欢划独木舟。我猜想当你们听到我说自己特别喜欢在月光下划独木舟时，你们一定会笑起来的。说实话，我确实无法看见月亮从松影后冉冉升上天空，悄悄地在天际穿行，为我们映照出一条闪闪发光的小径。但是，我知道月亮就在那里。当我倚靠在垫子里，把手放入水中时，月光洒落，我就想象自己触摸到了月亮那熠熠生辉的外衣。有时，一条鲁莽的小鱼会从我指间溜过，一朵羞涩的睡莲也会碰到我的手。往往当我们从一处遮蔽的屏障或小河湾里划出来时，我也会突然感到扑面而来的宽阔。一股融融的暖意拥着我，但我却搞不清它是来自被阳光照耀的树林，还是来自水面。甚至在城市中心，我也会同样产生这种奇异的感觉。而在狂风凛冽的日子里，以及在夜间，我都曾有过这种感觉，就仿佛是有一对温暖的双唇亲吻着我的脸颊。

　　我最喜爱的娱乐是乘船航行。1901年夏，我游览了新斯科舍，第一次有机会认识了大海。在伊凡吉琳的故乡①住了几天，朗费罗的精彩诗句为这里增添了迷人魅力。之后，我和沙利文小姐还去了哈利法克斯，而整个夏天的剩余时光，我们几乎都是在这里度过的。这座港口给了我们许多欢乐，它是我们的乐园。我们乘船游览了贝德福德流域、麦克纳布的海岛、约克堡，还到了西北湾，这是一次多么辉煌的航行啊！晚上，战舰那庞大而宁静的阴影笼罩着我们，哦，所有的一切都是那么的有趣而美好！那欢愉的回忆将永远铭刻在我脑海里。

　　一天，我们经历了惊心动魄的一幕。那天在西北湾举行了一场赛艇会，参赛小艇是由各式各样的军舰派出的。我们随同众人一起乘坐一条帆船去观看比赛。上百条小船在我们身边往返穿梭，海面上风平浪静。就在比赛结束，

---

① 参见美国诗人亨利·沃兹沃思·朗费罗（1807—1882）的作品《伊凡吉琳》。

我们调转船头准备回家时，有人注意到一片乌云从海上飘过来，这云不断地膨胀扩展，越来越黑，渐渐遮住了整个天空。刹那间，狂风大作，波涛汹涌。我们的小船勇敢地迎战暴风骤雨，她鼓起风帆，绷紧缆绳，在风中飘摇。她时而在巨浪上盘旋，时而在惊涛中跳跃，伴着狂风的怒吼艰难前行。主桅帆落下了，帆船抢风行驶，左冲右突。风怒气冲冲地把我们吹得东倒西歪，但我们仍然迎风搏击。我们由于激动而心跳加速，双手颤抖，但我们毫不畏惧，因为我们有着海盗的大无畏精神，我们也深知我们的船长是对付风浪的行家里手，他凭借坚毅的双手和受过航海历练的慧眼，曾多次驾船勇闯风暴。港口中的巨型船舶和炮艇在经过我们的船侧时，都纷纷向我们致意；水兵们也为这唯一一艘小帆船的船长能在风暴中化险为夷而鼓掌欢呼。最后，我们又冷又饿，疲惫不堪地回到了码头。

去年夏天，我是在新英格兰一个幽静宜人的村庄里度过的。马萨诸塞州的伦瑟姆是一个与我所有的喜悦和悲伤息息相关的地方。多年来，J.E. 张伯伦先生和他的家人一直住在菲利普国王池塘边的瑞德农场，那也曾是我的家。每当我想起这些朋友们的友爱之情，以及我们一起度过的美好时光，我心中总是充满了诚挚的谢意。与他们孩子之间建立的亲密友谊对我而言是弥足珍贵的。我和他们一起运动，到树林中散步，在水中嬉戏。幼小的孩子们天真无邪地围着我聊天，他们喜欢听我讲那些有关小精灵和侏儒、英雄和狡猾的熊的故事，这些都是令人愉快的回忆。张伯伦先生还教我辨认神秘的树种和野花，后来，凭借着爱的神奇小耳朵，我似乎听到了橡树中树液的流动声，也看到了层层树叶间闪烁的阳光。正如诗中所描述的：

当树根被关在阴暗的泥土中时，

仁慈的大自然也会让它分享树梢的欢乐，

想象明媚的阳光、无垠的天空和成群的飞鸟，

我亦如树根一般，感知到了看不见的事物。[2]

---

[2] 参见詹姆斯·拉塞尔·洛威尔的《大教堂》。

在我看来，自人类出现以来，我们每一个人的内心深处就已经具备感知各种情绪的经验。在每个人的潜意识中，都保存着对绿色大地和汩汩流水的记忆。即使是失明和失聪的人，也具有这种代代相传的天赋。这种源自遗传的能力是一种第六感觉——一种集视觉、听觉和触觉于一体的心灵感应。

我在伦瑟姆有很多"树友"，其中一棵是一株伟岸的橡树，它是我心中的骄傲。我会带着所有的朋友去看这棵树王。它屹立在一块峭壁上，俯视着菲利普国王[3]的池塘。那些博学多才的树木专家说，这棵树已在此矗立了800年至1000年。传说在这棵树下，菲利普国王，这位英勇的印第安首领最后凝视了一眼大地和天空，然后就牺牲了。

我还有另外一位树友，与那棵大橡树相比，它更温柔，也更易于靠近——这是一株长在瑞德农场庭院里的美洲椴。一天下午，在一场雷电交加的暴风雨中，我觉得房子的一侧似乎受到了剧烈撞击，在别人告诉我之前，我就明白那棵美洲椴已经被雷击倒了。我们跑到院子里察看这棵英雄树，它曾多次经历暴风雨而傲然挺立。但这次，它虽奋力拼搏，却仍然轰然倒下。看到它倒伏在地上，我不禁心痛不已。

我不会忘记自己特别要写写发生在去年夏天的事。我的考试刚一结束，沙利文小姐和我就匆匆赶到了这个"绿色幽境"。伦瑟姆有三个著名的湖，我们的小屋就坐落在其中的一个湖上。在这里，我们可以尽情享受充足而明媚的阳光，把所有有关学业的烦恼、学院和嘈杂的城市生活，统统抛入九霄云外。当然在伦瑟姆，我们照样能了解世上发生的一些事情——战争、联盟和社会冲突等等。我们听说了那残酷而不必要的、在遥远太平洋爆发的战争[4]，

---

[3] 梅塔康（1639？－1676），也被称为菲利普国王，是一名印第安瓦帕浓人的酋长，他领导了反抗殖民者侵占土地权的斗争。

[4] 指日俄战争（1904－1905）。

也了解到了资本家和劳工之间持续不断的斗争。我们知道，在我们的伊甸园之外，许多人正在辛勤劳动创造着历史，而没有去悠闲地享受假期。但是我们几乎没去关注过那些事。终究，所有的世事终将随风而逝；只有这里的湖泊、森林、开满繁星般雏菊的无垠田野和芬芳的草地，将会永恒地存在。

那些认为我们所有的感受都应该是通过眼睛和耳朵而获得的人们，在得知我在城市街道和在乡村道路上散步时，除了能注意到人行道的不同之外，竟然还能分辨出其他不同之处，总是感到大为惊奇。他们忘了我的整个身体对周围的环境都很敏感。城市的嘈杂和喧嚣会碰撞我的面部神经，我可以感觉到一大群看不见的人那无休止的沉重步伐，那种不协调的喧嚣会使我心烦意乱。对那些看得见的人来说，如果他的注意力没有被这嘈杂街头发生的其他事所吸引，那么沉甸甸的运货马车碾过坚硬人行道的隆隆声和机器单调的叮当声一定会使他的神经备受折磨。

而在乡村，人们看到的则是大自然的杰作。人们不必经受在拥挤城市里为生存而进行的残酷斗争，在这里，人们郁郁寡欢的心境会荡然无存。我曾好几次走过穷人居住的狭窄而肮脏的街道，我不由得会很激动，并愤愤不平地想，那些权贵阶层住着精美的房子，他们强大而衣冠楚楚，应该感到知足了；而另一些人却只能住在阴暗简陋的出租房里，衣衫褴褛、面容憔悴、卑躬屈膝，这绝不是理所当然的事。孩子们挤在那些肮脏的小巷里，他们衣不蔽体、食不果腹，对你伸出的手躲躲闪闪，仿佛怕你打他似的。这些可怜的小生命一直蜷缩在我的心中，常常让痛苦萦绕着我。这里的男人和女人，全都骨节粗大，弓腰驼背。我曾摸过他们那坚硬而粗糙的手，我意识到了他们为生存所必须进行的无尽的挣扎——那不过是些徒劳无益的小打小闹而已。他们的生活在奋斗和机遇之间似乎有着巨大的反差。我们会说，阳光和空气是上帝给所有人的免费礼物，但对他们也是如此吗？在城市的那些破败小巷，阳光照不进来，空气也是污浊的。哦，人啊，你们怎么能对你们的手足弟兄如此冷漠呢？当你们祈祷说"感谢主赐予我们今日之食，天天皆然"，而你们的弟兄却一无所有！哦，人们真应该离开城市，舍弃它的浮华、喧嚣和财富，去回归森林和田野，过一种简单而真实的生活！那么，他们的孩子一定会像那些高大的树木一样茁壮成长，而他们的思想也会像路边的野花一样纯洁芬芳。这些就是我在城里学习了一年，回到乡村后自然而然产生的想法。

再一次感受到脚下那松软而富有弹性的土地是多么令人兴奋啊！沿着长满青草的小道，我们来到蕨草茂盛的小溪边，在这里，我可以在那弹奏着绝妙音符、叮咚作响的急流中浸泡手指；也可以爬过一堵石墙进入绿茵茵的草地，尽情翻滚、跳跃、奔跑，这是多么自由自在的欢愉啊！

除了悠闲地散步之外，我还喜欢骑着我的双人自行车"飞驰"。风从脸上吹过，我的铁骏马轻快地转动，那种感觉真爽！驾车疾驰，带给了我力量感和悬浮感的美妙感受，这项运动还令我脉搏欢舞，心儿歌唱。

在我散步、骑车或航行时，只要有可能，我的狗都会陪伴着我。我曾有过很多狗狗朋友——马士提夫獒犬、目光温柔的西班牙猎狗、顽皮聪明的塞特种猎狗和忠良顾家的牛头梗。而目前我的宠物之王就是一只牛头梗。他有着源远流长的纯种血统、一条弯曲的尾巴和一张在狗世界中最滑稽可笑的"脸"。我的狗狗朋友们似乎都明白我身体上的缺陷，当我独自一人时，他们总是紧紧跟在我身旁。我感受着它们的深情厚谊，也喜欢它们欢蹦乱跳地摇尾巴。

下雨的时候，我就被困在了室内，我会像其他姑娘那样找些事情自娱自乐。我喜欢用棒针编织东西，也会用钩针钩花；我会随意而自在地浏览书籍，这里看一行，那里看一行；偶尔还会同朋友玩一场游戏，或下两盘西洋跳棋或国际象棋。我有一块专用棋板，可以在上面玩这些游戏。棋盘上的方格都被切削过，以使棋子能稳稳地立在上面。黑跳棋是平的，而白跳棋的顶部则弯曲成弧形；每个跳棋中间都有一个孔，带黄铜旋钮的是国王棋子。而国际

象棋的棋子也有两种规格，白棋比黑棋更大，这样每走完一步，我只需用手轻轻地抚摸，就能毫不费力地了解对手的棋局。当把棋子从一个格子移到另一个格子时会发出震动声，由此我就可以判断是否轮到自己走棋了。

如果碰巧只有我独自一人，且又感到百无聊赖时，我就会玩单人纸牌游戏，这是我非常喜欢的一项娱乐。我使用的纸牌右上角都有盲文符号，用以标明纸牌的花色。

如果周围有小孩子，那么我最高兴的就是同他们一起嬉戏。我发现即便是很小的孩子，也能成为我的好伙伴，并且，我很荣幸地说，孩子们通常都很喜欢我。他们领着我到处走，把他们感兴趣的东西指给我。当然，那些太小的孩子还不会用手指拼写，但我可以努力去读懂他们的嘴唇。如果我不能成功地领会其意，他们就采取演哑剧的方式来帮助我。有时，我出错了，做得牛头不对马嘴。孩子们就会对我的疏忽报以纯真的笑声，又从头再演一遍哑剧。我经常给他们讲故事或者教他们做游戏，时间飞驰而过，留给我们的则是美好和快乐。

博物馆和艺术品商店也是我的快乐和灵感的源泉。许多人都觉得如果仅凭双手，不借助视觉，就想从一块冷冰冰的大理石上感知出形态、情感和美，那简直是不可思议的。但我的确能通过触摸伟大的艺术作品，寻找到真正的快乐。当我的指尖追踪着那些起伏的线条时，它们能发现艺术家作画时的思想和感情。我能从诸神和英雄们的脸上感知出憎恨、勇气和爱恋，就如同我经某人允许，去触摸其生动脸庞时所能感受到的那些情感。我在黛安娜的姿势⑤中触摸到了森林里的优雅和自由，以及她驯服美洲狮和征服狂暴激情的精神。维纳斯宁静优美的曲线，使我的心灵充满了欢悦；而巴

⑤黛安娜是罗马神话中行动敏捷的狩猎女神。

列的青铜艺术品⑥则向我揭示了丛林的秘密。

在我书房的墙壁上，悬挂着荷马⑦的圆形雕像，它挂得很低，我一伸手就可以满怀崇敬地触摸到那英俊而忧伤的脸庞。雕像的面部表情很庄严，我深谙那容颜里的每一根线条——生活的轨迹，挣扎的苦涩与忧伤；而那双没有视力的眼睛，即使被镶嵌在冰冷的石膏里，依然在寻找他所深爱的古希腊的光明和蓝天，但这样的寻找却一无所获。雕像的嘴唇轮廓优美，闪现着坚毅、真诚和温柔。这是一张诗人的脸，也是一位饱经沧桑的男人的脸。啊！我是多么理解他所失去的一切啊——他将被留在永恒的黑夜中——

哦，黑暗，黑暗，在正午灿烂的阳光中，

无法弥补的黑暗，遮天蔽日，

将生活所有希望化为乌有！⑧

在想象中，我能听到荷马的吟唱，他跌跌撞撞，脚步踟蹰，从一个营地摸索到另一个营地——歌唱着生命、爱情、战争和一个高尚民族的辉煌成就。这是一首恢宏而美妙的颂歌，它为这位盲诗人赢得了一顶不朽的桂冠，也赢得了人们世世代代的崇敬。

有时，我也想知道手在感知雕塑的美感方面是不是比眼睛更敏锐。我觉得触摸应该比亲眼看更能精妙地感受出线条和曲线的流畅性和优美的韵律。无论如何，我知道自己能从那些古希腊诸神的大理石雕像中，充分感受到古希腊人的激情。

---

⑥法国雕塑家安托万-路易斯·巴列（1795－1875）因其创作的动物雕塑而闻名。

⑦荷马是双目失明的古希腊诗人（公元前9世纪－公元前8世纪），他因创作了史诗《奥德赛》和《伊利亚特》而举世闻名。

⑧参看英国诗人约翰·弥尔顿（1608－1674）所著的《力士参孙》。参孙是圣经里的英雄，被非利士人弄瞎了双眼。弥尔顿本人后来也双目失明。

我的另一大乐事就是去剧院看戏，但我很少有机会去。当一幕戏正在舞台上演出时，我喜欢旁边有人能给我讲述剧情，而不愿意去阅读剧本，因为唯有如此，我才能融入那激动人心的剧情里。我凭着特许权，曾见过几位卓越的男女演员，这些演员的表演有着神奇的魅力，会令人心醉神迷，恍如忘了时空，重新生活在那浪漫的往昔。当埃伦·特里小姐⑨出神入化地扮演了一位人们心目中的理想王后时，我曾被允许抚摸她的脸和服装。我能感受到她赋予角色一种庄严的神圣感，以及驱散无尽悲伤的高贵气质。站在她身边的是亨利·欧文爵士⑩，他穿着象征王权的袍服，举手投足间，都透着睿智和威严。他的脸上的每一根线条都蕴涵着胜利者的高贵气质。在国王的脸上，我似乎摸到了一副面具，那冷漠而遥不可及的忧伤，令我永生难忘。

我也认识杰弗逊先生⑪，我为有他这样的朋友而感到骄傲。无论何时，我去看他的时候他都有演出。我第一次观看他的演出是在纽约上学时，他演的是《瑞普·凡·温克尔》⑫。我经常读这个故事，但在读的时候却从来没有感觉到瑞普那慢吞吞、离奇有趣又质朴的行为方式有什么过人魅力。但杰弗逊先生那精妙绝伦、荡气回肠的表演令我着迷，让我感受到了人物的独特

---

⑨埃伦·特里，英国女演员（1847—1928）。

⑩英国演员亨利·欧文爵士（1838—1905），是埃伦·特里的专业搭档。

⑪约瑟夫·杰弗逊（1829—1905），美国演员，因在《瑞普·凡·温克尔》中塑造了主要角色，以及在谢立丹所著剧本《情敌》中饰演了鲍勃·埃克斯而闻名遐迩。

⑫《瑞普·凡·温克尔》是华盛顿·欧文的短篇小说，由出生于爱尔兰的美国演员和剧作家迪翁·鲍西考尔特（1820—1890）专门为约瑟夫·杰弗逊改编为剧本。

魅力。我的手指永远牢记着一幅"老瑞普"的肖像，我永远也不会忘记它。演出过后，沙利文小姐带我到后台去看望杰弗逊先生，我抚摸了他那奇特的装束、飘垂的头发和胡须。杰弗逊先生让我摸他的脸，这样我就能想象出他从那奇妙的一觉二十年中苏醒后的样子；而且，他还向我展示了可怜的老瑞普是如何摇晃着站起来的。

　　我也看过他表演的《情敌》。记得有一次是我在波士顿拜访他时，他专门为我表演了《情敌》中最扣人心弦的部分。我们见面的会客室被当成了临时舞台，他和他儿子在一张大桌子旁就座，他饰演的鲍勃·埃克斯写着决斗书。我用双手追随他的动作，捕捉他那跟跟跄跄的走路姿势中那逗人发笑的噱头。这些在某种程度上一直是我无法通过别人拼写的方式来领会的。接着，他们站起来进行决斗。我追踪着那迅捷的击刺和防守，当可怜的鲍勃的勇气慢慢从指尖流走时，他的身体开始摇摇晃晃。然后，这位伟大的演员把他的大衣猛地一拉，嘴角抽搐了一下，须臾之间，我仿佛就置身于落水山庄所在的村子，感受到狗儿谢利得那毛茸茸的头⑬正抵着我的膝盖。杰弗逊先生背诵了《瑞普·凡·温克尔》中最精彩的对白，其中溢满含泪的微笑。他要求我尽量比画一下和对白相配的姿势和动作。当然我对戏剧动作并无什么概念，只好胡乱猜测着做了几个动作。但是，他精湛的艺术功力使他赋予表演以生命力，正如瑞普喃喃自语"人离去后怎么这么快就被遗忘了？"后的长叹；在长睡之后，他怀着失魂落魄的心情寻找狗和枪；以及他在与德瑞克签合同时那令人发笑的优柔寡断——所有这些，似乎都脱离了生活本身。换句话说，理想的生活状态，应该按我们所想的样子而铺展。

---

⑬《瑞普·凡·温克尔》一剧是在落水山庄拍摄的；谢利得是瑞普·凡·温克尔的狗。

我清楚地记得自己第一次去剧院时的情景，那是12年前的事了。儿童演员艾尔希·莱斯利恰好在波士顿，于是沙利文小姐带我去看她演的《王子与贫儿》⑭。我永远也不会忘记这出精彩短剧中那悲喜交加、跌宕起伏的情节，以及那位在剧中扮演角色的可爱演员。演出结束后，我被允许到后台看看身着王室服装的她。艾尔希站在那里，肩上披着如云朵般飘逸的金发，灿烂地笑着。虽然刚刚在那么多观众面前进行了表演，但她脸上没有丝毫的羞怯或疲惫。在这世上，真的很难找到一位像她这么友好而可爱的孩子了！那时我刚开始学说话，于是我提前练习学说她的名字，直到我能流畅准确地说出来。你可以想象一下，当她听懂了我对她说的几个词，并毫不犹豫地伸出手来问候我时，我是多么得乐不可支啊！

尽管我的生命带有缺陷，但我依然从生活的不同角度触摸到了这个世界的美好，这难道不是真真切切的事吗？每件事物，即使是黑暗和寂静，也蕴涵着神奇。由此，我领悟到，无论自己可能会处于何种状态，都要知足常乐。

有时，当我独自坐在那道紧闭的生命之门旁等候时，的确会被一种与世隔绝的孤独感所笼罩，就像身处冷冰冰的雾霭之中。门内有光明、音乐、温馨的友情，但我却无法进入。冷酷无情的命运之手将我挡在了门外。我不得不质问它为何要下达如此专横的判决，因为我仍有一颗无拘无束、热情洋溢的心。但是，我的舌头并不会发出愤愤不平的抱怨。当徒劳的话语涌向嘴边时，它们会像那未流出的眼泪一样在我心中消融。当我的心中一片宁静，希望就会微笑着喃喃细语："忘却自我才能得到快乐。"于是，我努力把心中的太阳照耀进别人的眼中，把自己心中的交响乐在别人的耳中奏响，把自己的快乐镌刻在别人的脸庞上。

⑭马克·吐温1881年所著的同名小说，讲述一位贫穷的男孩与一位王子互换身份的故事，由艾比·塞奇·理查森改编为剧本。

第 23 章

致我敬爱的朋友们

> 这里不是结束,却是一个完结。凯勒把这诗意的末尾篇章献给了自己最敬爱的朋友们,是的,他(她)们都是天才人物,发明家贝尔、大文豪马克·吐温……在这里,我们读到的是伟人们诚挚的平凡之爱,还有凯勒那颗依旧敏感而喜悦的心。

但愿我能把所有那些曾给我带来过幸福的人的名字都记下来,如此,一定会为我的文章增添许多瑰丽的色彩!他们中有些人的名字已被写入我们的文学史,成为世人瞩目的焦点。但对我的大多数读者来说,一些人的名字也许是闻所未闻的。虽然他们不可能闻名遐迩,但他们积极而崇高的生活态度温暖了周围人的心灵,这种影响是永恒的。在我们的生活中,每当我们有幸遇到那些像一首好诗般令我们怦然心动的人时,那就是我们的幸运日。他们的握手饱含无言的同情,他们那温和醇厚的性格为我们饥渴而烦躁的心灵注入了一种奇妙的宁静,而这种宁静的本质,就是崇高。那些曾困扰我们的迷惑、恼怒和忧虑都像不愉快的梦境一样流逝了,当我们醒来后,会耳目一新,用全新的眼睛和耳朵去感受真实世界里的美好与和谐。那些沉甸甸地充斥着我们日常生活的毫无趣味的琐事,也会突然大放异彩。总而言之,如果我们身边有这样的朋友,我们就会感到无比充实。也许以前我们从未见过他们,也许萍水相逢之后，我们也不会再与他们相遇，但他们那沉静而完美的个性，却像一杯祭奠用的酒，喷洒在我们的不满情绪上，使我们感受到了心灵的升华，如同大海能感受山间清泉冲淡了它那咸涩的海水一样。

常常有人问我："难道你不觉得有些人很烦吗？"我实在不太明白这是什么意思。但我认为那些无聊而古怪的来访，特别是报社记者的，往往是不合时宜的。我也不喜欢那些以高人一等姿态对我品头论足的人，其实他们和那些在跟你一起走路时，总是试图缩短步伐来迎合你的人是一样的。这两种人的伪善都令人无法容忍。

我所遇到的人们，他们的手无声地向我述说了一切。有些手的触摸是傲慢无礼的。我还遇到过一些非常缺乏快乐的人，当我握紧他们那冷若冰霜的指尖时，我感觉自己仿佛握住了东北的暴风雪。而有些人的手则溢满阳光，同他们牵手会使我心中充满温暖。哪怕只是被一个孩子依恋地拉着，我也会感受到潜在的阳光，如同别人能从一个爱恋的眼神中感受到温暖一样。一次热情的握手，或是一封友好的信件，都会带给我最真切的快乐。

我有许多从未谋面的远方的朋友。他们确实太多了，以至于我无法一一给他们回信。在此，我想说自己一直对他们那友善的言辞心怀感激，虽然我对他们知之甚少。

能够有幸结识许多天才人物，并与他们交谈，这被我视为生命中的无上荣耀。只有那些认识布鲁克斯主教①的人，才能体验到拥有他的友谊是多么令人快乐的事！当我还是一个小孩子的时候，就喜欢坐在他的膝上，用一只手紧紧抓住他的大手，同时，沙利文小姐则把他关于上帝和宗教世界的精妙言辞一一拼写在我的另一只手上。我怀着孩子的好奇和喜悦听得津津有味。

---

①菲利普斯·布鲁克斯（1835—1893），马萨诸塞州的主教。

虽然我的精神境界无法企及他的高度，但他确实让我领悟到了什么叫作真正快乐的生活。而且我每次总能从他那带回一种深邃的思想。随着我日益长大，我对这些思想也有了更深刻、更美好的感悟。曾有一次，我对为何有这么多种宗教而感到迷惑不解。于是，他对我说道："海伦，世间只有一种通用的宗教——那就是爱的宗教。要全心全意地去爱你的天父，要尽你所能去爱上帝的每一个孩子，要记住，善良的力量远远大过邪恶的力量，进入天堂的钥匙就掌握在你自己手中。"事实上，他的一生正是对这伟大真理最恰当的诠释。在他那高尚的爱心和广博的知识中，已经被深深地渗透了信仰的力量。他看到——

> 上帝存在于人类所有的解放和自由中，
> 存在于所有的谦逊、甜美和安慰中。②

布鲁克斯主教并没有教授我什么特殊的信条或教义，但是他把两种伟大的观念印在了我心上——上帝有着父亲般的慈爱、人类有着兄弟般的情谊。他还使我认识到，这些真理是构成一切信条和崇拜形式的基础。上帝是爱，上帝是我们的天父，我们都是他的孩子。有了这样的信念，最黑暗的乌云也会被驱散，虽然正确可能会变成错误，但邪恶决不会胜利。

在这个世界上，我过得非常快乐，以至于很少考虑将来的事；但我也会记起自己有一些值得珍爱的好友已在天堂的某个美丽的地方等着我了。尽管岁月流逝，但他们似乎依然近在咫尺。假如他们什么时候握紧我的手，如同他们生前那样对我述说知心话语，那我也不会觉得惊奇。

自从布鲁克斯主教去世后，我通读了《圣经》，以及其他一些有关宗教的哲学著作。其中包括斯韦登伯格的《天堂与地狱》③和德拉蒙德的《人类

---

②参见詹姆斯·拉塞尔·洛威尔的《大教堂》。
③伊曼纽·斯韦登伯格（1688－1772）是瑞典的宗教神秘主义者。凯勒在她的《我的宗教》（1927）一书中，提到了她对斯韦登伯格宗教学说的看法。

的攀登》，但我发现，除布鲁克斯主教的"爱的信条"外，其他的信条或教理都无法令人获得心灵的慰藉。我也认识亨利·德拉蒙德先生④，在我的记忆中，他那温暖有力的手给我的拥抱就像是一场祝福仪式。他是朋友中最富有同情心的人。他知识面很广，又和蔼可亲，只要有他在场，人们就绝不会感到乏味。

我还清晰地记得初次见到小奥利弗·温德尔·霍姆斯博士⑤时的情景。那是一个星期日的下午，他邀请我和沙利文小姐去他家做客。那是早春时节，我刚刚学会说话。我们很快被带到了他的书房，发现他正坐在一张大扶手椅里，旁边的壁炉火焰闪烁，噼啪作响。他说他正在回想以前的一些事。

我试探地问："是不是还倾听到了查尔斯河的喃喃细语？"

"是啊，"他答道，"查尔斯河同我有着许多不解之缘。"这房间里有一股油墨和皮革的味道，显然这里满是书籍，于是我本能地伸手摸索起来。我的指尖偶然发现了丁尼生的一册精美诗集，当沙利文小姐告诉我这书的名字时，我就开始背诵：

撞碎，撞碎，撞碎在
灰冷的石上吧，哦，大海！⑥

但我突然停住了。我感到有泪水落在了我手上。我竟然把自己所敬爱的诗人弄哭了，那一刻，我也无比悲伤。他让我坐在他的扶手椅上，又拿来各种有趣的东西让我把玩。在他的请求下，我还背诵了《珍珠鹦鹉螺》⑦，当时，这是我最喜欢的诗。后来，我又多次见过霍姆斯博士，从他身上我不但学会诗，也学到了爱。

---

④亨利·德拉蒙德先生（1851—1897）是苏格兰的宗教作家和科学家。

⑤小奥利弗·温德尔·霍姆斯（1841—1935）是美国著名的法学家、随笔作家和诗人。

⑥参见丁尼生的诗《撞碎，撞碎，撞碎》（Break，Break，Break）。

⑦由美国诗人老霍姆斯所著的一首流行一时的诗歌。

在见过霍姆斯博士不久之后的一个美好夏日，我和沙利文小姐在惠蒂尔先生[8]位于梅里马克的安静家中拜访了他。他彬彬有礼，说起话来优雅而不俗，这使我对他颇有好感。他有一本书收录了他的诗作并印成了盲文版，我朗读了其中的一首《校园时光》。我的发音很清晰，这使他很高兴，并表示他能毫不费力地理解我。随后我问了许多有关这首诗的问题，并把自己的手指放在他的嘴唇上，来"读"他的回答。他说他就是诗中的那个小男孩，而那个女孩的名字是萨莉，他还说了很多，但我都忘了。我还背诵了《荣耀归于上帝》[9]，当我背诵到结尾的诗行时，他在我手中放了一个奴隶的雕像，镣铐正从那奴隶蹲着的身体上落下，就像天使引领彼得逃离监狱，镣铐从彼得的四肢上脱落一样。后来，我们走进了他的书房，他为我的老师亲笔题词：您高尚的工作，使这可爱孩子的心灵挣脱了束缚，我对您深表敬意，我是您真诚的朋友。约翰·G. 惠蒂尔。通过这份题词，惠蒂尔先生表达了对沙利文小姐工作的钦佩。他又对我说："她是你心灵的解放者。"然后，他领着我来到门口，温柔地吻了我的额头。我答应第二年夏天还来看他，可是没等我实现诺言，他就去世了。

爱德华·埃弗雷特·黑尔博士[10]是我的一位老朋友，我八岁时就认识他了。随着年龄的增长，我对他的热爱也不断加深。每当我和沙利文小姐处于困苦和悲伤之际，他那睿智而温暖的安慰总会给我们许多支持；他那强有力的双手，帮助我们度过了许多难关；他把给予我们的一切，同样也给予了千千万万个像我们一样坎坷无助的人们。他在陈腐教条的皮囊里注入了新的爱的美酒，并向人们展示了信念、生存和自由的真谛。他所教给我们的已由他自己在生活中做了完美诠释——热爱祖国，善待他人，以及在生活中怀着

---

[8] 约翰·格林利夫·惠蒂尔（1807－1892），美国诗人、记者和废奴主义者。
[9] 一首由惠蒂尔所著的诗。
[10] 爱德华·埃弗雷特·黑尔博士（1822－1909）是波士顿的一位牧师和作家。

真诚的愿望全力以赴，奋勇直前。他是人类的一名先知，一位灵魂施救者，一位精进不怠的圣徒。所有认识他的朋友们啊——让我们祈祷上帝保佑他！

我已经提过自己初见亚历山大·格雷汉姆·贝尔博士时的情景。从那以后，我还与他一起在华盛顿和他那毗邻巴德克、位于布雷顿角岛腹地的美丽家中度过了很多快乐日子。巴德克村因查尔斯·达德利·沃纳的书[11]而名扬四海。我曾在位于这里的贝尔博士实验室，以及壮丽的布拉斯德奥尔海岸，兴味盎然地听贝尔博士讲述他的实验，一听就是好几小时。我还帮他放风筝，他期望借此能发现控制未来航空器的规律。贝尔博士不但精通多个学科，而且还能巧妙地把那些学科知识，甚至是最深奥的理论都变得妙趣横生。同他在一起会使你感到，哪怕你只有一点点时间，你也有可能成为一个发明者。此外，他还有幽默和富有诗意的一面。他最强烈的感情就是对孩子们深深的爱。当他把一个失聪的小孩子拥入怀中时，他会感到无比高兴。他为失聪者所做的不懈努力将会延续下去，并造福一代又一代的儿童。我们爱他，不仅是他所取得的丰硕成就，还因为他唤醒了别人心中的希望。

我在纽约度过的两年中，曾有很多机会同那些一直久仰却从未奢望谋面的著名人物交谈。我与他们中的大多数人的初次见面都是在我的好朋友劳伦斯·胡顿先生[12]的家中。能在胡顿先生那温馨的家中与他和优雅的胡顿夫人见面，参观他们的图书馆，阅读那些卓有天赋的朋友们写给他们的饱含深情与真知灼见的留言，对我来说真是无上的荣幸。说真的，胡顿先生具有从每一个人身上挖掘最优秀的思想和最善良情感的能力。你无须阅读《一位我所认识的男孩》一书，就能了解他——他是我迄今认识的最慷慨大方、最天真

---

[11] 参见《巴德克》（Baddeck）和《诸如此类》（That Sort of Thing）（1824），这是由沃纳（1829—1900）所著的关于在加拿大大西洋沿岸旅行的书籍。

[12] 劳伦斯·胡顿（1843—1904）是纽约的一名作家和新闻工作者。

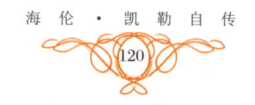

善良的男孩；也是一名在任何时候都对你不离不弃的好朋友。在生活中，他一路追随爱的足迹，对动物和同类都给予无尽的关怀。

胡顿夫人也是位真诚可靠的朋友。我之所以能拥有那么多甜美而珍贵的东西，这一切都要归功于她。在我读大学期间，她常常循循善诱，帮助我不断取得进步。当我在学习中遇到特殊困难并垂头丧气时，她就会写信鼓励我，给我注入了欢乐和勇气。她是那种能给予你启迪的人，从她身上，我们懂得了只有不畏艰辛地履行好自己的职责，以后的路才会平坦易行。

胡顿先生给我介绍了他的很多文学界的朋友，其中最著名的是威廉·迪安·豪威尔斯先生和马克·吐温先生。我见到了理查德·沃森·吉尔德先生和埃德蒙·克拉伦斯·斯特德曼先生[13]。还结识了查尔斯·达德利·沃纳先生，他是最令人开心的"讲故事的人"，也是我最亲爱的朋友；他有着博大的同情心，爱人如己。沃纳先生曾带我去拜会过可敬的"森林诗人"——约翰·巴勒斯先生[14]，他们都是温文尔雅且富有同情心的人，从他们的言行举止中，我能感受到与他们的散文和诗歌所散发出的一样的璀璨魅力。当然，当这些文学大师们在不同话题间纵横捭阖，进行深层次探讨，或是辩论中警句频现、妙语连珠之时，我是不可能跟上他们的步伐的。我就像小阿斯卡尼俄斯[15]一样，脚步蹒跚地跟在那昂首阔步、向着强大命运进发的英雄埃涅阿斯身后。但是，他们也会亲切和蔼地与我谈天说地。吉尔德先生曾向我讲述他在月光下穿过无垠沙漠，前往金字塔的旅程。在吉尔德先生写给我的一封信中，特意在他的签名下方做了一个深深的标记，以便我能感受到它。这使我记起黑尔博士在给我的信中，常常把他的签名用盲文刺在纸上，以便我能亲自触摸它。我

---

[13] 吉尔德（1844—1909）和斯特德曼（1833—1908）都是美国诗人和作家。

[14] 巴勒斯（1837—1921）是一名博物学家和随笔作家。

[15] 小阿斯卡尼俄斯是古罗马诗人维吉尔所著史诗《埃涅阿斯记》中的主人公埃涅阿斯之子。

还从马克·吐温的嘴唇上"阅读"了他的一两个有趣的故事。马克·吐温有着自己独特的思维方式，无论讲话、做事都个性鲜明。在同他握手时，我能感觉到他的眼神闪烁着睿智的光芒。即使当他用一种不可名状的滑稽声音愤世嫉俗地说出至理名言时，你仍能感觉到他的心是一部温馨的《伊利亚特》叙事诗，充满了柔情。

在纽约，我还遇到了其他许多风趣的人物：比如《圣尼古拉斯》那位受人爱戴的编辑玛丽·梅普斯·道奇夫人；还有《替罪羊》一书的可爱作者里格斯夫人（即凯特·道格拉斯·威金）。我不但感受到了她们的爱心，还收到了包含她们个人思想的书籍、启迪心灵的信件，以及那些我愿意反复描述的照片等。可是因篇幅所限，我无法在此一一提及我所有的朋友。实际上，关于他们的许多故事都掩藏在了小天使的羽翼之下，这些记忆是如此的神圣，以致我无法用冰冷的笔墨将其详尽地阐述出来。甚至当提到劳伦斯·胡顿夫人时，我也颇感踌躇。

我还要提及我的另外两位朋友。其中一位是匹兹堡的威廉·肖夫人⑯，我常去她那位于林德赫斯特的家中拜访。她总是做一些让人感到开心的事。自从我和老师认识她之后，多年来，她那宽大的胸怀和睿智的教导一直激励着我们不断前行。

我还有另一位于我有恩的朋友⑰，他因善用有效手段管理大型企业而闻名，他卓越的才能使他赢得了所有人的尊重。他待人友善，悄然无声地到处做好事。为信守承诺我不能提及他那高尚的名字；但是，我仍要欣然感谢他的慷慨大方和深情厚谊，使我实现了上大学的梦想。

不妨这样讲，是我的朋友们成就了我生活的故事。他们千方百计地把我的缺陷转变成一种美好的特权，使我能在失聪失明的阴影里，沉着而快乐地前行。

---

⑯ 一位著名的慈善家。

⑰ 这位朋友很可能是慈善家约翰·P.斯伯丁。

THE STORY OF MY LIFE

Chapter 1

IT IS WITH a kind of fear that I begin to write the history of my life. I have, as it were, a superstitious ***hesitation*** in lifting the veil that clings about my childhood like a golden mist. The task of writing an ***autobiography*** is a difficult one. When I try to classify my earliest impressions, I find that fact and fancy look alike across the years that link the past with the present. The woman paints the child's experiences in her own fantasy. A few impressions stand out vividly from the first years of my life; but "the shadows of the prison-house are on the rest."Besides, many of the joys and sorrows of childhood have lost their ***poignancy***; and many incidents of vital importance in my early education have been forgotten in the excitement of great discoveries. In order, therefore, not to be ***tedious*** I shall try to present in a series of sketches only the episodes that seem to me to be the most interesting and important.

I was born on June 27, 1880, in Tuscumbia, a little town of northern Alabama.

hesitation n. 犹豫；踌躇
autobiography n.自传；自传文学
poignancy n. 强烈；尖锐
tedious adj. 沉闷的；冗长乏味的

The family on my father's side is—descended from Caspar Keller, a native of Switzerland, who settled in Maryland. One of my Swiss ancestors was the first teacher of the deaf in Zurich and wrote a book on the subject of their education—rather a singular coincidence; though it is true that there is no king who has not had a slave among his ancestors, and no slave who has not had a king among his.

My grandfather, Caspar Keller's son, "entered" large tracts of land in Alabama and finally settled there. I have been told that once a year he went from Tuscumbia to Philadelphia on horseback to purchase supplies for the plantation, and my aunt has in her possession many of the letters to his family, which give charming and vivid accounts of these trips.

My Grandmother Keller was a daughter of one of Lafayette's aides, Alexander Moore, and granddaughter of Alexander Spotswood, an early Colonial Governor of Virginia. She was also second cousin to Robert E. Lee.

My father, Arthur H. Keller, was a captain in the Confederate Army, and my mother, Kate Adams, was his second wife and many years younger. Her grandfather, Benjamin Adams, married Susanna E. Goodhue, and lived in Newbury, Massachusetts, for many years. Their son, Charles Adams, was born in Newburyport, Massachusetts, and moved to Helena, Arkansas. When the Civil War broke out, he fought on the side of the South and became a brigadier-general. He married Lucy Helen Everett, who belonged to the same family of Everetts as Edward Everett and Dr. Edward Everett Hale. After the war was over the family moved to Memphis, Tennessee.

I lived, up to the time of the illness that deprived me of my sight and hearing, in a tiny house consisting of a large square room and a small one, in which the servant slept. It is a custom in the South to build a small house near the homestead as an annex to be used on occasion. Such a house my father built after the Civil War, and when he married my mother they went to live in it. It was completely covered with vines, climbing roses and honeysuckles. From the garden it looked like an arbor. The little porch was hidden from view by a screen of yellow roses and southern smilax. It was the favorite ***haunt*** of hummingbirds and bees.

The Keller homestead, where the family lived, was a few steps from our little rose-bower. It was called "Ivy Green" because the house and the surrounding trees and fences were covered with beautiful English ivy. Its old-fashioned garden was the paradise of my childhood.

Even in the days before my teacher came, I used to feel along the square ***stiff*** boxwood hedges, and, guided by the sense of smell, would find the first violets and lilies. There, too, after a fit of temper, I went to find comfort and to hide my hot face in the cool leaves and grass. What joy it was to lose myself in that garden of flowers, to wander happily from spot to spot, until, coming suddenly upon a beautiful vine, I recognized it by its leaves and blossoms, and knew it was the vine which covered the tumble-down summer-house at the farther end of the garden! Here, also, were trailing clematis, drooping jessamine, and some rare sweet flowers called butterfly lilies, because their ***fragile*** petals ***resemble*** butterflies' wings. But the roses—they were loveliest of all. Never have I found in the greenhouses of the North such heart-satisfying roses as the climbing roses of my southern home. They used to hang in long festoons from our porch, filling the whole air with their fragrance, untainted by any earthy smell; and in the early morning, washed in the dew, they felt so soft, so pure, I could not help wondering if they did not resemble the asphodels of God's garden.

The beginning of my life was simple and much like every other little life. I came, I saw, I conquered, as the first baby in the family always does. There was the usual amount of discussion as to a name for me. The first baby in the family was not to be lightly named, every one

haunt n. 栖息地；常去的地方　　stiff adj. 呆板的；坚硬的
fragile adj. 脆的；易碎的　　　　resemble vt. 类似；像

was **emphatic** about that. My father suggested the name of Mildred Campbell, an ancestor whom he highly **esteemed**, and he declined to take any further part in the discussion. My mother solved the problem by giving it as her wish that I should be called after her mother, whose maiden name was Helen Everett. But in the excitement of carrying me to church my father lost the name on the way, very naturally, since it was one in which he had declined to have a part. When the minister asked him for it, he just remembered that it had been decided to call me after my grandmother, and he gave her name as Helen Adams.

I am told that while I was still in long dresses I showed many signs of an eager, self-asserting disposition. Everything that I saw other people do I insisted upon imitating. At six months I could pipe out "How d'ye," and one day I attracted everyone's attention by saying "Tea, tea, tea" quite plainly. Even after my illness I remembered one of the words I had learned in these early months. It was the word "water," and I continued to make some sound for that word after all other speech was lost. I ceased making the sound "wah-wah" only when I learned to spell the word.

They tell me I walked the day I was a year old. My mother had just taken me out of the bath-tub and was holding me in her lap, when I was suddenly attracted by the flickering shadows of leaves that danced in the sunlight on the smooth floor. I slipped from my mother's lap and almost ran toward them. The impulse gone, I fell down and cried for her to take me up in her arms.

These happy days did not last long. One brief spring, musical with the song of robin and mockingbird, one summer rich in fruit and roses, one autumn of gold and crimson sped by and left their gifts at the feet of an eager, delighted child. Then, in the **dreary** month of February, came the illness which closed my eyes and ears and plunged me into the

emphatic adj. 着重的；加强语气的
esteemed adj. 受人尊敬的   dreary adj. 沉闷的；令人沮丧的

unconsciousness of a newborn baby. They called it acute congestion of the stomach and brain. The doctor thought I could not live. Early one morning, however, the fever left me as suddenly and mysteriously as it had come. There was great rejoicing in the family that morning, but no one, not even the doctor, knew that I should never see or hear again.

I fancy I still have confused recollections of that illness. I especially remember the ***tenderness*** with which my mother tried to soothe me in my waking hours of fret and pain, and the agony and bewilderment with which I awoke after a tossing half sleep, and turned my eyes, so dry and hot, to the wall, away from the once-loved light, which came to me dim and yet more dim each day. But, except for these fleeting memories, if, indeed, they be memories, it all seems very unreal, like a nightmare. Gradually I got used to the silence and darkness that surrounded me and forgot that it had ever been different, until she came—my teacher—who was to set my spirit free. But during the first nineteen months of my life I had caught glimpses of broad, green fields, a ***luminous*** sky, trees and flowers which the darkness that followed could not wholly blot out. If we have once seen, "the day is ours, and what the day has shown."

unconsciousness n. 无意识；意识不清；人事不省
tenderness n. 亲切；柔软；柔和
luminous adj. 发光的；明亮的；清楚的

Chapter 2

I CANNOT RECALL what happened during the first months after my illness. I only know that I sat in my mother's lap or clung to her dress as she went about her household duties. My hands felt every object and observed every motion, and in this way I learned to know many things. Soon I felt the need of some communication with others and began to make crude signs. A shake of the head meant "No" and a nod, "Yes," a pull meant "Come" and a push "Go." Was it bread that I wanted? Then I would *imitate* the acts of cutting the slices and buttering them. If I wanted my mother to make ice-cream for dinner I made the sign for working the freezer and shivered, indicating cold. My mother, more-over, succeeded in making me understand a good deal. I always knew when she wished me to bring her something, and I would run upstairs or anywhere else she indicated. Indeed, I owe to her loving wisdom all that was bright and good in my long night.

I understood a good deal of what was going on about me. At five I learned to fold and put away the clean clothes when they were brought in from the *laundry*, and I distinguished my own from the rest. I knew

---

imitate vt. 模仿；仿效　　laundry n. 洗衣店

by the way my mother and aunt dressed when they were going out, and I ***invariably*** begged to go with them. I was always sent for when there was company, and when the guests took their leave, I waved my hand to them, I think with a vague remembrance of the meaning of the ***gesture***. One day some gentlemen called on my mother, and I felt the shutting of the front door and other sounds that indicated their arrival. On a sudden thought I ran upstairs before any one could stop me, to put on my idea of a company dress. Standing before the mirror, as I had seen others do, I anointed mine head with oil and covered my face thickly with powder. Then I pinned a veil over my head so that it covered my face and fell in folds down to my shoulders, and tied an ***enormous*** bustle round my small waist, so that it dangled behind, almost meeting the hem of my skirt. Thus attired I went down to help ***entertain*** the company.

I do not remember when I first realized that I was different from other people; but I knew it before my teacher came to me. I had noticed that my mother and my friends did not use signs as I did when they wanted anything done, but talked with their mouths. Sometimes I stood between two persons who were conversing and touched their lips. I could not understand, and was vexed. I moved my lips and gesticulated frantically without result. This made me so angry at times that I kicked and screamed until I was exhausted.

I think I knew when I was naughty, for I knew that it hurt Ella, my nurse, to kick her, and when my fit of temper was over I had a feeling akin to regret. But I cannot remember any instance in which this feeling prevented me from repeating the naughtiness when I failed to get what I wanted.

In those days a little colored girl, Martha Washington, the child of our cook, and Belle, an old setter and a great hunter in her day, were my constant companions. Martha Washington understood my signs, and I

invariably adv. 总是；不变地；一定　　gesture n. 姿态；手势
enormous adj. 庞大的　　entertain vt. 招待

seldom had any difficulty in making her do just as I wished. It pleased me to domineer over her, and she generally submitted to my **_tyranny_** rather than risk a hand-to-hand encounter. I was strong, active, indifferent to consequences. I knew my own mind well enough and always had my own way, even if I had to fight tooth and nail for it. We spent a great deal of time in the kitchen, kneading dough balls, helping make ice-cream, grinding coffee, quarreling over the cake-bowl, and feeding the hens and turkeys that swarmed about the kitchen steps. Many of them were so **_tame_** that they would eat from my hand and let me feel them. One big gobbler snatched a tomato from me one day and ran away with it. Inspired, perhaps, by Master Gobbler's success, we carried off to the **_woodpile_** a cake which the cook had just frosted, and ate every bit of it. I was quite ill afterward, and I wonder if retribution also overtook the turkey.

The guinea-fowl likes to hide her nest in out-of-the-way places, and it was one of my greatest delights to hunt for the eggs in the long grass. I could not tell Martha Washington when I wanted to go egg-hunting, but I would double my hands and put them on the ground, which meant something round in the grass, and Martha always understood. When we were fortunate enough to find a nest I never allowed her to carry the eggs home, making her understand by emphatic signs that she might fall and break them.

The sheds where the corn was stored, the stable where the horses were kept, and the yard where the cows were milked morning and evening were unfailing sources of interest to Martha and me. The milkers would let me keep my hands on the cows while they milked, and I often got well switched by the cows for my curiosity.

The making ready for Christmas was always a delight to me. Of

tyranny n. 暴政；专横；严酷　　tame adj. 驯服的；平淡的；顺从的
woodpile n. 柴堆；木料堆

course I did not know what it was all about, but I enjoyed the pleasant odors that filled the house and the tidbits that were given to Martha Washington and me to keep us quiet. We were sadly in the way, but that did not interfere with our pleasure in the least. They allowed us to ***grind*** the spices, pick over the raisins and lick the stirring spoons. I hung my stocking because the others did; I cannot remember, however, that the ceremony interested me especially, nor did my curiosity cause me to wake before daylight to look for my gifts.

Martha Washington had as great a love of mischief as I. Two little children were seated on the veranda steps one hot July afternoon. One was black as ebony, with little bunches of fuzzy hair tied with shoestrings sticking out all over her head like corkscrews. The other was white, with long golden curls. One child was six years old, the other two or three years older. The younger child was blind—that was I—and the other was Martha Washington. We were busy cutting out paper dolls; but we soon wearied of this amusement, and after cutting up our shoestrings and clipping all the leaves off the honeysuckle that were within reach. I turned my attention to Martha's corkscrews. She objected at first, but finally submitted. Thinking that turn and turn about is fair play, she seized the ***scissors*** and cut off one of my curls, and would have cut them all off but for my mother's timely interference.

Belle, our dog, my other companion, was old and lazy and liked to sleep by the open fire rather than to romp with me. I tried hard to teach her my sign language, but she was dull and ***inattentive***. She sometimes started and quivered with excitement, then she became perfectly rigid, as dogs do when they point a bird. I did not then know why Belle acted in this way; but I knew she was not doing as I wished. This vexed me and the lesson always ended in a one-sided boxing match. Belle would

grind vt. 磨碎　　scissors n. 剪刀
inattentive adj. 疏忽的；怠慢的；不注意的

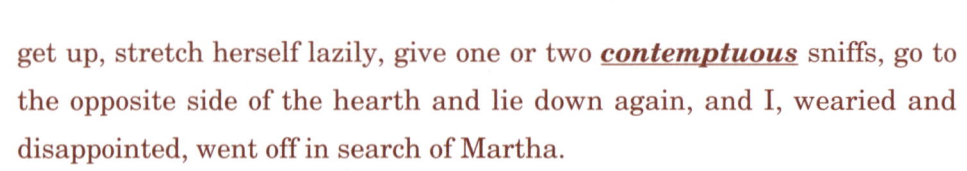

get up, stretch herself lazily, give one or two **contemptuous** sniffs, go to the opposite side of the hearth and lie down again, and I, wearied and disappointed, went off in search of Martha.

Many incidents of those early years are fixed in my memory, isolated, but clear and distinct, making the sense of that silent, aimless, dayless life all the more intense.

One day I happened to spill water on my apron, and I spread it out to dry before the fire which was flickering on the sitting-room hearth. The apron did not dry quickly enough to suit me, so I drew nearer and threw it right over the hot ashes. The fire leaped into life; the flames encircled me so that in a moment my clothes were blazing. I made a terrified noise that brought Viny, my old nurse, to the rescue. Throwing a blanket over me, she almost suffocated me, but she put out the fire. Except for my hands and hair I was not badly burned.

About this time I found out the use of a key. One morning I locked my mother up in the **pantry**, where she was obliged to remain three hours, as the servants were in a detached part of the house. She kept pounding on the door, while I sat outside on the porch steps and laughed with glee as I felt the jar of the pounding. This most naughty prank of mine convinced my parents that I must be taught as soon as possible. After my teacher, Miss Sullivan, came to me, I sought an early opportunity to lock her in her room. I went upstairs with something which my mother made me understand I was to give to Miss Sullivan; but no sooner had I given it to her than I slammed the door to, locked it, and hid the key under the **wardrobe** in the hall. I could not be induced to tell where the key was. My father was obliged to get a ladder and take Miss Sullivan out through the window—much to my delight. Months after I produced the key.

contemptuous adj. 轻蔑的；侮辱的
pantry n. 餐具室；食品室；食品储藏室　　wardrobe n. 衣柜

When I was about five years old we moved from the little vine-covered house to a large new one. The family consisted of my father and mother, two older half-brothers, and, afterward, a little sister, Mildred. My earliest distinct recollection of my father is making my way through great drifts of newspapers to his side and finding him alone, holding a sheet of paper before his face. I was greatly puzzled to know what he was doing. I imitated this action, even wearing his spectacles, thinking they might help solve the mystery. But I did not find out the secret for several years. Then I learned what those papers were, and that my father edited one of them.

My father was most loving and **_indulgent_**, devoted to his home, seldom leaving us, except in the hunting season. He was a great hunter, I have been told, and a celebrated shot. Next to his family he loved his dogs and gun. His hospitality was great, almost to a fault, and he seldom came home—without bringing a guest. His special pride was the big garden where, it was said, he raised the finest watermelons mad strawberries in the country; and to me he brought the first ripe grapes and the choicest berries. I remember his caressing touch as he led me from tree to tree, from vine to vine, and his eager delight in whatever pleased me.

He was a famous story-teller; after I had acquired language he used to spell **_clumsily_** into my hand his cleverest anecdotes, and nothing pleased him more than to have me repeat them at an opportune moment.

I was in the North, enjoying the last beautiful days of the summer of 1896, when I heard the news of my father's death. He had had a short illness, there had been a brief time of acute suffering, then all was over. This was my first great sorrow—my first personal experience with death.

How shall I write of my mother? She is so near to me that it almost seems indelicate to speak of her.

For a long time I regarded my little sister as an intruder. I knew

indulgent adj. 宽容的；任性的   clumsily adv. 笨拙地；粗陋地

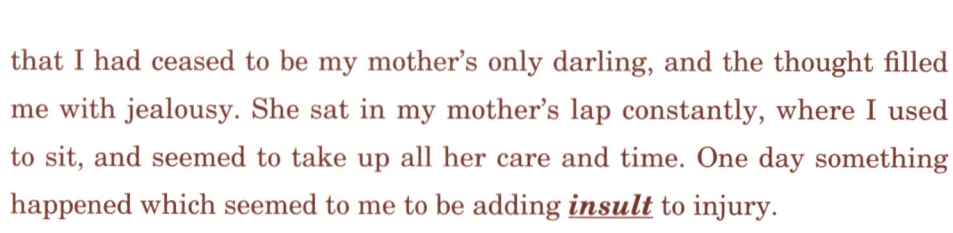

that I had ceased to be my mother's only darling, and the thought filled me with jealousy. She sat in my mother's lap constantly, where I used to sit, and seemed to take up all her care and time. One day something happened which seemed to me to be adding ***insult*** to injury.

At that time I had a much-petted, much-abused doll, which I afterward named Nancy. She was, alas, the helpless victim of my outbursts of temper and of affection, so that she became much the worse for wear, I had dolls which talked, and cried, and opened and shut their eyes; yet I never loved one of them as I loved poor Nancy. She had a cradle, and I often spent an hour or more rocking her. I guarded both doll and cradle with the most jealous care; but once I discovered my little sister sleeping peacefully in the cradle. At this ***presumption*** on the part of one to whom as yet no tie of love bound me I grew angry. I rushed upon the cradle and overturned it, and the baby might have been killed had my mother not caught her as she fell. Thus it is that when we walk in the valley of twofold solitude we know little of the tender affections that grow out of endearing words and actions and companionship. But afterward, when I was restored to my human heritage, Mildred and I grew into each other's hearts, so that we were content to go hand-in-hand wherever ***caprice*** led us, although she could not understand my finger language, nor I her childish ***prattle***.

insult n. 侮辱；凌辱；无礼　　presumption n. 推测
caprice n. 反复无常　　　　　prattle n. 咿咿呀呀声

Chapter 3

MEANWHILE, THE DESIRE to express myself grew. The few signs I used became less and less ***adequate***, and my failures to make myself understood were invariably followed by outbursts of passion. I felt as if invisible hands were holding me, and I made frantic efforts to free myself. I struggled—not that struggling helped matters, but the spirit of resistance was strong within me; I generally broke down in tears and physical exhaustion. If my mother happened to be near I crept into her arms, too ***miserable*** even to remember the cause of the tempest. After awhile the need of some means of communication became so urgent that these outbursts occurred daily, sometimes hourly.

My parents were deeply grieved and ***perplexed***. We lived a long way from any school for the blind or the deal, and it seemed unlikely that any one would come to such all out-of-the-way place as Tuscumbia to teach a child who was both deaf and blind. Indeed, my friends and relatives sometimes doubted whether I could be taught. My mother's only ray of hope came from Dickens's "American Notes." She had read his account of

adequate adj. 充足的；适当的　　miserable adj. 悲惨的；痛苦的
perplexed adj. 困惑的；不知所措的

Laura Bridgman, and remembered vaguely that she was deaf and blind, yet had been educated. But she also remembered with a hopeless pang that Dr. Howe, who had discovered the way to teach the deaf and blind, had been dead many years. His methods had probably died with him; and if they had not, how was a little girl in a far-off town in Alabama to receive the benefit of them?

When I was about six years old, my father heard of an eminent oculist in Baltimore, who had been successful in many eases that had seemed hopeless. My parents at once determined to take me to Baltimore to see if anything could be done for my eyes.

The journey, which I remember well, was very pleasant. I made friends with many people on the train. One lady gave me a box of shells. My father made holes in these so that I could string them, and for a long time they kept me happy and contented. The conductor, too, was kind. Often when he went his rounds I clung to his coat tails while he collected and punched the tickets. His **punch**, with which he let me play, was a delightful toy. Curled up in a corner of the seat I amused myself for hours making funny little holes in bits of cardboard.

My aunt made me a big doll out of towels. It was the most comical, shapeless thing, this **improvised** doll, with no nose, mouth, ears or eves—nothing that even the imagination of a child could convert into a face. Curiously enough, the absence of eyes struck me more than all the other defects put together. I pointed this out to everybody with provoking **persistency**, but no one seemed equal to the task of providing the doll with eyes. A bright idea, however, shot into my mind, and the problem was solved. I tumbled off the seat and searched under it until I found my aunt's cape, which was trimmed with large beads. I pulled two beads off and indicated to her that I wanted her to sew them on my doll. She raised my hand to her eyes in a questioning way, and I nodded energetically.

punch n. 打洞器；钻孔机　　improvised adj. 即兴的；临时准备的
persistency n. 持续；固执；坚韧

The beads were sewed in the right place and I could not contain myself for joy; but immediately I lost all interest in the doll. During the whole trip I did not have one fit of temper, there were so many things to keep my mind and fingers busy.

When we arrived in Baltimore, Dr. Chisholm received us kindly: but he could do nothing. He said, however, that I could be educated, and advised my father to consult Dr. Alexander Graham Bell, of Washington, who would be able to give him information about schools and teachers of deaf or blind children. Acting on the doctor's advice, we went immediately to Washington to see Dr. Bell, my father with a sad heart and many misgivings, I wholly unconscious of his **_anguish_**, finding pleasure in the excitement of moving from place to place. Child as I was, I at once felt the tenderness and sympathy which endeared Dr. Bell to so many hearts, as his wonderful achievements enlist their admiration. He held me on his knee while I examined his watch, and he made it strike for me. He understood my signs, and I knew it and loved him at once. But I did not dream that that interview would be the door through which I should pass from darkness into light, from isolation to friendship, companionship, knowledge, love.

Dr. Bell advised my father to write to Mr. Anagnos, director of the Perkins Institution in Boston, the scene of Dr. Howe's great labors for the blind, and ask him if he had a teacher competent to begin my education. This my father did at once, and in a few weeks there came a kind letter from Mr. Anagnos with the comforting assurance that a teacher had been found. This was in the summer of 1886. But Miss Sullivan did not arrive until the following March.

Thus I came up out of Egypt and stood before Sinai, and a power divine touched my spirit and gave it sight, so that I beheld many wonders. And from the **_sacred_** mountain I heard a voice which said, "Knowledge is love and light and vision."

anguish n. 痛苦；苦恼　　sacred adj. 神的；神灵的；宗教的；庄严的

Chapter 4

THE MOST IMPORTANT day I remember in all my life is the one on which my teacher, Anne Mansfield Sullivan, came to me. I am filled with wonder when I consider the immeasurable contrasts between the two lives which it connects. It was the third of March, 1887, three months before I was seven years old.

On the afternoon of that eventful day, I stood on the porch, dumb, expectant. I guessed vaguely from my mother's signs and from the hurrying to and ***fro*** in the house that something unusual was about to happen, so I went to the door and waited on the steps. The afternoon sun penetrated the mass of honeysuckle that covered the porch, and fell on my upturned face. My fingers lingered almost unconsciously on the familiar leaves and blossoms which had just come forth to greet the sweet southern spring. I did not know what the future held of ***marvel*** or surprise for me. Anger and bitterness had preyed upon me continually for weeks and a deep languor had succeeded this passionate struggle.

Have you ever been at sea in a dense fog, when it seemed as if a ***tangible*** white darkness shut you in, and the great ship, tense and

---

fro adv. 向后；向那边　　marvel n. 奇迹

anxious, groped her way toward the shore with plummet and sounding-line, and you waited with beating heart for something to happen? I was like that ship before my education began, only I was without compass or sounding-line, and had no way of knowing how near the harbor was. "Light! give me light!" was the wordless cry of my soul, and the light of love shone on me in that very hour.

I felt approaching footsteps. I stretched out my hand as I supposed to my mother. Some one took it, and I was caught up and held close in the arms of her who had come to **_reveal_** all things to me, and, more than all things else, to love me.

The morning after my teacher came she led me into her room and gave me a doll. The little blind children at the Perkins Institution had sent it and Laura Bridgman had dressed it; but I did not know this until afterward. When I had played with it a little while, Miss Sullivan slowly spelled into my hand the word "d-o-l-l." I was at once interested in this finger play and tried to imitate it. When I finally succeeded in making the letters correctly I was flushed with childish pleasure and pride. Running downstairs to my mother I held up my hand and made the letters for doll. I did not know that I was spelling a word or even that words existed; I was simply making my fingers go in monkey-like imitation. In the days that followed I learned to spell in this uncomprehending way a great many words, among them *pin*, *hat*, *cup* and a few verbs like *sit*, *stand* and *walk*. But my teacher had been with me several weeks before I understood that everything has a name.

One day, while I was playing with my new doll, Miss Sullivan put my big **_rag_** doll into my lap also, spelled, "d-o-l-l" and tried to make me understand that "d-o-l-l" applied to both. Earlier in the day we had had a tussle over the words "m-u-g" and "w-a-t-e-r". Miss Sullivan had tried to

tangible adj. 有形的；切实的；可触摸的
reveal vt. 显示；透露；揭露   rag n. 破布；碎屑

impress upon me that "m-u-g" is *mug* and that "w-a-t-e-r" is *water*, but I persisted in confounding the two. In despair she had dropped the subject for the time, only to renew it at the first opportunity. I became impatient at her repeated attempts and, seizing the new doll, I dashed it upon the floor. I was keenly delighted when I felt the fragments of the broken doll at my feet. Neither sorrow nor regret followed my passionate outburst. I had not loved the doll. In the still, dark world in which I lived there was no strong sentiment or tenderness. I felt my teacher sweep the fragments to one side of the hearth and I had a sense of satisfaction that the cause of my discomfort was removed. She brought me my hat, and I knew I was going out into the warm sunshine. This thought, if a wordless sensation may be called a thought, made me hop and skip with pleasure.

We walked down the path to the well-house, attracted by the **fragrance** of the honeysuckle with which it was covered. Someone was drawing water and my teacher placed my hand under the spout. As the cool stream gushed over one hand she spelled into the other the word *water*, first slowly, then rapidly. I stood still, my whole attention fixed upon the motions of her fingers. Suddenly I felt a **misty** consciousness as of something forgotten—a thrill of returning thought; and somehow the mystery of language was revealed to me. I knew then that "w-a-t-e-r" meant the wonderful cool something that was flowing over my hand. That living word awakened my soul, gave it light, hope, joy, set it free! There were barriers still, it is true, but barriers that could in time be swept away.

I left the well-house eager to learn. Everything had a name, and each name gave birth to a new thought. As we returned to the house every object which I touched seemed to quiver with life. That was because I saw everything with the strange, new sight that had come to me. On

fragrance n. 香味；芬芳   misty adj. 模糊的；有雾的

entering the door I remembered the doll I had broken. I felt my way to the hearth and picked up the pieces. I tried vainly to put them together. Then my eyes filled with tears; for I realized what I had done, and for the first time I felt repentance and sorrow.

I learned a great many new words that day. I do not remember what they all were; but I do know that *mother*, *father*, *sister*, *teacher* were among them—words that were to make the world blossom for me, "like Aaron's rod, with flowers." It would have been difficult to find a happier child than I was as I lay in my crib at the close of that eventful day and lived over the joys it had brought me, and for the first time longed for a new day to come.

Chapter 5

I RECALL MANY incidents of the summer of 1887 that followed my soul's sudden awakening. I did nothing but explore with my hands and learn the name of every object that I touched; and the more I handled things and learned their names and uses, the more **_joyous_** and confident grew my sense of **_kinship_** with the rest of the world.

When the time of daisies and buttercups came Miss Sullivan took me by the hand across the fields, where men were preparing the earth for the seed, to the banks of the Tennessee River, and there, sitting on the warm grass, I had my first lesson in the beneficence of nature. I learned how the sun and the rain make to grow out of the ground every tree that is pleasant to the sight and good for food, how birds build their nests and live and thrive from land to land, how the squirrel, the deer, the lion and every other creature finds food and shelter. As my knowledge of things grew I felt more and more the delight of the world I was in. Long before I learned to do a sum in arithmetic or describe the shape of the earth, Miss Sullivan had taught me to find beauty in the fragrant woods, in every **_blade_** of grass, and in the curves and dimples of my baby sister's hand.

joyous adj. 令人高兴的；充满快乐的　　kinship n. 亲密关系
blade n. 叶片

She linked my earliest thoughts with nature, and made me feel that "birds and flowers and I were happy peers."

But about this time I had an experience which taught me that nature is not always kind. One day my teacher and I were returning from a long ***ramble***. The morning had been fine, but it was growing warm and sultry when at last we turned our faces homeward. Two or three times we stopped to rest under a tree by the wayside. Our last halt was under a wild cherry tree a short distance from the house. The shade was grateful, and the tree was so easy to climb that with my teacher's assistance I was able to scramble to a seat in the branches. It was so cool up in the tree that Miss Sullivan proposed that we have our luncheon there. I promised to keep still while she went to the house to fetch it.

Suddenly a change passed over the tree. All the sun's warmth left the air. I knew the sky was black, because all the heat, which meant light to me, had died out of the atmosphere. A strange odor came up from the earth. I knew it, it was the odor that always precedes a thunderstorm, and a nameless fear clutched at my heart. I felt absolutely alone, cut off from my friends and the firm earth. The immense, the unknown, enfolded me. I remained still and expectant; a chilling ***terror*** crept over me. I longed for my teacher's return; but above all things I wanted to get down from that tree.

There was a moment of sinister silence, then a multitudinous stirring of the leaves. A shiver ran through the tree, and the wind sent forth a blast that would have knocked me off had I not clung to the branch with might and main. The tree swayed and strained. The small twigs snapped and fell about me in showers. A wild impulse to jump seized me, but terror held me fast. I crouched down in the fork of the tree. The branches lashed about me. I felt the intermittent jarring that came now and then, as if something heavy had fallen and the shock had traveled up till it reached the limb I sat on. It worked my suspense up

ramble n. 漫步；漫游   terror n. 恐怖；恐惧

to the highest point, and just as I was thinking the tree and I should fall together, my teacher seized my hand and helped me down. I clung to her, trembling with joy to feel the earth under my feet once more. I had learned a new lesson—that nature "wages open war against her children, and under softest touch hides treacherous claws."

After this experience it was a long time before I climbed another tree. The mere thought filled me with terror. It was the sweet allurement of the mimosa tree in full bloom that finally overcame my fears. One beautiful spring morning when I was alone in the summer-house, reading, I became aware of a wonderful **subtle** fragrance in the air. I started up and instinctively stretched out my hands. It seemed as if the spirit of spring had passed through the summer-house. "What is it?" I asked, and the next minute I recognized the odor of the mimosa blossoms. I felt my way to the end of the garden, knowing that the mimosa tree was near the fence, at the turn of the path. Yes, there it was, all quivering in the warm sunshine, its blossom-laden branches almost touching the long grass. Was there ever anything so exquisitely beautiful in the world before! Its delicate blossoms shrank from the slightest earthly touch; it seemed as if a tree of paradise had been transplanted to earth. I made my way through a shower of petals to the great trunk and for one minute stood *irresolute*; then, putting my foot in the broad space between the forked branches, I pulled myself up into the tree. I had some difficulty in holding on, for the branches were very large and the bark hurt my hands. But I had a delicious sense that I was doing something unusual and wonderful, so I kept on climbing higher and higher, until I reached a little seat which somebody had built there so long ago that it had grown part of the tree itself. I sat there for a long, long time, feeling like a fairy on a rosy cloud. After that I spent many happy hours in my tree of paradise, thinking fair thoughts and dreaming bright dreams.

subtle adj. 微妙的；精细的；稀薄的   irresolute adj. 优柔寡断的；踌躇不定的

Chapter 6

I HAD NOW the key to all language, and I was eager to learn to use it. Children who hear acquire language without any particular effort; the words that fall from others' lips they catch on the wing, as it were, delightedly, while the little deaf child must trap them by a slow and often painful process. But whatever the process, the result is wonderful. Gradually from naming an object we advance step by step until we have traversed the vast distance between our first stammered ***syllable*** and the sweep of thought in a line of Shakespeare.

At first, when my teacher told me about a new thing I asked very few questions. My ideas were vague, and my vocabulary was inadequate; but as my knowledge of things grew, and I learned more and more words, my field of inquiry broadened, and I would return again and again to the same subject, eager for further information. Sometimes a new word revived an image that some earlier expericnce had ***engraved*** on my brain.

I remember the morning that I first asked the meaning of the word, "love." This was before I knew many words. I had found a few early

---

syllable n. 音节   engraved v. 雕刻

violets in the garden and brought them to my teacher. She tried to kiss me; but at that time I did not like to have any one kiss me except my mother. Miss Sullivan put her arm gently round me and spelled into my hand, "I love Helen."

"What is love?" I asked.

She drew me closer to her and said, "It is here," pointing to my heart, whose beats I was conscious of for the first time. Her words puzzled me very much because I did not then understand anything unless I touched it.

I smelt the violets in her hand and asked, half in words, half in signs, a question which meant, "Is love the sweetness of flowers?"

"No," said my teacher.

Again I thought. The warm sun was shining on us.

"Is this not love?" I asked, pointing in the direction from, which the heat came. "Is this not love?"

It seemed to me that there could be nothing more beautiful than the sun, whose warmth makes all things grow. But Miss Sullivan shook her head, and I was greatly puzzled and disappointed. I thought it strange that my teacher could not show me love.

A day or two afterward I was stringing beads of different sizes in **symmetrical** groups—two large beads, three small ones, and so on. I had made many mistakes, and Miss Sullivan had pointed them out again and again with gentle patience. Finally I noticed a very obvious error in the **sequence** and for an instant I concentrated my attention on the lesson and tried to think how I should have arranged the beads. Miss Sullivan touched my forehead and spelled with decided emphasis, "Think."

In a flash I knew that the word was the name of the process that was going on in my head. This was my first conscious perception of an abstract idea.

For a long time I was still—I was not thinking of the beads in

symmetrical adj. 匀称的；对称的   sequence n. 序列；顺序

my lap, but trying to find a meaning for "love" in the light of this new idea. The sun had been under a cloud all day, and there had been brief showers; but suddenly the sun broke forth in all its southern splendor.

Again I asked my teacher, "Is this not love?"

"Love is something like the clouds that were in the sky before the sun came out."she replied. Then in simpler words than these, which at that time I could not have understood, she explained: "You cannot touch the clouds, you know; but you feel the rain and know how glad the flowers and the thirsty earth are to have it after a hot day. You cannot touch love either; but you feel the sweetness that it pours into everything. Without love you would not be happy or want to play."

The beautiful truth burst upon my mind—I felt that there were invisible lines stretched between my spirit and the spirits of others.

From the beginning of my education Miss Sullivan made it a practice to speak to me as she would speak to any hearing child; the only difference was that she spelled the sentences into my hand instead of speaking them. If I did not know the words and idioms necessary to express my thoughts she supplied them, even suggesting conversation when I was unable to keep up my end of the dialogue.

This process was continued for several years; for the deaf child does not learn in a month, or even in two or three years, the numberless idioms and expressions used in the simplest daily intercourse. The little hearing child learns these from constant repetition and imitation. The conversation he hears in his home stimulates his mind and suggests topics and calls forth the **spontaneous** expression of his own thoughts. This natural exchange of ideas is denied to the deaf child. My teacher, realizing this, determined to supply the kinds of stimuli I lacked. This she did by repeating to me as far as possible, verbatim, what she heard, and by showing me how I could take part in the conversation. But it was

spontaneous adj. 自发的；自然的；无意识的

a long time before I ventured to take the initiative, and still longer before I could find something appropriate to say at the right time.

The deaf and the blind find it very difficult to acquire the amenities of conversation. How much more this difficulty, must be augmented in the case of those who are both deaf and bind! They cannot ***distinguish*** the tone of the voice or, without assistance, go up and down the gamut of tones that give significance to words; nor can they watch the expression of the speaker's face, and a look is often the very soul of what one says.

distinguish vt. 区分；辨别

Chapter 7

THE NEXT IMPORTANT step in my education was learning to read.

As soon as I could spell a few words my teacher gave me slips of cardboard on which were printed words in raised letters. I quickly learned that each printed word stood for an object, an act, or a quality. I had a frame in which I could arrange the words in little sentences; but before I ever put sentences in the frame I used to make them in objects. I found the slips of paper which represented, for example, "doll," "is," "on," "bed" and placed each name on its object; then I put my doll on the bed with the words *is*, *on*, *bed* arranged beside the doll, thus making a sentence of the words, and at the same time carrying out the idea of the sentence with the things themselves.

One day, Miss Sullivan tells me, I pinned the word *girl* on my pinafore and stood in the wardrobe. On the shelf I arranged the words, *is*, *in*, *wardrobe*. Nothing delighted me so much as this game. My teacher and I played it for hours at a time. Often everything in the room was arranged in object sentences.

From the printed slip it was but a step to the printed book. I took my "Reader for Beginners" and hunted for the words I knew; when I found them my joy was like that of a game of hide-and-seek. Thus I began to read. Of the time when I began to read connected stories I shall speak later.

For a long time I had no regular lessons. Even when I studied most earnestly it seemed more like play than work. Everything Miss Sullivan taught me she illustrated by a beautiful story or a poem. Whenever anything delighted or interested me she talked it over with me just as if she were a little girl herself. What many children think of with dread, as a painful **_plodding_** through grammar, hard sums and harder definitions, is today one of my most precious memories.

I cannot explain the peculiar sympathy Miss Sullivan had with my pleasures and desires. Perhaps it was the result of long association with the blind. Added to this she had a wonderful faculty for description. She went quickly over uninteresting details, and never nagged me with questions to see if I remembered the day-before-yesterday's lesson. She introduced dry technicalities of science little by little, making every subject so real that I could not help remembering what she taught.

We read and studied out of doors, preferring the sunlit woods to the house. All my early lessons have in them the breath of the woods—the fine, resinous odor of pine needles, blended with the perfume of wild grapes. Seated in the gracious shade of a wild tulip tree, I learned to think that everything has a lesson and a suggestion. "The loveliness of things taught me all their use." Indeed, everything that could hum, or buzz, or sing, or bloom, had a part in my education—noisy-throated frogs, katydids and crickets held in my hand until, forgetting their embarrassment, they trilled their reedy note, little downy chickens and wildflowers, the dogwood blossoms, **_meadow_**-violets and budding fruit trees. I felt the bursting cotton-bolls and fingered their soft fiber and fuzzy seeds; I felt the low soughing of the wind through the cornstalks,

plodding adj. 单调乏味的　　meadow n. 草场；牧场

the silky rustling of the long leaves, and the indignant snort of my pony, as we caught him in the pasture and put the bit in his mouth—ah me! how well I remember the spicy, clovery smell of his breath!

Sometimes I rose at dawn and stole into the garden while the heavy dew lay on the grass and flowers. Few know what joy it is to feel the roses pressing softly into the hand, or the beautiful motion of the lilies as they sway in the morning breeze. Sometimes I caught an insect in the flower I was plucking, and I felt the faint noise of a pair of wings rubbed together in a sudden terror, as the little creature became aware of a pressure from without.

Another favorite haunt of mine was the **orchard**, where the fruit ripened early in July. The large, downy peaches would reach themselves into my hand, and as the joyous breezes flew about the trees the apples tumbled at my feet. Oh, the delight with which I gathered up the fruit in my pinafore, pressed my face against the smooth cheeks of the apples, still warm from the sun, and skipped back to the house!

Our favorite walk was to Keller's Landing, an old tumble-down **lumber**-wharf on the Tennessee River, used during the Civil War to land soldiers. There we spent many happy hours and played at learning geography. I built dams of pebbles, made islands and lakes, and dug river-beds, all for fun, and never dreamed that I was learning a lesson. I listened with increasing wonder to Miss Sullivan's descriptions of the great round world with its burning mountains, buried cities, moving rivers of ice, and many other things as strange. She made raised maps in **clay**, so that I could feel the mountain ridges and valleys, and follow with my fingers the devious course of rivers. I liked this, too; but the division of the earth into zones and poles confused and teased my mind. The illustrative strings and the orange sticks representing the poles seemed so real that even to this day the mere mention of temperature zone

orchard n. 果园；果树林　　lumber n. 木材；废物；无用的杂物
clay n. 黏土；泥土

suggests a series of twine circles; and I believe that if any one should set about it he could convince me that white bears actually climb the North Pole.

Arithmetic seems to have been the only study I did not like. From the first I was not interested in the science of numbers. Miss Sullivan tried to teach me to count by stringing beads in groups, and by arranging kindergarten straws I learned to add and subtract. I never had patience to arrange more than five or six groups at a time. When I had accomplished this my conscience was at rest for the day, and I went out quickly to find my playmates.

In the same leisurely manner I studied zoölogy and **botany**.

Once a gentleman, whose name I have forgotten, sent me a collection of fossils—tiny mollusk shells beautifully marked, and bits of sandstone with the print of birds' claws, and a lovely **fern** in bas-relief. These were the keys which unlocked the treasures of the antediluvian world for me. With trembling fingers I listened to Miss Sullivan's descriptions of the terrible beasts with uncouth, unpronounceable names, which once went tramping through the primeval forests, tearing down the branches of gigantic trees for food, and died in the dismal swamps of an unknown age. For a long time these strange creatures haunted my dreams, and this gloomy period formed a **somber** back-ground to the joyous Now, filled with sunshine and roses and echoing with the gentle beat of my pony's hoof.

Another time a beautiful shell was given me, and with a child's surprise and delight I learned how a tiny mollusk had built the **lustrous** coil for his dwelling place, and how on still nights, when there is no breeze stirring the waves, the Nautilus sails on the blue waters of the Indian Ocean in his "ship of pearl." After I had learned a great many

---

botany n. 植物学；地区植物总称　　fern n. 蕨；蕨类植物
somber adj. 忧郁的；昏暗的；阴天的　　lustrous adj. 有光泽的；光辉的

interesting things about the life and habits of the children of the sea—how in the midst of dashing waves the little polyps build the beautiful coral isles of the Pacific, and the foraminifera have made the chalkhills of many a land—my teacher read me "The Chambered Nautilus," and showed me that the shell-building process of the mollusks is symbolical of the development of the mind. Just as the wonder-working mantle of the Nautilus changes the material it absorbs from the water and makes it a part of itself, so the bits of knowledge one gathers undergo a similar change and become pearls of thought.

Again, it was the growth of a plant that furnished the text for a lesson. We bought a lily and set it in a sunny window. Very soon the green, pointed buds showed signs of opening. The **_slender_**, fingerlike leaves on the outside opened slowly, reluctant, I thought, to reveal the loveliness they hid; once having made a start, however, the opening process went on rapidly, but in order and systematically. There was always one bud larger and more beautiful than the rest, which pushed her outer covering back with more pomp, as if the beauty in soft, silky robes knew that she was the lily-queen by right divine, while her more timid sisters doffed their green hoods shyly, until the whole plant was one nodding bough of loveliness and fragrance.

Once there were eleven tadpoles in a glass globe set in a window full of plants. I remember the eagerness with which I made discoveries about them. It was great fun to plunge my hand into the bowl and feel the tadpoles frisk about, and to let them slip and slide between my fingers. One day a more ambitious fellow leaped beyond the edge of the bowl and fell on the floor, where I found him to all appearance more dead than alive. The only sign of life was a slight wriggling of his tail. But no sooner had he returned to his element than he darted to the bottom, swimming round and round in joyous activity. He had made his leap, he had seen

slender adj. 细长的；苗条的

the great world, and was content to stay in his pretty glass house under the big fuchsia tree until he attained the dignity of froghood. Then he went to live in the leafy pool at the end of the garden, where he made the summer nights musical with his *quaint* love-song.

Thus I learned from life itself. At the beginning I was only a little mass of possibilities. It was my teacher who unfolded and developed them. When she came, everything about me breathed of love and joy and was full of meaning. She has never since let pass an opportunity to point out the beauty that is in everything, nor has she ceased trying in thought and action and example to make my life sweet and useful.

It was my teacher's genius, her quick sympathy, her loving *tact* which made the first years of my education so beautiful. It was because she seized the right moment to impart knowledge that made it so pleasant and acceptable to me. She realized that a child's mind is like a shallow brook which ripples and dances merrily over the stony course of its education and reflects here a flower, there a bush yonder a fleecy cloud; and she attempted to guide my mind on its way, knowing that like a brook it should be fed by mountain streams and hidden springs, until it broadened out into a deep river, capable of reflecting in its *placid* surface, billowy hills, the luminous shadows of trees and the blue heavens, as well as the sweet face of a little flower.

Any teacher can take a child to the classroom, but not every teacher can make him learn. He will not work joyously unless he feels that liberty is his, whether he is busy or at rest; he must feel the flush of victory and the heart-sinking of disappointment before he takes with a will the tasks distasteful to him and resolves to dance his way bravely through a dull routine of textbooks.

My teacher is so near to me that I scarcely think of myself apart

---

quaint adj. 奇怪的；离奇有趣的   tact n. 机智；老练

placid adj. 平静的；温和的；沉着的

from her. How much of my delight in all beautiful things is innate, and how much is due to her influence, I can never tell. I feel that her being is inseparable from my own, and that the footsteps of my life are in hers. All the best of me belongs to her—there is not a talent, or an inspiration or a joy in me that has not awakened by her loving touch.

Chapter 8

THE FIRST CHRISTMAS after Miss Sullivan came to Tuscumbia was a great event. Every one in the family prepared surprises for me, but what pleased me most, Miss Sullivan and I prepared surprises for everybody else. The mystery that surrounded the gifts was my greatest delight and amusement. My friends did all they could to excite my curiosity by hints and half-spelled sentences which they pretended to break off in the nick of time. Miss Sullivan and I kept up a game of guessing which taught me more about the use of language than any set lessons could have done. Every evening, seated round a glowing wood fire, we played our guessing game, which grew more and more exciting as Christmas approached.

On Christmas Eve the Tuscumbia schoolchildren had their tree, to which they invited me. In the center of the schoolroom stood a beautiful tree ablaze and shimmering in the soft light, its branches loaded with strange, wonderful fruit. It was a moment of supreme happiness. I danced and capered round the tree in an **_ecstasy_**. When I learned that there was a gift for each child, I was delighted, and the kind people who

---

ecstasy n. 狂喜；入迷；忘形

had prepared the tree permitted me to hand the presents to the children. In the pleasure of doing this, I did not stop to look at my own gifts; but when I was ready for them. my ***impatience*** for the real Christmas to begin almost got beyond control. I knew the gifts I already had were not those of which friends had thrown out such tantalizing hints, and my teacher said the presents I was to have would be even nicer than these. I was persuaded, however, to content myself with the gifts from the tree and leave the others until morning.

That night, after I had hung my stocking, I lay awake a long time, pretending to be asleep and keeping alert to see what Santa Claus would do when he came. At last I fell asleep with a new doll and a white bear in my arms. Next morning it was I who waked the whole family with my first "Merry Christmas!" I found surprises, not in the stocking only, but on the table, on all the chairs, at the door, on the very window-sill; indeed, I could hardly walk without stumbling on a bit of Christmas wrapped up in tissue paper. But when my teacher presented me with a ***canary***, my cup of happiness overflowed.

Little Tim was so tame that he would hop on my finger and eat candied cherries out of my hand. Miss Sullivan taught me to take all the care of my new pet. Every morning after breakfast I prepared his bath, made his cage clean and sweet, filled his cups with fresh seed and water from the well-house, and hung a spray of chickweed in his swing.

One morning I left the cage on the window-seat while I went to fetch water for his bath. When I returned I felt a big cat brush past me as I opened the door. At first I did not realize what had happened; but when I put my hand in the cage and Tim's pretty wings did not meet my touch or his small pointed claws take hold of my finger, I knew that I should never see my sweet little singer again.

impatience n. 急躁；无耐心   canary n. 金丝雀

Chapter 9

THE NEXT IMPORTANT event in my life was my visit to Boston, in May 1888. As if it were yesterday I remember the preparations, the departure with my teacher and my mother, the journey, and finally the arrival in Boston. How different this journey was from the one I had made to Baltimore two years before! I was no longer a restless, excitable little creature, requiring the attention of everybody on the train to keep me amused. I sat quietly beside Miss Sullivan, taking in with eager interest all that she told me about what she saw out of the car window: the beautiful Tennessee River, the great cottonfields, the hills and woods, and the crowds of laughing negroes at the stations, who waved to the people on the train and brought delicious candy and popcorn balls through the car. On the seat opposite me sat my big rag doll, Nancy, in a new gingham dress and a beruffled sunbonnet, looking at me out of two ***bead*** eyes. Some times, when I was not absorbed in Miss Sullivan's descriptions, I remembered Nancy's existence and took her up in my arms, but I generally calmed my conscience by making myself believe that she was asleep.

bead n. 珠子

As I shall not have occasion to refer to Nancy again, I wish to tell here a sad experience she had soon after our arrival in Boston. She was covered with dirt—the remains of mud pies I had compelled her to eat, although she had never shown any special liking for them. The laundress at the Perkins Institution secretly carried her off to give her a bath. This was too much for poor Nancy. When I next saw her she was a formless heap of cotton, which I should not have recognized at all except for the two bead eyes which looked out at me reproachfully.

When the train at last pulled into the station at Boston it was as if a beautiful fairy tale had come true. The "once upon a time" was now; the "far-away country" was here.

We had scarcely arrived at the Perkins Institution for the Blind when I began to make friends with the little blind children. It delighted me inexpressibly to find that they knew the ***manual*** alphabet. What joy to talk with other children in my own language! Until then I had been like a foreigner speaking through an ***interpreter***. In the school where Laura Bridgman was taught I was in my own country. It took me some time to appreciate the fact that my new friends were blind. I knew I could not see; but it did not seem possible that all the eager, loving children who gathered round me and joined heartily in my frolics were also blind. I remember the surprise and the pain I felt as I noticed that they placed their hands over mine when I talked to them and that they read books with their fingers. Although I had been told this before, and although I understood my own deprivations, yet I had thought vaguely that since they could hear, they must have a sort of "second sight," and I was not prepared to find one child and another and yet another deprived of the same precious gift. But they were so happy and contented that I lost all sense of pain in the pleasure of their companionship.

One day spent with the blind children made me feel thoroughly at

manual adj. 手工的；体力的   interpreter n. 解释者；口译者

home in my new environment, and I looked eagerly from one pleasant experience to another as the days flew swiftly by. I could not quite convince myself that there was much world left, for I regarded Boston as the beginning and the end of creation.

While we were in Boston we visited Bunker Hill, and there I had my first lesson in history. The story of the brave men who had fought on the spot where we stood excited me greatly. I climbed the monument, counting the steps, and wondering as I went higher and yet higher if the soldiers had climbed this great stairway and shot at the enemy on the ground below.

The next day we went to Plymouth by water. This was my first trip on the ocean and my first voyage in a steam-boat. How full of life and motion it was! But the rumble of the machinery made me think it was thundering, and I began to cry, because I feared if it rained we should not be able to have our picnic out of doors. I was more interested, I think, in the great rock on which the Pilgrims landed than in anything else in Plymouth. I could touch it, and perhaps that made the coming of the Pilgrims and their toils and great deeds seem more real to me. I have often held in my hand a little model of the Plymouth Rock which a kind gentleman gave me at Pilgrim Hall, and I have fingered its curves, the split in the center and the embossed figures "1620," and turned over in my mind all that I knew about the wonderful story of the Pilgrims.

How my childish imagination glowed with the splendor of their enterprise! I idealized them as the bravest and most generous men that ever sought a home in a strange land. I thought they desired the freedom of their fellow men as well as their own. I was **_keenly_** surprised and disappointed years later to learn of their acts of persecution that make us tingle with shame, even while we glory in the courage and energy that gave us our "Country Beautiful."

keenly adv. 敏锐地；强烈地

Among the many friends I made in Boston were Mr. William Endicott and his daughter. Their kindness to me was the seed from which many pleasant memories have since grown. One day we visited their beautiful home at Beverly Farms. I remember with delight how I went through their rose-garden, how their dogs, big Leo and little curly-haired Fritz with long ears, came to meet me, and how Nimrod, the swiftest of the horses, poked his nose into my hands for a pat and a lump of sugar. I also remember the beach, where for the first time I played in the sand. It was hard, smooth sand, very different from the loose, sharp sand, mingled with kelp and shells, at Brewster. Mr. Endicott told me about the great ships that came sailing by from Boston, bound for Europe. I saw him many times after that, and he was always a good friend to me; indeed, I was thinking of him when I called Boston "the City of Kind Hearts."

Chapter 10

JUST BEFORE THE Perkins Institution closed for the summer, it was arranged that my teacher and I should spend our vacation at Brewster, on Cape Code, with our dear friend, Mrs. Hopkins. I was delighted, for my mind was full of the prospective joys and of the wonderful stories I had heard about the sea.

My most vivid recollection of that summer is the ocean. I had always lived far inland and had never had so much as a whiff of salt air; but I had read in a big book called "Our World" a description of the ocean which filled me with wonder and an intense longing to touch the **_mighty_** sea and feel it roar. So my little heart leaped high with eager excitement when I knew that my wish was at last to be realized.

No sooner had I been helped into my bathing-suit than I sprang out upon the warm sand and without thought of fear plunged into the cool water. I felt the great billows rock and sink. The **_buoyant_** motion of the water filled me with an exquisite, quivering joy. Suddenly my ecstasy gave place to terror; for my foot struck against a rock and the next instant there was a rush of water over my head. I thrust out my hands

mighty adj. 有力的；强有力的   buoyant adj. 轻快的；有浮力的；上涨的

to grasp some support. I clutched at the water and at the seaweed which the waves tossed in my face. But all my frantic efforts were in vain. The waves seemed to be playing a game with me, and tossed me from one to another in their wild frolic. It was fearful! The good, firm earth had slipped from my feet, and everything seemed shut out from this strange, all-enveloping element—life, air, warmth and love. At last, however, the sea, as if weary of its new toy, threw me back on the shore, and in another instant I was clasped in my teacher's arms. Oh, the comfort of the long, tender embrace! As soon as I had recovered from my panic sufficiently to say anything, I demanded: "Who put salt in the water?"

After I had recovered from my first experience in the water, I thought it great fun to sit on a big rock in my bathing-suit and feel wave after wave dash against the rock, sending up a shower of spray which quite covered me. I felt the pebbles rattling as the waves threw their **_ponderous_** weight against the shore; the whole beach seemed racked by their terrific onset, and the air throbbed with their pulsations. The breakers would swoop back to gather themselves for a mightier leap, and I clung to the rock, tense, fascinated, as I felt the dash and roar of the rushing sea!

I could never stay long enough on the shore. The tang of the untainted, fresh and free sea air was like a cool, quieting thought, and the shells and pebbles and the seaweed with tiny living creatures attached to it never lost their **_fascination_** for me. One day Miss Sullivan attracted my attention to a strange object which she had captured basking in the shallow water. It was a great horseshoe crab—the first one I had ever seen. I felt of him and thought it very strange that he should carry his house on his back. It suddenly occurred to me that he might make a delightful pet; so I seized him by the tail with both hands and carried him home. This feat pleased me highly, as his body was very

ponderous adj. 笨重的　　fascination n. 魅力；魔力

heavy, and it took all my strength to drag him half a mile. I would not leave Miss Sullivan in peace until she had put the crab in a trough near the well where I was confident he would be secure. But next morning I went to the trough, and lo, he had disappeared! Nobody knew where he had gone, or how he had escaped. My disappointment was bitter at the time; but little by little I came to realize that it was not kind or wise to force this poor dumb creature out of his element, and after awhile I felt happy in the thought that perhaps he had returned to the sea.

Chapter 11

IN THE AUTUMN I returned to my southern home with a heart full of joyous memories. As I recall that visit North I am fitted with wonder at the richness and variety of the experiences that cluster about it. It seems to have been the beginning of everything. The treasures of a new, beautiful world were laid at my feet, and I took in pleasure and information at every turn. I lived myself into all things. I was never still a moment; my life was as full of motion as those little insects that crowd a whole existence into one brief day. I met many people who talked with me by spelling into my hand, and thought in joyous sympathy leaped up to meet thought, and behold, a miracle had been wrought! The ***barren*** places between my mind and the minds of others blossomed like the rose.

I spent the autumn months with my family at our summer cottage, on a mountain about fourteen miles from Tuscumbia. It was called Fern Quarry, because near it was a limestone quarry, long since abandoned. Three frolicsome little streams ran through it from springs in the rocks above, leaping here and tumbling there in laughing cascades wherever the rocks tried to bar their way. The opening was filled with ferns which

barren adj. 贫瘠的；不生育的

completely covered the beds of **_limestone_** and in places hid the streams. The rest of the mountain was thickly wooded. Here were great oaks and splendid ever-greens with trunks like mossy pillars, from the branches of which hung garlands of ivy and mistletoe, and persimmon trees, the odor of which pervaded every nook and corner of the wood—an illusive, fragrant something that made the heart glad. In places the wild muscadine and scuppernong vines stretched from tree to tree, making arbors which were always full of butterflies and buzzing insects. It was delightful to lose ourselves in the green hollows of that tangled wood in the late afternoon, and to smell the cool, delicious odors that came up from the earth at the close of the day.

Our cottage was a sort of rough camp, beautifully situated on the top of the mountain among oaks and pines. The small rooms were arranged on each side of a long open hall. Round the house was a wide piazza, where the mountain winds blew, sweet with all wood-scents. We lived on the piazza most of the time—there we worked, ate and played. At the back door there was a great butternut tree, round which the steps had been built, and in front the trees stood so close that I could touch them and feel the wind shake their branches, or the leaves twirl downward in the autumn blast.

Many visitors came to Fern Quarry. In the evening, by the campfire, the men played cards and whiled away the hours in talk and sport. They told stories of their wonderful feats with fowl, fish and quadruped—how many wild ducks and turkeys they had shot, what "savage trout" they had caught, and how they had bagged the craftiest foxes, out-witted the most clever 'possums and overtaken the fleetest deer, until I thought that surely the lion, the tiger, the bear and the rest of the wild tribe would not be able to stand before these **_wily_** hunters. "To-morrow to the chase!" was their good-night shout as the circle of merry friends broke up for the night. The men slept in the hall outside our door, and I could

limestone n. 石灰岩　　　wily adj. 狡猾的；诡计多端的

feel the deep breathing of the dogs and the hunters as they lay on their improvised beds.

At dawn I was awakened by the smell of coffee, the rattling of guns, and the heavy footsteps of the men as they strode about, promising themselves the greatest luck of the season. I could also feel the stamping of the horses, which they had ridden out from town and hitched under the trees, where they stood all night, neighing loudly, impatient to be off. At last the men mounted, and, as they say in the old songs, away went the steeds with bridles ringing and whips cracking and hounds racing ahead, and away went the champion hunters "with hark and whoop and wild halloo!"

Later in the morning we made preparations for a barbecue. A fire was kindled at the bottom of a deep hole in the ground, big sticks were laid crosswise at the top, and meat was hung from them and turned on spits. Around the fire squatted negros, driving away the flies with long branches. The savory odor of the meat made me hungry long before the tables were set.

When the bustle and excitement of preparation was at its height, the hunting party made its appearance, struggling in by twos and threes, the men hot and **_weary_**, the horses covered with foam, and the jaded hounds panting and dejected—and not a single kill! Every man declared that he had seen at least one deer, and that the animal had come very close; but however hotly the dogs might Pursue the game, however well the guns might be aimed, at the snap of the trigger there was not a deer in sight. They had been as fortunate as the little boy who said he came very near seeing a rabbit—he saw his tracks. The party soon forgot its disappointment, however, and we sat down, not to venison, but to a tamer feast of veal and roast pig.

One summer I had my pony at Fern Quarry. I called him Black

weary adj. 疲倦的

Beauty, as I had just read the book, and he resembled his namesake in every way, from his glossy black coat to the white star on his forehead. I spent many of my happiest hours on his back. Occasionally, when it was quite safe, my teacher would let go of the leading-rein, and the pony sauntered on or stopped at his sweet will to eat grass or **nibble** the leaves of the trees that grew beside the narrow trail.

On mornings when I did not care for the ride, my teacher and I would start after breakfast for a ramble in the woods, and allow ourselves to get lost amid the trees and vines, with no road to follow except the paths made by cows and horses. Frequently we came upon impassable thickets which forced us to take a roundabout way. We always returned to the cottage with armfuls of laurel, goldenrod, ferns and gorgeous swamp-flowers such as grow only in the South.

Sometimes I would go with Mildred and my little cousins to gather persimmons. I did not eat them; but I loved their fragrance and enjoyed hunting for them in the leaves and grass. We also went nutting, and I helped them open the chestnut burrs and break the shells of hickory-nuts and walnuts—the big, sweet walnuts!

At the foot of the mountain there was a railroad, and the children watched the trains whiz by. Sometimes a terrific whistle brought us to the steps, and Mildred told me in great excitement that a cow or a horse had strayed on the track. About a mile distant there was a trestle spanning a deep **gorge**. It was very difficult to walk over, the ties were wide apart and so narrow that one felt as if one were walking on knives. I had never crossed it until one day Mildred, Miss Sullivan and I were lost in the woods, and wandered for hours without finding a path.

Suddenly Mildred pointed with her little hand and exclaimed, "There's the trestle!" We would have taken any way rather than this; but it was late and growing dark, and the trestle was a short cut home. I had

nibble　vt. 细咬；一点点地咬　　　gorge　n. 峡谷

to feel for the rails with my toe; but I was not afraid, and got on very well, until all at once there came a faint "puff, puff" from the distance.

"I see the train!" cried Mildred. and in another minute it would have been upon us had we not climbed down on the crossbraces while it rushed over our heads. I felt the hot breath from the engine on my face, and the smoke and ashes almost choked us. As the train rumbled by, the trestle shook and swayed until I thought we should be dashed to the chasm below. With the utmost difficulty we regained the track. Long after dark we reached home and found the cottage empty; the family were all out hunting for us.

Chapter 12

AFTER MY FIRST visit to Boston, I spent almost every winter in the North. Once I went on a visit to a New England village with its frozen lakes and vast snow fields. It was then that I had opportunities such as had never been mine to enter into the treasures of the snow.

I recall my surprise on discovering that a mysterious hand had stripped the trees and bushes, leaving only here and there a wrinkled leaf. The birds had flown, and their empty nests in the bare trees were filled with snow. Winter was on hill and field. The earth seemed benumbed by his icy touch, and the very spirits of the trees had withdrawn to their roots, and there, curled up in the dark, lay fast asleep. All life seemed to have ebbed away, and even when the sun shone the day was

> Shrunk and cold,
> As if her veins were sapless and old.
> And she rose up decrepitly
> For a last dim look at earth and sea.

The withered grass and the bushes were transformed into a forest of icicles.

Then came a day when the chill air portended a snowstorm. We rushed out of doors to feel the first few tiny flakes descending. Hour by hour the flakes dropped silently, softly from their airy height to the earth, and the country became more and more level. A snowy night closed upon the world, and in the morning one could scarcely recognize a feature of the landscape. All the roads were hidden, not a single landmark was visible, only a waste of snow with trees rising out of it.

In the evening a wind from the northeast sprang up, and the flakes rushed hither and thither in furious mêlée. Around the great fire we sat and told merry tales, and frolicked, and quite forgot that we were in the midst of a desolate ***solitude***, shut in from all communication with the outside world. But during the night the fury of the wind increased to such a degree that it thrilled us with a vague terror. The rafters creaked and strained, and the branches of the trees surrounding the house rattled and beat against the windows, as the winds rioted up and down the country.

On the third day after the beginning of the storm the snow ceased. The sun broke through the clouds and shone upon a vast, undulating white plain. High mounds, pyramids heaped in fantastic shapes, and ***impenetrable*** drifts lay scattered in every direction.

Narrow paths were shoveled through the drifts. I put on my cloak and hood and went out. The air stung my cheeks like fire. Half walking in the paths, half working our way through the lesser drifts, we succeeded in reaching a pine grove just outside a broad pasture. The trees stood motionless and white like figures in a marble frieze. There was no odor of pine-needles. The rays of the sun fell upon the trees, so that the twigs sparkled like diamonds and dropped in showers when we touched them. So dazzling was the light, it penetrated even the darkness that veils my eyes.

solitude n. 孤独；隐居；荒僻的地方
impenetrable adj. 费解的；不接纳的

As the days wore on, the drifts gradually shrunk, but before they were wholly gone another storm came, so that I scarcely felt the earth under my feet once all winter. At intervals the trees lost their icy covering, and the bulrushes and underbrush were bare; but the lake lay frozen and hard beneath the sun.

Our favorite amusement during that winter was tobogganing. In places the shore of the lake rises **_abruptly_** from the water's edge. Down these steep slopes we used to coast. We would get on our toboggan, a boy would give us a **_shove_**, and off we went! Plunging through drifts, leaping hollows, swooping down upon the lake, we would shoot across its gleaming surface to the opposite bank. What joy! What exhilarating madness! For one wild, glad moment we snapped the chain that binds us to earth, and joining hands with the winds we felt ourselves divine!

abruptly adv. 突然地；唐突地　　shove n. 推；挤

Chapter 13

IT WAS IN the spring of 1890 that I learned to speak. The impulse to utter **_audible_** sounds had always been strong within me. I used to make noises, keeping one hand on my throat while the other hand felt the movements of my lips. I was pleased with anything that made a noise and liked to feel the cat purr and the dog bark. I also liked to keep my band on a singer's throat, or on a piano when it was being played. Before I lost my sight and hearing, I was fast learning to talk, but after my illness it was found that I had ceased to speak because I could not hear. I used to sit in my mother's lap all day long and keep my hands on her face because it amused me to feel the motions of her lips; and I moved my lips, too, although I had forgotten what talking was. My friends say that I laughed and cried naturally, and for awhile I made many sounds and word-elements, not because they were a means of communication, but he cause the need of exercising my vocal organs was imperative. There was, however, one word the meaning of which I still remembered, *water*. I pronounced it, "wa-wa." Even this became less and less intelligible until the time when Miss Sullivan began to teach me. I stopped using it only

audible adj. 听得见的

after I had learned to spell the word on my fingers.

I had known for a long time that the people about me used a method of communication different from mine; and even before I knew that a deaf child could be taught to speak, I was conscious of dissatisfaction with the means of communication I already possessed. One who is entirely dependent upon the manual alphabet has always a sense of restraint, of narrowness. This feeling began to **agitate** me with a vexing, forward-reaching sense of a lack that should be filled. My thoughts would often rise and beat up like birds against the wind; and I persisted in using my lips and voice. Friends tried to discourage this tendency, fearing lest it would lead to disappointment. But I persisted, and an accident soon occurred which resulted in the breaking down of this great barrier—I heard the story of Ragnhild Kaata.

In 1890 Mrs. Lamson, who had been one of Laura Bridgman's teachers, and who had just returned from a visit to Norway and Sweden, came to see me, and told me of Ragnhild Kaata, a deaf and blind girl in Norway who had actually been taught to speak. Mrs. Lamson had scarcely finished telling me about this girl's success before I was on fire with eagerness. I resolved that I, too, would learn to speak. I would not rest satisfied until my teacher took me, for advice and assistance, to Miss Sarah Fuller, principal of the Horace Mann School. This lovely, sweet-natured lady offered to teach me herself, and we began the twenty-sixth of March, 1890.

Miss Fuller's method was this: she passed my hand lightly over her face, and let me feel the position of het tongue and lips when she made a sound. I was eager to imitate every motion and in an hour had learned six elements of speech: M, P, A, S, T, I. Miss Fuller gave me eleven lessons in all. I shall never forget the surprise and delight I felt when I uttered my first connected sentence, "It is warm." True, they were broken and

agitate vt. 摇动；骚动；使⋯激动

stammering syllables; but they were human speech. My soul, conscious of new strength, came out of **_bondage_**, and was reaching through those broken symbols of speech to all knowledge and all faith.

No deaf child who has earnestly tried to speak the words which he has never heard—to come out of the prison of silence, where no tone of love, no song of bird, no strain of music ever pierces the stillness—can forget the thrill of surprise, the joy of discovery which came over him when he uttered his first word. Only such a one can appreciate the eagerness with which I talked to my toys, to stones, trees, birds and dumb animals, or the delight I felt when at my call Mildred ran to me or my dogs obeyed my commands. It is an unspeakable boon to me to be able to speak in winged words that need no interpretation. As I talked, happy thoughts fluttered up out of my words that might perhaps have struggled in vain to escape my fingers.

But it must not be supposed that I could really talk in this short time. I had learned only the elements of speech. Miss Fuller and Miss Sullivan could understand me, but most people would not have understood one word in a hundred. Nor is it true that, after I had learned these elements. I did the rest of the work myself. But for Miss Sullivan's genius, untiring perseverance and devotion, I could not have progressed as far as I have toward natural speech. In the first place, I labored night and day before I could be understood even by my most intimate friends; in the second place, I needed Miss Sullivan's assistance constantly in my efforts to articulate each sound clearly and to combine all sounds in a thousand ways. Even now she calls my attention every day to mispronounced words.

All teachers of the deaf know what this means, and only they can at all appreciate the peculiar difficulties with which I had to contend.

bondage n. 奴役；束缚

I had to use the sense of touch in catching the vibrations of the throat, the movements of the mouth and the expression of the face; and often this sense was at fault. In such eases I was forced to repeat the words or sentences, sometimes for hours, until I felt the proper ring in my own voice. My work was practice, practice, practice. Discouragement and weariness cast me down frequently; but the next moment the thought that I should soon be at home and show my loved ones what I had accomplished spurred me on, and I eagerly looked forward to their pleasure in my achievement.

"My little sister will understand me now," was a thought stronger than all obstacles. I used to repeat ecstatically, "I am not dumb now." I could not be despondent while I anticipated the delight of talking to my mother and reading her responses from her lips. It ***astonished*** me to find how much easier it is to talk than to spell with the fingers, and I discarded the manual alphabet as a medium of communication on my part; but Miss Sullivan and a few friends still use it in speaking to me, for it is more convenient and more rapid than lip-reading.

Just here, perhaps, I had better explain our use of the manual alphabet, which seems to puzzle people who do not know us. One who reads or talks to me spells with his hand, using the single-hand manual alphabet generally employed by the deaf. I place my hand on the hand of the speaker so lightly as not to ***impede*** its movements. The position of the hand is as easy to feel as it is to see. I do not feel each letter any more than you see each letter separately when you read. Constant practice makes the fingers very flexible, and some of my friends spell rapidly— about as fast as an expert writes on a typewriter. The mere spelling is, of course, no more a conscious act than it is in writing.

When I had made speech my own, I could not wait to go home. At

astonished vt. 使惊讶   impede vt. 阻碍；妨碍；阻止

last the happiest of happy moments arrived. I had made my homeward journey, talking constantly to Miss Sullivan, not for the sake of talking, but determined to improve to the last minute. Almost before I knew it, the train stopped at the Tuscumbia station, and there on the platform stood the whole family. My eyes fill with tears now as I think how my mother pressed me close to her, speechless and trembling with delight, taking in every syllable that I spoke, while little Mildred seized my free hand and kissed it and danced, and my father expressed his pride and affection in a big silence. It was as if Isaiah's prophecy had been fulfilled in me. "The mountains and the hills shall break forth before you into singing, and all the trees of the field shall clap their hands!"

Chapter 14

THE WINTER OF 1892 was darkened by the one cloud in my childhood's bright sky. Joy deserted my heart, and for a long, long time I lived in doubt, anxiety and fear. Books lost their charm for me, and even now the thought of those dreadful days chills my heart. A little story called "The Frost King," which I wrote and sent to Mr. Anagnos, of the Perkins Institution for the Blind, was at the root of the trouble. In order to make the matter clear, I must set forth the facts connected with this *episode*, which justice to my teacher and to myself compels me to write.

I wrote the story when I was at home, the autumn after I had learned to speak. We had stayed up at Fern Quarry later than usual. While we were there, Miss Sullivan had described to me the beauties of the late foliage, and it seems that her descriptions revived the memory of a story, which must have been read to me, and which I must have unconsciously retained. I thought then that I was "making up a story," as children say, and I eagerly sat down to write it before the ideas should slip from me. My thoughts flowed easily; I felt a sense of joy in the composition. Words and images came tripping to my finger ends, and as

episode n. 插曲；一段情节

I thought out sentence after sentence. I wrote them on my braille ***slate***. Now, if words and images come to me without effort, it is a pretty sure sign that they are not the offspring of my own mind, but stray waifs that I regretfully dismiss. At that time I eagerly absorbed everything I read without a thought of authorship, and even now I cannot be quite sure of the boundary line between my ideas and those I find in books. I suppose that is because so many of my impressions come to me through the medium of others' eyes and ears.

When the story was finished, I read it to my teacher, and I recall now vividly the pleasure I felt in the more beautiful passages, and my annoyance at being interrupted to have the pronunciation of a word corrected. At dinner it was read to the assembled family, who were surprised that I could write so well. Some one asked me if I had read it in a book.

This question surprised me very much; for I had not the faintest recollection of having had it read to me. I spoke up and said. "Oh, no, it is my story, and I have written it for Mr. Anagnos."

Accordingly I copied the story and sent it to him for his birthday. It was suggested that I should change the title from "Autumn Leaves" to "The Frost King," which I did. I carried the little story to the post-office myself, feeling as if I were walking on air. I little dreamed how cruelly I should pay for that birthday gift.

Mr. Anagnos was delighted with "The Frost King," and published it in one of the Perkins Institution reports. This was the pinnacle of my happiness, from which I was in a little while dashed to earth. I had been in Boston only a short time when it was discovered that a story similar to "The Frost King," called "The Frost Fairies," by Miss Margaret T. Canby, had appeared before I was born in a book called "Birdie and His Friends." The two stories were so much alike in thought and language that it was

slate n. 石板；石片

evident Miss Canby's story had been read to me. and that mine was—a **plagiarism**. It was difficult to make me understand this; but when I did understand I was astonished and grieved. No child ever drank deeper of the cup of bitterness than I did. I had disgraced myself; I had brought suspicion upon those I loved best. And yet how could it possibly have happened? I racked my brain until I was weary to recall anything about the frost that I had read before I wrote "The Frost King"; but I could remember nothing, except the common reference to Jack Frost, and a poem for children, "The Freaks of the Frost," and I knew I had not used that in my composition.

At first Mr. Anagnos, though deeply troubled, seemed to believe me. He was unusually tender and kind to me, and for a brief space the shadow lifted. To please him I tried not to be unhappy, and to make myself as pretty as possible for the celebration of Washington's birthday, which took place very soon after I received the sad news.

I was to be Ceres in a kind of masque given by the blind girls. How well I remember the graceful draperies that enfolded me, the bright autumn leaves that wreathed my head, and the fruit and grain at my feet and in my hands, and beneath all the gaiety of the masque the oppressive sense of coming ill that made my heart heavy.

The night before the celebration one of the teachers of the Institution had asked me a question connected with "The Frost King," and I was telling her that Miss Sullivan had talked to me about Jack Frost and his wonderful works. Something I said made her think she detected in my words a confession that I did remember Miss Canby's story of "The Frost Fairies," and she laid her conclusions before Mr. Anagnos, although I had told her most **emphatically** that she was mistaken.

Mr. Anagnos, who loved me tenderly, thinking that he had been deceived, turned a deaf ear to the pleadings of love and innocence. He

---

plagiarism n. 剽窃；剽窃物　　　emphatically adv. 着重地；强调地；断然地

believed, or at least suspected, that Miss Sullivan and I had deliberately stolen the bright thoughts of another and imposed them on him to win his admiration. I was brought before a court of investigation composed of the teachers and officers of the Institution, and Miss Sullivan was asked to leave me. Then I was questioned and cross-questioned with what seemed to me a determination on the part of my judges to force me to acknowledge that I remembered having had "The Frost Fairies" read to me. I felt in every question the doubt and suspicion that was in their minds, and I felt, too, that a loved friend was looking at me reproachfully, although I could not have put all this into words. The blood pressed about my thumping heart, and I could scarcely speak, except in monosyllables. Even the consciousness that it was only a dreadful mistake did not lessen my suffering, and when at last I was allowed to leave the room, I was dazed and did not notice my teacher's caresses, or the tender words of my friends, who said I was a brave little girl and they were proud of me.

As I lay in my bed that night. I wept as I hope few children have wept. I felt so cold. I imagined I should die before morning, and the thought comforted me. I think if this sorrow had come to me when I was older, it would have broken my spirit beyond repairing. But the angel of forgetfulness has gathered up and carried away much of the misery and all the bitterness of those sad days.

Miss Sullivan had never heard of "The Frost Fairies" or of the book in which it was published. With the assistance of Dr. Alexander Graham Bell, she investigated the matter carefully, and at last it came out that Mrs. Sophia C. Hopkins had a copy of Miss Canby's "Birdie and His Friends" in 1888, the year that we spent the summer with her at Brewster. Mrs. Hopkins was unable to find her copy; but she has told me that at that time, while Miss Sullivan was away on a vacation, she tried to amuse me by reading from various books, and although she could not remember reading "The Frost Fairies" any more than I, yet she felt sure that "Birdie and His Friends" was one of them. She explained the disappearance of the book by the fact that she had a short time before she sold her house and disposed of many juvenile books, such as old school-books and fairy tales, and that "Birdie and His Friends" was probably among them.

The stories had little or no meaning for me then; but the mere spelling of the strange words was sufficient to amuse a little child who could do almost nothing to amuse herself; and although I do not recall a single circumstance connected with the reading of the stories, yet I cannot help thinking that I made a great effort to remember the words, with the intention of having my teacher explain them when she returned. One thing is certain, the language was ineffaceably stamped upon my brain, though for a long time no one knew it, least of all myself.

When Miss Sullivan came back, I did not speak to her about "The Frost Fairies," probably because she began at once to read "Little Lord Fauntleroy," which filled my mind to the exclusion of everything else. But the fact remains that Miss Canby's story was read to me once, and that long after I had forgotten it, it came back to me so naturally that I never suspected that it was the child of another mind.

In my trouble I received many messages of love and sympathy. All the friends I loved best, except one, have remained my own to the present time.

Miss Canby herself wrote kindly, "Some day you will write a great story out of your own head, that will be a comfort and help to many," But this kind **prophecy** has never been fulfilled. I have never played with words again for the mere pleasure of the game. Indeed, I have ever since been tortured by the fear that what I write is not my own. For a long time, when I wrote a letter, even to my mother, I was seized with a sudden feeling of terror, and I would spell the sentences over and over, to make sure that I had not read them in a book. Had it not been for the

---

prophecy n. 预言；预言能力

persistent encouragement of Miss Sullivan, I think I should have given up trying to write altogether.

I have read "The Frost Fairies" since, also the letters I wrote in which I used other ideas of Miss Canby's. I find in one of them, a letter to Mr. Anagnos, dated September 29, 1891, words and sentiments exactly like those of the book. At the time I was writing "The Frost King," and this letter, like many others, contains phrases which show that my mind was **saturated** with the story. I represent my teacher as saying to me of the golden autumn leaves, "Yes, they are beautiful enough to comfort us for the flight of summer" an idea direct from Miss Canby's story.

This habit of assimilating what pleased me and giving it out again as my own appears in much of my early correspondence and my first attempts at writing. In a composition which I wrote about the old cities of Greece and Italy, I borrowed my glowing descriptions, with variations, from sources I have forgotten. I knew Mr. Anagnos's great love of antiquity and his enthusiastic appreciation of all beautiful sentiments about Italy and Greece. I therefore gathered from all the books I read every bit of poetry or of history that I thought would give him pleasure. Mr. Anagnos, in speaking of my composition on the cities, has said, "These ideas are poetic in their essence." But I do not understand how he ever thought a blind and deaf child of eleven could have invented them. Yet I cannot think that because I did not originate the ideas, my little composition is therefore quite devoid of interest. It shows me that I could express my appreciation of beautiful and poetic ideas in clear and animated language.

Those early compositions were mental gymnastics. I was learning, as all young and inexperienced persons learn, by assimilation and imitation, to put ideas into words. Everything I found in books that pleased me I retained in my memory, consciously or unconsciously, and adapted it. The

saturated v. 使渗透

young writer, as Stevenson has said, instinctively tries to copy whatever seems most admirable, and he shifts his admiration with astonishing versatility. It is only after years of this sort of practice that even great men have learned to marshal the legion of words which come thronging through every byway of the mind.

I am afraid I have not fet completed this process. It is certain that I cannot always distinguish my own thoughts from those I read, because what I read becomes the very substance and texture of my mind. Consequently, in nearly all that I write, I produce something which very much resembles the crazy patchwork I used to make when I first learned to sew. This patchwork was made of all sorts of odds and ends—pretty bits of silk and velvet; but the *coarse* pieces that were not pleasant to touch always predominated. Likewise my compositions are made up of crude notions of my own, inlaid with the brighter thoughts and riper opinions of the authors I have read. It seems to me that the great difficulty of writing is to make the language of the educated mind express our confused ideas, half feelings, half thoughts, when we are little more than bundles of instinctive tendencies. Trying to write is very much like trying to put a Chinese puzzle together. We have a pattern in mind which we wish to work out in words; but the words will not fit the spaces, or, if they do, they will not match the design. But we keep on trying because we know that others have succeeded, and we are not willing to acknowledge defeat.

"There is no way to become original, except to be born so," says Stevenson, and although I may not be original, I hope sometime to outgrow my artificial, periwigged compositions. Then, perhaps, my own thoughts and experiences will come to the surface. Meanwhile I trust and hope and persevere, and try not to let the bitter memory of "The Frost King" trammel my efforts.

coarse adj. 粗糙的

So this sad experience may have done me good and set me thinking on some of the problems of composition. My only regret is that it resulted in the loss of one of my dearest friends, Mr. Anagnos.

Since the publication of "The Story of My Life" in the *Ladies' Home Journal*, Mr. Anagnos has made a statement, in a letter to Mr. Macy, that at the time of the "Frost King" matter, he believed I was innocent. He says, the court of investigation before which I was brought consisted of eight people: four blind, four seeing persons. Four of them, he says, thought I knew that Miss Canby's story had been read to me, and the others did not hold this view. Mr. Anagnos states that he cast his vote with those who were favorable to me.

But, however the case may have been, with whichever side he may have cast his vote, when I went into the room where Mr. Anagnos had so often held me on his knee and, forgetting his many cares, had shared in my frolics, and found there persons who seemed to doubt me, I felt that there was something hostile and menacing in the very atmosphere, and subsequent events have borne out this impression. For two years he seems to have held the belief that Miss Sullivan and I were innocent. Then he evidently retracted his favorable judgment, why I do not know. Nor did I know the details of the investigation. I never knew even the names of the members of the "court" who did not speak to me. I was too excited to notice anything, too frightened to ask questions. Indeed, I could scarcely think what I was saying, or what was being said to me.

I have given this account of the "Frost King" affair because it was important in my life and education; and, in order that there might be no misunderstandings, I have set forth all the facts as they appear to me, without a thought of defending myself or of laying blame on any one.

Chapter 15

THE SUMMER AND winter following the "Frost King" incident I spent with my family in Alabama. I recall with delight that home-going. Everything had budded and blossomed. I was happy "The Frost King" was forgotten.

When the ground was strewn with the crimson and golden leaves of autumn, and the musk-scented grapes that covered the arbor at the end of the garden were turning golden brown in the sunshine, I began to write a sketch of my life—a year after I had written "The Frost King."

I was still excessively **scrupulous** about everything I wrote. The thought that what I wrote might not be absolutely my own tormented me. No one knew of these fears except my teacher. A strange sensitiveness prevented me from referring to the "Frost King"; and often when an idea flashed out in the course of conversation I would spell softly to her, "I am not sure it is mine." At other times, in the midst of a paragraph I was writing, I said to myself, "Suppose it should be found that all this was written by some one long ago!" An impish fear clutched my hand, so that I could not write any more that day. And even now I sometimes feel the

---

scrupulous adj. 细心的；小心谨慎的；一丝不苟的

same uneasiness and disquietude. Miss Sullivan consoled and helped me in every way she could think of; but the terrible experience I had passed through left a lasting impression on my mind, the significance of which I am only just beginning to understand. It was with the hope of restoring my self-confidence that she persuaded me to write for the *Youth's Companion* a brief account of my life. I was then twelve years old. As I look back on my struggle to write that little story, it seems to me that I must have had a prophetic vision of the good that would come of the undertaking, or I should surely have failed.

I wrote timidly, fearfully, but resolutely, urged on by my teacher, who knew that if I persevered, I should find my mental foothold again and get a grip on my faculties. Up to the time of the "Frost King" episode, I had lived the unconscious life of a little child; now my thoughts were turned inward, and I beheld things invisible. Gradually I emerged from the penumbra of that experience with a mind made clearer by trial and with a truer knowledge of life.

The chief events of the year 1893 were my trip to Washington during the ***inauguration*** of President Cleveland, and visits to Niagara and the World's Fair. Under such circumstances my studies were constantly interrupted and often put aside for many weeks, so that it is impossible for me to give a connected account of them.

We went to Niagara in March, 1893. It is difficult to describe my emotions when I stood on the point which overhangs the American Falls and felt the air vibrate and the earth tremble.

It seems strange to many people that I should be impressed by the wonders and beauties of Niagara. They are always asking: "What does this beauty or that music mean to you? You cannot see the waves rolling up the beach or hear their roar. What do they mean to you?" In the most evident sense they mean everything. I cannot fathom or define their meaning any

inauguration n. 就职典礼

more than I can fathom or define love or religion or goodness.

During the summer of 1893, Miss Sullivan and I visited the World's Fair with Dr. Alexander Graham Bell. I recall with unmixed delight those days when a thousand childish fancies became beautiful realities. Every day in imagination I made a trip round the world, and I saw many wonders from the uttermost parts of the earth—marvels of invention, treasuries of industry and skill and all the activities of human life actually passed under my finger tips.

I liked to visit the Midway Plaisance. It seemed like the "Arabian Nights," it was crammed so full of novelty and interest. Here was the India of my books in the curious **bazaar** with its Shivas and elephant-gods; there was the land of the Pyramids concentrated in a model Cairo with its mosques and its long processions of camels; yonder were the lagoons of Venice, where we sailed every evening when the city and the fountains were illuminated. I also went on board a viking ship which lay a short distance from the little **craft**. I had been on a man-of-war before, in Boston, and it interested me to see, on this viking ship, how the seaman was once all in all—how he sailed and took storm and calm alike with undaunted heart, and gave chase to whosoever reëchoed his cry, "We are of the sea!" and fought with brains and sinews, self-reliant, self-sufficient, instead of being thrust into the background by unintelligent machinery, as Jack is to-day. So it always is— "man only is interesting to man."

At a little distance from this ship there was a model of the *Santa Maria*, which I also examined. The captain showed me Columbus's cabin and the desk with an hourglass on it. This small instrument impressed me most because it made me think how weary the heroic navigator must have felt as he saw the sand dropping grain by grain while desperate men were plotting against his life.

Mr. Higinbotham, President of the World's Fair, kindly gave me

---

bazaar n. 集市；市场；义卖市场   craft n. 工艺；手艺

permission to touch the exhibits, and with an eagerness as insatiable as that with which Pizarro seized the treasures of Peru, I took in the glories of the Fair with my fingers. It was a sort of tangible kaleidoscope, this white city of the West. Everything fascinated me, especially the French bronzes. They were so lifelike, I thought they were angel visions which the artist had caught and bound in earthly forms.

At the Cape of Good Hope exhibit, I learned much about the processes of mining diamonds. Whenever it was possible, I touched the machinery while it was in motion, so as to get a clearer idea how the stones were weighed, cut, and polished. I searched in the washings for a diamond and found it myself—the only true diamond, they said, that was ever found in the United States.

Dr. Bell went everywhere with us and in his own delightful way described to me the objects of greatest interest. In the electrical building we examined the telephones, autophones, phonographs, and other inventions, and he made me understand how it is possible to send a message on wires that ***mock*** space and outrun time, and, like Prometheus, to draw fire from the sky. We also visited the anthropological department, and I was much interested in the relies of ancient Mexico, in the rude stone implements that are so often the only record of an age—the simple monuments of nature's unlettered children (so I thought as I fingered them) that seem bound to last while the memorials of kings and sages crumble in dust away—and in the Egyptian mummies, which I shrank from touching. From these relics I learned more about the progress of man than I have heard or read since.

All these experiences added a great many new terms to my vocabulary, and in the three weeks I spent at the Fair I took a long leap from the little child's interest in fairy tales and toys to the appreciation of the real and the earnest in the workaday world.

mock adj. 模拟的

Chapter 16

BEFORE OCTOBER, 1893, I had studied various subjects by myself in a more or less desultory manner. I read the histories of Greece, Rome and the United States. I had a French grammar in raised print, and as I already knew some French, I often amused myself by composing in my head short exercises, using the new words as I came across them, and ignoring rules and other technicalities as much as possible. I even tried, without aid, to master the French pronunciation, as I found all the letters and sounds described in the book. Of course this was tasking slender powers for great ends; but it gave me something to do on a rainy day, and I acquired a sufficient knowledge of French to read with pleasure La Fontaine's "Fables," "Le Médecin Malgré Lui" and passages from "Athalie."

I also gave considerable time to the improvement of my speech. I read aloud to Miss Sullivan and recited passages from my favorite poets, which I had committed to memory; she corrected my pronunciation and helped me to phrase and inflect. It was not, however, until October, 1893, after I had recovered from the fatigue and excitement of my visit to the World's Fair, that I began to have lessons in special subjects at fixed hours.

Miss Sullivan and I were at that time in Hulton, Penn—sylvania, visiting the family of Mr. William Wade. Mr. Irons, a neighbor of theirs, was a good Latin scholar; it was arranged that I should study under him. I remember him as a man of rare, sweet nature and of wide experience. He taught me Latin grammar principally; but he often helped me in arithmetic, which I found as troublesome as it was uninteresting. Mr. Irons also read with me Tennyson's "In Memoriam." I had read many books before, but never from a critical point of view. I learned for the first time to know an author, to recognize his style as I recognize the clasp of a friend's hand.

At first I was rather unwilling to study Latin grammar. It seemed absurd to waste time analyzing every word I came across—noun, genitive, singular, feminine—when its meaning was quite plain. I thought I might just as well describe my pet in order to know it—order, vertebrate; division, quadruped; class, mammalia; genus, felinus; species, cat, individual, Tabby. But as I got deeper into the subject, I became more interested, and the beauty of the language delighted me. I often amused myself by reading Latin passages, picking up words I understood and trying to make sense. I have never ceased to enjoy this pastime.

There is nothing more beautiful, I think, than the ***evanescent*** fleeting images and sentiments presented by a language one is just becoming familiar with—ideas that flit across the mental sky, shaped and tinted by ***capricious*** fancy. Miss Sullivan sat beside me at my lessons, spelling into my hand whatever Mr. Irons said, and looking up new words for me. I was just beginning to read Caesar's "Gallic War" when I went to my home in Alabama.

evanescent adj. 容易消散的；逐渐消失的
capricious adj. 反复无常的，任性的

Chapter 17

IN THE SUMMER of 1894, I attended the meeting at Chautauqua of the American Association to Promote the Teaching of Speech to the Deaf. There it was arranged that I should go to the Wright-Humason School for the Deaf in New York City. I went there in October, 1894, accompanied by Miss Sullivan. This school was chosen especially for the purpose of obtaining the highest advantages in vocal culture and training in lip-reading. In addition to my work in these subjects, I studied, during the two years I was in the school, arithmetic, physical geography, French and German.

Miss Reamy, my German teacher, could use the manual alphabet, and after I had acquired a small vocabulary, we talked together in German whenever we had a chance, and in a few months I could understand almost everything she said. Before the end of the first year I read "Wilhelm Tell" with the greatest delight. Indeed, I think I made more progress in German than in any of my other studies. I found French much more difficult. I studied it with Madame Olivier, a French lady who did not know the manual alphabet, and who was obliged to give her instruction orally. I could not read her lips easily; so my progress was much slower than in German. I managed, however, to read "Le Médecin

Malgré Lui" again. It was very amusing but I did not like it nearly so well as "Wilhelm Tell."

My progress in lip-reading and speech was not what my teachers and I had hoped and expected it would be. It was my ambition to speak like other people, and my teachers believed that this could be accomplished; but, although we worked hard and faithfully, yet we did not quite reach our goal. I suppose we aimed too high, and disappointment was therefore inevitable. I still regarded arithmetic as a system of pitfalls. I hung about the dangerous frontier of "guess," avoiding with infinite trouble to myself and others the broad valley of reason. When I was not guessing, I was jumping at conclusions, and this fault, in addition to my dullness, aggravated my difficulties more than was right or necessary.

But although these disappointments caused me great depression at times, I pursued my other studies with unflagging interest, especially physical geography. It was a joy to learn the secrets of nature: how—in the picturesque language of the Old Testament—the winds are made to blow from the four corners of the heavens, how the vapors ascend from the ends of the earth, how rivers are cut out among the rocks, and mountains overturned by the roots, and in what ways man may overcome many forces mightier than himself. The two years in New York were happy ones, and I look back to them with genuine pleasure.

I remember especially the walks we all took together every day in Central Park, the only part of the city that was ***congenial*** to me. I never lost a jot of my delight in this great park. I loved to have it described every time I entered it; for it was beautiful in all its aspects, and these aspects were so many that it was beautiful in a different way each day of the nine months I spent in New York.

In the spring we made excursions to various places of interest. We sailed on the Hudson River and wandered about on its green banks,

congenial adj. 意气相投的；性格相似的

of which Bryant loved to sing. I liked the simple wild grandeur of the palisades. Among the places I visited were West Point, Tarrytown, the home of Washington Irving, where I walked through "Sleepy Hollow."

The teachers at the Wright-Humason School were always planning how they might give the pupils every advantage that those who hear enjoy—how, they might make much of few tendencies and passive memories in the cases of the little ones—and lead them out of the cramping circumstances in which their lives were set.

Before I left New York, these bright days were darkened by the greatest sorrow that I have ever borne, except the death of my father. Mr. John P. Spaulding, of Boston, died in February, 1896. Only those who knew and loved him best can understand what his friendship meant to me. He, who made every one happy in a beautiful, unobtrusive way, was most kind and tender to Miss Sullivan and me. So long as we felt his loving presence and knew that he took a watchful interest in our work, fraught with so many difficulties, we could not be discouraged. His going away left a vacancy in our lives that has never been filled.

Chapter 18

IN OCTOBER, 1896, I entered the Cambridge School for Young Ladies, to be prepared for Radcliffe.

When I was a little girl, I visited Wellesley and surprised my friends by the announcement, "Some day I shall go to college—but I shall go to Harvard!" When asked why I would not go to Wellesley, I replied that there were only girls there. The thought of going to college took root in my heart and became an earnest desire, which impelled me to enter into competition for a degree with seeing and hearing girls, in the face of the strong opposition of many true and wise friends. When I left New York the idea had become a fixed purpose; and it was decided that I should go to Cambridge. This was the nearest approach I could get to Harvard and to the fulfillment of my childish ***declaration***.

At the Cambridge School the plan was to have Miss Sullivan attend the classes with me and interpret to me the instruction given.

Of course my instructors had had no experience in teaching any but normal pupils, and my own means of conversing with them was reading their lips. My studies for the first year were English history, English

declaration n. 申报；宣布；公告

literature, German, Latin, arithmetic, Latin composition and occasional themes. Until then I had never taken a course of study with the idea of preparing for college; but I had been well drilled in English by Miss Sullivan, and it soon became evident to my teachers that I needed no special instruction in this subject beyond a critical study of the books prescribed by the college. I had had, moreover, a good start in French, and received six months' instruction in Latin; but German was the subject with which I was most familiar.

In spite, however, of these advantages, there were serious drawbacks to my progress. Miss Sullivan could not spell out in my hand all that the books required, and it was very difficult to have the text-books embossed in time to be of use to me, although my friends in London and Philadelphia were willing to hasten the work. For a while, indeed, I had to copy my Latin in braille, so that I could recite with the other girls. My instructors soon became sufficiently familiar with my imperfect speech to answer my questions readily and correct mistakes. I could not make notes in class or write exercises; but I wrote all my compositions and translations at home on my typewriter.

Each day Miss Sullivan went to the classes with me and spelled into my hand with infinite patience all that the teachers said. In study hours she had to look up new words for me and read and reread notes and books I did not have in raised print. The tedium of that work is hard to conceive. Frau Gröte, my German teacher, and Mr. Gilman, the principal, were the only teachers in the school who learned the finger alphabet to give me instruction. No one realized more fully than dear Frau Gröte how slow and inadequate her spelling was. Nevertheless, in the goodness of her heart she laboriously spelled out her instructions to me in special lessons twice a week, to give Miss Sullivan a little rest. But, though everybody was kind and ready to help us, there was only one hand that could turn drudgery into pleasure.

That year I finished arithmetic, reviewed my Latin grammar, and read three chapters of Caesar's "Gallic War." In German I read, partly with my fingers and partly with Miss Sullivan's assistance, Schiller's "Lied von der Glocke" and "Taucher," Heine's "Harzreise," Freytag's "Aus dem Staat Friedrichs des Grossen," Riehl's "Fluch Der Schonheit," Lessing's "Minna von Barnhelm," and Goethe's "Aus meinem Leben." I took the greatest delight in these German books, especially Schiller's wonderful lyrics, the history of Frederick the Great's magnificent achievements and the account of Goethe's life. I was sorry to finish "Die Harzreise," so full of happy witticisms and charming descriptions of vine-clad hills, streams that sing and ripple in the sunshine, and wild regions, sacred to tradition and legend, the gray sisters of a long-vanished, imaginative age—descriptions such as can be given only by those to whom nature is "a feeling, a love and an appetite."

Mr. Gilman instructed me part of the year in English literature. We read together, "As You Like It," Burke's "Speech on Conciliation with America," and Macaulay's "Life of Samuel Johnson." Mr. Gilman's broad views of history and literature and his clever explanations made my work easier and pleasanter than it could have been had I only read notes mechanically with the necessarily brief explanations given in the classes.

Burke's speech was more instructive than any other book on a political subject that I had ever read. My mind stirred with the stirring times, and the characters round which the life of two contending nations centered seemed to move right before me. I wondered more and more, while Burke's masterly speech rolled on in ***mighty*** surges of eloquence, how it was that King George and his ministers could have turned a deaf ear to his warning prophecy of our victory and their humiliation. Then I entered into the melancholy details of the relation in which the great statesman stood to his party and to the representatives of the people. I thought how strange it was that such precious seeds of truth and wisdom

mighty adj. 有力的；强有力的

should have fallen among the tares of ignorance and corruption.

In a different way Macaulay's "Life of Samuel Johnson" was interesting. My heart went out to the lonely man who ate the bread of affliction in Grub Street, and yet, in the midst of toil and cruel suffering of body and soul, always had a kind word, and lent a helping hand to the poor and despised. I rejoiced over all his successes, I shut my eyes to his faults, and wondered, not that he had them, but that they had not crushed or dwarfed his soul. But in spite of Macaulay's brilliancy and his admirable faculty of making the commonplace seem fresh and picturesque, his positiveness wearied me at times, and his frequent sacrifices of truth to effect kept me in a questioning attitude very unlike the attitude of reverence in which I had listened to the Demosthenes of Great Britain.

At the Cambridge school, for the first time in my life, I enjoyed the companionship of seeing and hearing girls of my own age. I lived with several others in one of the pleas ant houses connected with the school, the house where Mr. Howells used to live, and we all had the advantage of home life. I joined them in many of their games, even blind man's buff and frolics in the snow; I took long walks with them; we discussed our studies and read aloud the things that interested us. Some of the girls learned to speak to me, so that Miss Sullivan did not have to repeat their conversation.

At Christmas, my mother and little sister spent the holidays with me, and Mr. Gilman kindly offered to let Mildred study in his school. So Mildred stayed with me in Cambridge, and for six happy months we were hardly ever apart. It makes me most happy to remember the hours we spent helping each other in study and sharing our recreation together.

I took my preliminary examinations for Radcliffe from the 29th of June to the 3rd of July in 1897. The subjects I offered were ***Elementary***

Elementary　adj. 基本的；初级的

and Advanced German, French, Latin, English, and Greek and Roman history, making nine hours in all. I passed in everything, and received "honors" in German and English.

Perhaps an explanation of the method that was in use when I took my examinations will not be amiss here. The student was required to pass in sixteen hours—twelve hours being called elementary and four advanced. He had to pass five hours at a time to have them counted. The examination papers were given out at nine o'clock at Harvard and brought to Radcliffe by a special messenger. Each candidate was known, not by his name, but by a number. I was No. 233, but, as I had to use a typewriter, my identity could not be concealed.

It was thought advisable for me to have my examinations in a room by myself, because the noise of the typewriter might disturb the other girls. Mr. Gilman read all the papers to me by means of the manual alphabet. A man was placed on guard at the door to prevent interruption.

The first day I had German, Mr. Gilman sat beside me and read the paper through first, then sentence by sentence, while I repeated the words aloud, to make sure that I understood him perfectly. The papers were difficult, and I felt very anxious as I wrote out my answers on the type-writer. Mr. Gilman spelled to me what I had written, and I made such changes as I thought necessary, and he inserted them. I wish to say here that I have not had this advantage since in any of my examinations. At Radcliffe no one reads the papers to me after they are written, and I have no opportunity to correct errors unless I finish before the time is up. In that case I correct only such mistakes as I can recall in the few minutes allowed, and make notes of these corrections at the end of my paper. If I passed with higher credit in the preliminaries than in the finals, there are two reasons. In the finals, no one read my work over to me, and in the preliminaries I offered subjects with sonic of which I was in a measure familiar before my work in the Cambridge school; for at the beginning of the year I had passed examinations in English, History,

French and German, which Mr. Gilman gave me from previous Harvard papers.

Mr. Gilman sent my written work to the examiners with a certificate that I, candidate No. 233, had written the papers.

All the other preliminary examinations were conducted in the same manner, None of them was so difficult as the first. I remember that the day the Latin paper was brought to us, Professor Schilling came in and informed me I had passed satisfactorily in German. This encouraged me greatly, and I sped on to the end of the ordeal with a light heart and a steady hand.

Chapter 19

WHEN I BEGAN my second year at the Gilman school, I was full of hope and determination to succeed. But during the first few weeks I was confronted with unforeseen difficulties. Mr. Gilman had agreed that that year I should study mathematics principally. I had physics, algebra, geometry, ***astronomy***, Greek and Latin. Unfortunately, many of the books I needed had not been embossed in time for me to begin with the classes, and I lacked important ***apparatus*** for sonic of my studies. The classes I was in were very large and it was impossible for the teachers to give me special instruction. Miss Sullivan was obliged to read all the books to me, and interpret for the instructors, and for the first time in eleven years it seemed as if her dear hand would not be equal to the task.

It was necessary for me to write algebra and geometry in class and solve problems in physics, and this I could not do until we bought a braille writer, by means of which I could put down the steps and processes of my work. I could not follow with my eyes the geometrical figures drawn on the blackboard, and my only means of getting a clear idea of them was to make them on a cushion with straight and curred

astronomy n. 天文学　　apparatus n. 装置；设备；仪器

wires, which had bent and pointed ends. I had to carry in my mind, as Mr. Keith says in his report, the lettering of the figures, the hypothesis and conclusion, the construction and the process of the proof. In a word, every study had its obstacles. Sometimes I lost all courage and betrayed my feelings in a way I am ashamed to remember, especially as the signs of my trouble were afterward used against Miss Sullivan, the only person of all the kind friends I had there, who could make the crooked straight and the rough places smooth.

Little by little, however, my difficulties began to disappear. The embossed books and other apparatus arrived, and I threw myself into the work with renewed confidence. Algebra and geometry were the only studies that continued to defy my efforts to comprehend them. As I have said before, I had no **aptitude** for mathematics; the different points were not explained to me as fully as I wished. The geometrical diagrams were particularly **vexing** because I could not see the relation of the different parts to one another, even on the cushion. It was not until Mr. Keith taught me that I had a clear idea of mathematics.

I was beginning to overcome these difficulties when an event occurred which changed everything.

Just before the books came, Mr. Gilman had begun to remonstrate with Miss Sullivan on the ground that I was working too hard, and in spite of my earnest protestations, he reduced the number of my recitations. At the beginning we had agreed that I should, if necessary, take five years to prepare for college, but at the end of the first year the success of my examinations showed Miss Sullivan, Miss Harbaugh (Mr. Gilman's head teacher), and one other, that I could without too much effort complete my preparation in two years more. Mr. Gilman at first agreed to this; but when my tasks had become somewhat perplexing, he insisted that I was overworked, and that I should remain at his school

aptitude n. 天资   vexing adj. 令人烦恼的

three years longer. I did not like his plan, for I wished to enter college with my class.

On the seventeenth of November I was not very well, and did not go to school. Although Miss Sullivan knew that my indisposition was not serious, yet Mr. Gilman, on hearing of it, declared that I was breaking down and made changes in my studies which would have rendered it impossible for me to take my final examinations with my class. In the end the difference of opinion between Mr. Gilman and Miss Sullivan resulted in my mother's withdrawing my sister Mildred and me from the Cambridge School.

After some delay it was arranged that I should continue my studies under a tutor, Mr. Merton S. Keith, of Cambridge. Miss Sullivan and I spent the rest of the winter with our friends, the Chamberlins in Wrentham, twenty-five miles from Boston.

From February to July 1898, Mr. Keith came out to Wrentham twice a week, and taught me ***algebra***, geometry, Greek and Latin. Miss Sullivan interpreted his instruction.

In October, 1898, we returned to Boston. For eight months Mr. Keith gave me lessons five times a week, in periods of about an hour. He explained each time what I did not understand in the previous lesson, assigned new work, and took home with him the Greek exercises which I had written during the week on my typewriter, corrected them fully, and returned them to me.

In this way my preparation for college went on without interruption. I found it much easier and pleasanter to be taught by myself than to receive instruction in class. There was no hurry, no confusion. My tutor had plenty of time to explain what I did not understand, so I got on faster and did better work than I ever did in school. I still found more difficulty in mastering problems in mathematics than I did in any other

algebra n. 代数学

of my studies. I wish algebra and geometry had been half as easy as the languages and literature. But even mathematics Mr. Keith made interesting; he succeeded in whittling problems small enough to get through my brain . He kept my mind alert and eager, and trained it to reason clearly, and to seek conclusions calmly and logically, instead of jumping wildly into space and arriving nowhere. He was always gentle and **_forbearing,_** no matter how dull I might be, and believe me, my stupidity would often have exhausted the patience of Job.

On the 29th and 30th of June, 1899, I took my final examinations for Radcliffe College. The first day I had Elementary Greek and Advanced Latin, and the second day Geometry, Algebra and Advanced Greek.

The college authorities did not allow Miss Sullivan to read the examination papers to me; so Mr. Eugene C. Vining, one of the instructors at the Perkins Institution for the Blind, was employed to copy the papers for me in American braille. Mr. Vining was a stranger to me, and could not communicate with me, except by writing braille. The **_proctor_** was also a stranger, and did not attempt to communicate with me in any way.

The braille worked well enough in the languages, but when it came to geometry and algebra, difficulties rose. I was sorely perplexed, and felt discouraged wasting much precious time, especially in algebra. It is true that I was familiar with all literary braille in common use in this country—English, American, and New York Point; but the various signs and symbols in geometry and algebra in the three systems are very different, and I had used only the English braille in my algebra.

Two days before the examinations, Mr. Vining sent me a braille copy of one of the old Harvard papers in algebra. To my **_dismay_** I found that it was in the American notation. I sat down immediately and wrote to

---

forbearing adj. 宽容的；忍耐的　　proctor n. 代理人；学监
dismay n. 沮丧；灰心；惊慌

Mr. Vining, asking him to explain the signs. I received another paper and a table of signs by return mail, and I set to work to learn the notation. But on the night before the algebra examination, while I was struggling over some very complicated examples, I could not tell the combinations of bracket, brace and radical. Both Mr. Keith and I were distressed and full of forebodings for the morrow; but we went over to the college a little before the examination began, and had Mr. Vining explain more fully the American symbols.

In geometry my chief difficulty was that I had always been accustomed to read the propositions in line print, or to have them spelled into my hand; and somehow, although the propositions were right before me, I found the braille confusing, and could not fix clearly in my mind what I was reading. But when I took up algebra I had a harder time still. The signs, which I had so lately learned, and which I thought I knew, perplexed me. Besides, I could not see what I wrote on my typewriter. I had always done my work in braille or in my head. Mr. Keith had relied too much on my ability to solve problems mentally, and had not trained me to write examination papers. Consequently my work was painfully slow, and I had to read the examples over and over before I could form any idea of what I was required to do. Indeed, I am not sure now that I read all the signs correctly. I found it very hard to keep my wits about me.

But I do not blame any one. The administrative board of Radcliffe did not realize how difficult they were making my examinations, nor did they understand the peculiar difficulties I had to ***surmount***. But if they unintentionally placed obstacles in my way, I have the consolation of knowing that I overcame them all.

surmount vt. 克服；越过；战胜

Chapter 20

THE STRUGGLE FOR admission to college was ended, and I could now enter Radcliffe whenever I pleased. Before I entered college, however, it was thought best that I should study another year under Mr. Keith. It was not, therefore, until the fall of 1900 that my dream of going to college was realized.

I remember my first day at Radcliffe. It was a day full of interest for me. I had looked forward to it for years. A potent force within me, stronger than the persuasion of my friends, stronger even than the pleadings of my heart, had impelled me to try my strength by the standards of those who see and hear. I knew that there were obstacles in the way; but I was eager to overcome them. I had taken to heart the words of the wise Roman who said, "To be banished from Rome is but to live outside of Rome." Debarred from the great highways of knowledge, I was compelled to make the journey across country by unfrequented roads—that was all; and I knew that in college there were many bypaths where I could touch hands with girls who were thinking, loving and struggling like me.

I began my studies with eagerness. Before me I saw a new world opening in beauty and light, and I felt within me the capacity to know all things. In the wonderland of Mind I should be as free as another. Its people, scenery, manners, joys, tragedies should be living, tangible interpreters of the real world. The lecture-halls seemed filled with the spirit of the great and the wise, and I thought the professors were the embodiment of wisdom. If I have since learned differently, I am not going to tell anybody.

But I soon discovered that college was not quite the romantic lyceum I had imagined. Many of the dreams that had delighted my young inexperience became beautifully less and "faded into the light of common day." Gradually I began to find that there were disadvantages in going to college.

The one I felt and still feel most is lack of time. I used to have time to think, to reflect, my mind and I. We would sit together of an evening and listen to the inner melodies of the spirit, which one hears only in leisure moments when the words of some loved poet touch a deep, sweet ***chord*** in the soul that until then had been silent. But in college there is no time to commune with one's thoughts. One goes to college to learn, it seems, not to think. When one enters the portals of learning, one leaves the dearest pleasures—solitude, books and imagination—outside with the whistling pines. I suppose I ought to find some comfort in the thought that I am laying up treasures for future enjoyment, but I am improvident enough to prefer present joy to hoarding riches against a rainy day.

My studies the first year were French, German, history, English composition and English literature. In the French course I read some of the works of Corneille, Molière, Racine, Alfred de Musset and Sainte-Beuve, and in the German those of Goethe and Schiller. I reviewed rapidly the whole period of history from the fall of the Roman Empire to the eighteenth century, and in English literature studied critically Milton's poems and "Areopagitica."

chord n. 弦；和弦

I am frequently asked how I overcome the peculiar conditions under which I work in college. In the classroom I am of course practically alone. The professor is as remote as if he were speaking through a telephone. The lectures are spelled into my hand as rapidly as possible, and much of the individuality of the lecturer is lost to me in the effort to keep in the race. The words rush through my hands like hounds in pursuit of a hare which they often miss. But in this respect I do not think I am much worse off than the girls who take notes. If the mind is occupied with the mechanical process of hearing and putting words on paper at pell-mell speed, I should not think one could pay much attention to the subject under consideration or the manner in which it is presented. I cannot make notes during the lectures, because my hands are busy listening. Usually I jot down what I can remember of them when I get home. I write the exercises, daily themes, criticisms and hour-tests, the mid-year and final examinations, on my typewriter, so that the professors have no difficulty in finding out how little I know. When I began the study of Latin prosody, I devised and explained to my professor a system of signs indicating the different meters and quantities.

I use the Hammond typewriter. I have tried many machines, and I find the Hammond is the best adapted to the peculiar needs of my work. With this machine movable type shuttles can be used, and one can have several shuttles, each with a different set of characters—Greek, French, or mathematical, according to the kind of writing one wishes to do on the typewriter. Without it, I doubt if I could go to college.

Very few of the books required in the various courses are printed for the blind, and I am obliged to have them spelled into my hand. Consequently I need more time to prepare my lessons than other girls. The manual part takes longer, and I have perplexities which they have not. There are days when the close attention I must give to details chafes my spirit, and the thought that I must spend hours reading a few chapters, while in the world without other girls are laughing and singing and dancing, makes me rebellious; but I soon recover my buoyancy and laugh the discontent out of my heart. For, after all, every one who wishes to gain true knowledge must climb the Hill Difficulty alone, and since there is no royal road to the summit, I must zigzag it in my own way. I slip back many times, I fall, I stand still, I run against the edge of hidden obstacles, I lose my temper and find it again and keep it better. I trudge on, I gain a little, I feel encouraged, I get more eager and climb higher and begin to see the widening horizon. Every struggle is a victory. One more effort and I reach the luminous cloud, the blue depths of the sky, the uplands of my desire. I am not always alone, however, in these struggles. Mr. William Wade and Mr. E. E. Allen, Principal of the Pennsylvania Institution for the Instruction of the Blind, get for me many of the books I need in raised print. Their thoughtfulness has been more of a help and encouragement to me than they can ever know.

Last year, my second year at Radcliffe, I studied English composition, the Bible as English literature, the governments of America and Europe, the Odes of Horace, and Latin comedy. The class in composition was the pleasantest. It was very lively. The lectures were always interesting, **_vivacious_**, **_witty_**; for the instructor, Mr. Charles Townsend Copeland, more than any one else I have had until this year, brings before you literature in all its original freshness and power. For one short hour you are permitted to drink in the eternal beauty of the old masters without needless interpretation or exposition. You revel in their fine thoughts. You enjoy with all your soul the sweet thunder of the Old Testament, forgetting the existence of Jahweh and Elohim; and you go home feeling that you have had "a glimpse of that perfection in which spirit and form dwell in immortal harmony; truth and beauty bearing a new growth on the ancient stem of time."

This year is the happiest because I am studying subjects that

vivacious adj. 活泼的；快活的；有生气的   witty adj. 诙谐的；富于机智的

especially interest me, economics, Elizabethan literature, Shakespeare under Professor George L. Kittredge, and the History of Philosophy under Professor Josiah Royce. Through philosophy one enters with sympathy of comprehension into the traditions of remote ages and other modes of thought, which erewhile seemed alien and without reason.

But college is not the universal Athens I thought it was, There one does not meet the great and the wise face to face; one does not even feel their living touch. They are there, it is true; but they seem mummified. We must extract them from the crannied wall of learning and dissect and analyze them before we can be sure that we have a Milton or an Isaiah. and not merely a clever imitation. Many scholars forget, it seems to me, that our enjoyment of the great works of literature depends more upon the depth of our sympathy than upon our understanding. The trouble is that very few of their laborious explanations stick in the memory. The mind drops them as a branch drops its overripe fruit. It is possible to know a flower, root and stem and all, and all the processes of growth, and yet to have no appreciation of the flower flesh bathed in heaven's dew. Again and again I ask impatiently, "Why concern myself with these explanations and hypotheses?" They fly hither and thither in my thought like blind birds beating the air with ineffectual wings. I do not mean to object to a thorough knowledge of the famous works we read. I object only to the interminable comments and **_bewildering_** criticisms that teach but one thing: there are as many opinions as there are men. But when a great scholar like Professor Kittredge interprets what the master said. it is "as if new sight were given the blind." He brings back Shakespeare, the poet.

There are, however, times when I long to sweep away half the things I am expected to learn; for the overtaxed mind cannot enjoy the treasure it has secured at the greatest cost. It is impossible, I think, to read in

bewildering adj. 使人困惑的；令人产生混乱的

one day four or five different books in different languages and treating of widely different subjects, and not lose sight of the very ends for which one reads. When one reads hurriedly and nervously, having in mind written tests and examinations, one's brain becomes encumbered with a lot of choice bric-a-brac for which there seems to be little use. At the present time my mind is so full of **heterogeneous** matter that I almost despair of ever being able to put it in order. Whenever I enter the region that was the kingdom of my mind I feel like the proverbial bull in the china shop. A thousand odds and ends of knowledge come crashing about my head like hailstones, and when I try to escape them, theme-goblins and college nixies of all sorts pursue me, until I wish—oh, may I be forgiven the wicked wish!—that I might smash the idols I came to worship.

But the examinations are the chief bugbears of my college life. Although I have faced them many times and cast them down and made them bite the dust, yet they rise again and menace me with pale looks, until like Bob Acres I feel my courage oozing out at my finger ends. The days before these ordeals take place are spent in cramming your mind with mystic formulae and indigestible dates—unpalatable diets, until you wish that books and science and you were buried in the depths of the sea.

At last the dreaded hour arrives, and you are a favored being indeed if you feel prepared, and are able at the right time to call to your standard thoughts that will aid you in that supreme effort. It happens too often that your **trumpet** call is unheeded. It is most perplexing and exasperating that just at the moment when you need your memory and a nice sense of discrimination, these faculties take to themselves wings and fly away. The facts you have garnered with such infinite trouble invariably fail you at a pinch.

"Give a brief account of Huss and his work." Huss? Who was he

heterogeneous adj. 多相的；由不同成分形成的
trumpet n. 喇叭；喇叭声

and what did he do? The name looks strangely familiar. You ransack your budget of historic facts much as you would hunt for a bit of silk in a ragbag. You are sure it is somewhere in your mind near the top—you saw it there the other day when you were looking up the beginnings of the Reformation. But where is it now? You fish out all manner of odds and ends of knowledge—revolutions, schisms, massacres, systems of government; but Huss—where is he? You are amazed at all the things yon know which are not on the examination paper. In desperation you seize the budget and dump everything out, and there in a corner is your man, serenely brooding on his own private thought, unconscious of the **catastrophe** which he has brought upon you.

Just then the proctor informs you that the time is up. With a feeling of intense disgust you kick the mass of rubbish into a corner and go home, your head full of revolutionary schemes to abolish the divine right of professors to ask questions without the consent of the questioned.

It comes over me that in the last two or three pages of this chapter I have used figures which will turn the laugh against me. Ah, here they are—the mixed metaphors mocking and strutting about before me, pointing to the bull in the china shop assailed by hailstones and the bugbears with pale looks, an unanalyzed species! Let them mock on. The words describe so exactly the atmosphere of jostling, tumbling ideas I live in that I will **wink** at them for once, and put on a deliberate air to say that my ideas of college have changed.

While my days at Radcliffe were still in the future, they were encircled with a hale of romance, which they have lost; but in the transition from romantic to actual I have learned many things I should never have known had I not tried the experiment. One of them is the precious science of patience, which teaches us that we should take our education as we would take a walk in the country, leisurely, our minds

catastrophe n. 大灾难；大祸；惨败　　　wink vi. 眨眼；使眼色

hospitably open to impressions of every sort. Such knowledge floods the soul unseen with a soundless tidal wave of deepening thought. "Knowledge is power." Rather, knowledge is happiness, because to have knowledge—broad, deep knowledge—is to know true ends from false, and lofty things from low. To know the thoughts and deeds that have marked man's progress is to feel the great heartthrobs of humanity through the centuries; and if one does not feel in these pulsations a heavenward striving, one must indeed be deaf to the harmonies of life.

Chapter 21

I HAVE THUS far sketched the events of my life, but I have not shown how much I have depended on books not only for pleasure and for the wisdom they bring to all who read, but also for that knowledge which comes to others through their eyes and their ears. Indeed, books have meant so much more in my education than in that of others, that I shall go back to the time when I began to read.

I read my first connected story in May 1887, when I was seven years old, and from that day to this I have devoured everything in the shape of a printed page that has come within the reach of my hungry finger tips. As I have said, I did not study regularly during the early years of my education; nor did I read according to rule.

At first I had only a few books in raised print— "readers" for beginners, a collection of stories for children, and a book about the earth called "Our World." I think that was all; but I read them over and over, until the words were so worn and pressed I could scarcely make them out. Sometimes Miss Sullivan read to me, spelling into my hand little stories and poems that she knew I should understand; but I preferred reading myself to being read to, because I liked to read again and again the things that pleased me.

It was during my first visit to Boston that I really began to read in good earnest. I was permitted to spend a part of each day in the Institution library, and to wander from bookcase to bookcase, and take down whatever book my fingers lighted upon. And read I did, whether I understood one word in ten or two words on a page. The words themselves fascinated me; but I took no conscious account of what I read. My mind must, however, have been very impressionable at that period, for it retained many words and whole sentences, to the meaning of which I had not the faintest clue; and afterward, when I began to talk and write, these words and sentences would flash out quite naturally, so that my friends wondered at the richness of my vocabulary. I must have read parts of many books (in those early days I think I never read any book through)and a great deal of poetry in this uncomprehending way, until I discovered "Little Lord Fauntleroy," which was the first book of any consequence I read understandingly.

One day my teacher found me in a corner of the library poring over the pages of "The Scarlet Letter." I was then about eight years old. I remember she asked me if I liked little Pearl, and explained some of the words that had puzzled me. Then she told me that she had a beautiful story about a little boy which she was sure I would like better than "The Scarlet Letter." The name of the story was "Little Lord Fauntleroy," and she promised to read it to me the following summer. But we did not begin the story until August; the first few weeks of my stay at the seashore were so full of discoveries and excitement that I forgot the very existence of books. Then my teacher went to visit some friends in Boston, leaving me for a short time.

When she returned almost the first thing we did was to begin the story of "Little Lord Fauntleroy." I recall distinctly the time and place when we read the first chapters of the fascinating child's story. It was a warm afternoon in August. We were sitting together in a **hammock**

hammock n. 吊床；吊铺

which swung from two ***solemn*** pines at a short distance from the house. We had hurried through the dish-washing after luncheon, in order that we might have as long an afternoon as possible for the story. As we hastened through the long grass toward the hammock, the grasshoppers swarmed about us and fastened themselves on our clothes, and I remember that my teacher insisted upon picking them all off before we sat down, which seemed to me an unnecessary waste of time. The hammock was covered with pine needles, for it had not been used while my teacher was away. The warm sun shone on the pine trees and drew out all their fragrance. The air was balmy, with a tang of the sea in it. Before we began the story Miss Sullivan explained to me the things that she knew I should not understand, and as we read on she explained the unfamiliar words, At first there were many words I did not know, and the reading was constantly interrupted; but as soon as I thoroughly comprehended the situation. I became too eagerly absorbed in the story to notice mere words. and I am afraid I listened impatiently to the explanations that Miss Sullivan felt to be necessary. When her fingers were too tired to spell another word, I had for the first time a keen sense of my deprivations. I took the book in my hands and tried to feel the letters with an intensity of longing that I can never forget.

  Afterward, at my eager request, Mr. Anagnos had this story embossed, and I read it again and again, until I almost knew it by heart; and all through my childhood "Little Lord Fauntleroy" was my sweet and gentle companion. I have given these details at the risk of being tedious, because they are in such vivid contrast with my vague, mutable and confused memories of earlier reading.

  From "Little Lord Fauntleroy" I date the beginning of my true interest in books. During the next two years I read many books at my home and on my visits to Boston. I cannot remember what they all were, or in what

solemn　adj. 庄严的；严肃的

order I read them; but I know that among them were "Greek Heroes," La Fontaine's "Fables," Hawthorne's "Wonder Book," "Bible Stories," Lamb's "Tales from Shakespeare," "A Child's History of England" by Dickens, "The Arabian Nights," "The Swiss Family Robinson," "The Pilgrim's Progress," "Robinson Crusoe," "Little Women," and "Heidi," a beautiful little story which I afterward read in German. I read them in the intervals between study and play with an ever-deepening sense of pleasure. I did not study nor analyze them—I did not know whether they were well written or not; I never thought about style or authorship. They laid their treasures at my feet, and I accepted them as we accept the sunshine and the love of our friends. I loved "Little Women" because it gave me a sense of kinship with girls and boys who could see and hear. Circumscribed as my life was in so many ways, I had to look between the covers of books for news of the world that lay outside my own.

I did not care especially for "The Pilgrim's Progress," which I think I did not finish, or for the "Fables." I read La Fontaine's "Fables" first in an English translation, and enjoyed them only after a halfhearted fashion. Later I read the book again in French, and I found that, in spite of the vivid word-pictures, and the wonderful mastery of language, I liked it no better. I do not know why it is, but stories in which animals are made to talk and act like human beings have never appealed to me very strongly. The **_ludicrous_** caricatures of the animals occupy my mind to the exclusion of the moral.

Then, again, La Fontaine seldom, if ever, appeals to our higher moral sense. The highest chords he strikes are those of reason and self-love. Through all the fables runs the thought that man's morality springs wholly from self-love, and that if that self-love is directed and restrained by reason, happiness must follow. Now, so far as I can judge, self-love is the root of all evil; but, of course, I may be wrong, for La Fontaine had

ludicrous adj. 滑稽的；荒唐的

greater opportunities of observing men than I am likely ever to have. I do not object so much to the cynical and satirical fables as to those in which momentous truths are taught by monkeys and foxes.

But I love "The Jungle Book" and "Wild Animals I Have Known." I feel a genuine interest in the animals themselves, because they are real animals and not caricatures of men. One sympathizes with their loves and hatreds, laughs over their comedies, and weeps over their tragedies. And if they point a moral, it is so subtle that we are not conscious of it.

My mind opened naturally and joyously to a conception of antiquity. Greece, ancient Greece, exercised a mysterious fascination over me. In my fancy the **pagan** gods and goddesses still walked on earth and talked face to face with men, and in my heart I secretly built shrines to those I loved best. I knew and loved the whole tribe of nymphs and heroes and demigods—no, not quite all, for the cruelty and greed of Medea and Jason were too monstrous to be forgiven, and I used to wonder why the gods permitted them to do wrong and then punished them for their wickedness. And the mystery is still unsolved. I often wonder how

God Can dumbness keep
While Sin creeps grinning through His house of Time.

It was the Iliad that made Greece my paradise. I was familiar with the story of Troy before I read it in the original, and consequently I had little difficulty in making the Greek words surrender their treasures after I had passed the borderland of grammar. Great poetry, whether written in Greek or in English, needs no other interpreter than a responsive heart. Would that the host of those who make the great works of the poets **odious** by their analysis, impositions and laborious comments

pagan adj. 异教徒的；异教的　n. 异教徒；无宗教信仰者
odious adj. 可憎的；讨厌的

might learn this simple truth! It is not necessary that one should be able to define every word and give it its principal pines and its grammatical position in the sentence in order to understand and appreciate a fine poem. I know my learned professors have found greater riches in the Iliad than I shall ever find; but I am not avaricious. I am content that others should be wiser than I. But with all their wide and comprehensive knowledge, they cannot measure their enjoyment of that splendid epic, nor can I. When I read the finest passages of the Iliad, I am conscious of a soul-sense that lifts me above the narrow, cramping circumstances of my life. My physical limitations are forgotten—my world lies upward, the length and the breadth and the sweep of the heavens are mine!

My admiration for the Aeneid is not so great, but it is none the less real. I read it as much as possible without the help of notes or dictionary, and I always like to translate the episodes that pleased me especially. The word-painting of Virgil is wonderful sometimes; but his gods and men move through the scenes of passion and strife and pity and love like the graceful figures in an Elizabethan mask, whereas in the Iliad they give three leaps and go on singing. Virgil is serene and lovely like a marble Apollo in the moonlight; Homer is a beautiful, **_animated_** youth in the full sunlight with the wind in his hair.

How easy it is to fly on paper wings! From "Greek Heroes" to the Iliad was no day's journey, nor was it altogether pleasant. One could have traveled round the world many times while I trudged my weary way through the **_labyrinthine_** mazes of grammars and dictionaries, or fell into those dreadful pitfalls called examinations, set by schools and colleges for the contusion of those who seek after knowledge. I suppose this sort of Pilgrim's Progress was justified by the end; but it seemed interminable to me, in spite of the pleasant surprises that met me now and then at a turn in the road.

animated adj. 活生生的；活泼的；愉快的   labyrinthine adj. 迷宫的；复杂的

I began to read the Bible long before I could understand it. Now it seems strange to me that there should have been a time when my spirit was deaf to its wondrous harmonies; but I remember well a rainy Sunday morning when, having nothing else to do, I begged my cousin to read me a story out of the Bible. Although she did not think I should understand, she began to spell into my hand the story of Joseph and his brother. Somehow it failed to interest me.The unusual language and repetition made the story seem unreal and far away in the land of Canaan, and I fell asleep and wandered off to the land of Nod, before the brothers came with the coat of many colors unto the tent of Jacob and told their wicked lie! I cannot understand why the stoties of the Greeks should have been so full of charm for me, and those of the Bible so devoid of interest, unless it was that I had made the acquaintance of several Greeks in Boston and been inspired by their enthusiasm for the stories of their country; whereas I had not met a single Hebrew or Egyptian, and therefore concluded that they were nothing more than barbarians, and the stories about them were probably all made up. Curiously enough, it never occurred to me to call Greek patronymics "queer."

But how shall I speak of the glories I have since discovered in the Bible? For years I have read it with an ever-broadening sense of joy and inspiration; and I love it as I love no other book. Still there is much in the Bible against which every instinct of my being rebels, so much that I regret the necessity which has compelled me to read it through from beginning to end. I do not think that the knowledge which I have gained of its history and sources compensates me for the unpleasant details it has forced upon my attention. For my part, I wish, with Mr. Howells, that the literature of the past might be purged of all that is ugly and barbarous in it, although I should object as much as any one to having these great works weakened or falsified.

There is something impressive, awful, in the simplicity and terrible directness of the Book of Esther. Could there be anything more dramatic than the scene in which Esther stands before her wicked lord? She knows her life is in his hands; there is no one to protect her from his wrath. Yet, conquering her woman's fear, she approaches him, animated by the noblest **_patriotism_**, having but one thought: "If I perish, I perish; but if I live, my people shall live."

The story of Ruth, too—how Oriental it is! Yet how different is the life of these simple country folks from that of the Persian capital! Ruth is so loyal and gentle-hearted, we cannot help loving her, as she stands with the reapers amid the waving corn. Her beautiful, unselfish spirit shines out like a bright star in the night of a dark and cruel age. Love like Ruth's, love which can rise above conflicting creeds and deep-seated racial prejudices, is hard to find in all the world.

The Bible gives me a deep, comforting sense that "things seen are temporal, and things unseen are eternal."

I do not remember a time since I have been capable of loving books that I have not loved Shakespeare. I cannot tell exactly when I began Lamb's "Tales from Shakespeare"; but I know that I read them at first with a child's understanding and a child's wonder. "Macbeth" seems to have impressed me most. One reading was sufficient to stamp every detail of the story upon my memory forever. For a long time the ghosts and witches pursued me even into Dreamland. I could see, absolutely see, the **_dagger_** and Lady Macbeth's little white hand—the dreadful stain was as real to me as to the grief-stricken queen.

I read "King Lear" soon after "Macbeth," and I shall never forget the feeling of horror when I came to the scene in which Gloster's eyes are put out. Anger seized me, my fingers refused to move, I sat rigid for one long moment, the blood throbbing in my temples, and all the hatred that a child can feel concentrated in my heart.

I must have made the acquaintance of Shylock and Satan about the

patriotism n. 爱国主义；爱国心；爱国精神　　dagger n. 匕首；短剑

same time, for the two characters were long associated in my mind. I remember that I was sorry for them. I felt vaguely that they could not be good even if they wished to, because no one seemed willing to help them or to give them a fair chance. Even now I cannot find it in my heart to condemn them utterly. There are moments when I feel that the Shylocks, the Judases, and even the Devil, are broken spokes in the great wheel of good which shall in due time be made whole.

It seems strange that my first reading of Shakespeare should have left me so many unpleasant memories. The bright, gentle, fanciful plays—the ones I like best now—appear not to have impressed me at first, perhaps because they reflected the habitual sunshine and gaiety of a child's life. But "there is nothing more capricious than the memory of a child: what it will hold, and what it will lose."

I have since read Shakespeare's plays many times and know parts of them by heart, but I cannot tell which of them I like best. My delight in them is as varied as my moods. The little songs and the sonnets have a meaning for me as fresh and wonderful as the dramas. But, with all my love for Shakespeare, it is often weary work to read all the meanings into his lines which critics and commentators have given them. I used to try to remember their interpretations, but they discouraged and vexed me; so I made a secret compact with myself not to try any more. This compact I have only just broken in my study of Shakespeare under Professor Kittredge. I know there are many things in Shakespeare, and in the world, that I do not understand; and I am glad to see veil after veil lift gradually, revealing new realms of thought and beauty.

Next to poetry I love history. I have read every historical work that I have been able to lay my hands on, from a catalogue of dry facts and dryer dates to Green's impartial, picturesque "History of the English People"; from Freeman's "History of Europe" to Emerton's "Middle Ages." The first book that gave me any real sense of the value of history was Swinton's "World's History," which I received on my thirteenth birthday.

Though I believe it is no longer considered valid, yet I have kept it ever since as one of my treasures. From it I learned how the races of men spread from land to land and built great cities, how a few great rulers, earthly Titans, put everything under their feet, and with a decisive word opened the gates of happiness for millions and closed them upon millions more; how different nations pioneered in art and knowledge and broke ground for the mightier growths of coming ages; how civilization underwent, as it were, the holocaust of a degenerate age, and rose again, like the Phoenix, among the nobler sons of the North; and how by liberty, tolerance and education the great and the wise have opened the way for the **salvation** of the whole world.

In my college reading I have become somewhat familiar with French and German literature. The German puts strength before beauty, and truth before convention, both in life and literature. There is a vehement, sledge-hammer vigor about everything that he does, When he speaks, it is not to impress others, but because his heart would burst if he did not find an outlet for the thoughts that burn in his soul.

Then, too, there is in German literature a fine reserve which I like; but its chief glory is the recognition I find in it of the redeeming potency of woman's self-sacrificing love. This thought pervades all German literature and is mystically expressed in Goethe's "Faust":

All things transitory
    But as symbols are sent.
Earth's insufficiency
    Here grows to event.
The indescribable
Here it is done.
The Woman Soul leads us upward and on!

salvation n. 拯救，救助

Of all the French writers that I have read. I like Molière and Racine best. There are fine things in Balzac and passages in Mérimée which strike one like a keen blast of sea air. Alfred de Musset is impossible! I admire Victor Hugo—I appreciate his genius, his brilliancy, his romanticism; though he is not one of my literary passions. But Hugo and Goethe and Schiller and all great poets of all great nations are interpreters of eternal things, and my spirit reverently follows them into the regions where Beauty and Truth and Goodness are one.

I am afraid I have written too much about my book-friends, and yet I have mentioned only the authors I love most; and from this fact one might easily suppose that my circle of friends was very limited and undemocratic, which would be a very wrong impression. I like many writers for many reasons—Carlyle for his ruggedness and scorn of shams; Wordsworth, who teaches the oneness of man and nature; I find an exquisite pleasure in the oddities and surprises of Hood, in Herrick's quaintness and the palpable scent of lily and rose in his verses; I like Whittier for his enthusiasms and moral rectitude. I knew him, and the gentle remembrance of our friendship doubles the pleasure I have in reading his poems. I love Mark Twain—who does not? The gods, too, loved him and put into his heart all manner of wisdom; then, fearing lest he should become a pessimist, they spanned his mind, with a rainbow of love and faith. I like Scott for his freshness, dash and large honesty. I love all writers whose minds, like Lowell's, bubble up in the sunshine of optimism—fountains of joy and good will, with occasionally a splash of anger and here and there a ***healing*** spray of sympathy and pity.

In a word, literature is my Utopia. Here I am not disfranchised. No barrier of the senses shuts me out from the sweet, gracious discourse of my book-friends. They talk to me without embarrassment or awkwardness. The things I nave learned and the things I have been taught seem of ridiculously little importance compared with their "large loves and heavenly charities."

healing adj. 能治愈的

Chapter 22

I TRUST THAT my readers have not concluded from the preceding chapter on books that reading is my only pleasure; my pleasures and amusements are many and varied.

More than once in the course of my story I have referred to my love of the country and out-of-door sports. When I was quite a little girl, I learned to row and swim, and during the summer, when I am at Wrentham, Massachusetts, I almost live in my boat. Nothing gives me greater pleasure than to take my friends out rowing when they come to visit me. Of course, I cannot guide the boat very well. Some one usually sits in the stern and manages the ***rudder*** while I row. Sometimes, however, I go rowing without the rudder. It is fun to try to steer by the scent of water-grasses and lilies, and of bushes that grow on the shore. I use oars with leather bands, which keep them in position in the oarlocks, and I know by the resistance of the water when the oars are ***evenly*** poised. In the same manner I can also tell when I am pulling against the current. I like to contend with wind and wave. What is more exhilarating than to make your staunch little boat, obedient to your will and muscle,

rudder n. 船舵　　evenly adv. 均匀地；平衡地

go slamming lightly over glistening, tilting waves, and to feel the steady, imperious surge of the water!

I also enjoy canoeing, and I suppose you will smile when I say that I especially like it on moonlight nights. I cannot, it is true, see the moon climb up the sky behind the pines and steal softly across the heavens, making a shining path for us to follow; but I know she is there, and as lie back among the pillows and put my hand in the water, I fancy that I feel the shimmer of her garments as she passes. Sometimes a daring little fish slips between my fingers, and often a pond-lily presses shyly against my hand. Frequently, as we emerge from the shelter of a cove or inlet, I am suddenly conscious of the spaciousness of the air about me. A luminous warmth seems to enfold me. Whether it comes from the trees which have been heated by the sun, or from the water, I can never discover. I have had the same strange sensation even in the heart of the city. I have felt it on cold, stormy days and at night. It is like the kiss of warm lips on my face.

My favorite amusement is sailing. In the summer of 1901 I visited Nova Scotia, and had opportunities such as I had not enjoyed before to make the acquaintance of the ocean. After spending a few days in Evangeline's country, about which Longfellow's beautiful poem has woven a spell of enchantment, Miss Sullivan and I went to Halifax, where we remained the greater part of the summer. The harbor was our joy,our paradise.What glorious sails we had to Bedford Basin, to McNabb's Island, to York Redoubt, and to the Northwest Arm! And at night what soothing, wondrous hours we spent in the shadow of the great, silent men-of-war, Oh, it was all so interesting, so beautiful! The memory of it is a joy forever.

One day we had a thrilling experience. There was a regatta in the Northwest Arm, in which the boats from the different warships were engaged. We went in a sail-boat along with many others to watch the races. Hundreds of little sail-boats swung to and fro close by, and the sea was calm. When the races were over, and we turned our faces homeward, one of the party noticed a black cloud drifting in from the sea, which grew and spread and thickened until it covered the whole sky. The wind rose, and the waves chopped angrily at unseen barriers. Our little boat confronted the gale fearlessly; with sails spread and ropes taut, she seemed to sit upon the wind. Now she swirled in the billows, now she sprang upward on a gigantic wave, only to be driven down with angry howl and hiss. Down came the mainsail. Tacking and jibbing, we wrestled with opposing winds that drove us from side to side with impetuous fury. Our hearts beat fast, and our hands trembled with excitement, not fear; for we had the hearts of vikings, and we knew that our skipper was master of the situation. He had steered through many a storm with firm hand and sea-wise eye. As they passed us, the large craft and the gunboats in the harbor saluted and the seamen shouted applause for the master of the only little sail-boat that ventured out into the storm. At last, cold, hungry and weary, we reached our pier.

Last summer I spent in one of the loveliest nooks of one of the most charming villages in New England. Wrentham, Massaehusetts, is associated with nearly all of my joys and sorrows. For many years Red Farm, by King Philip's Pond, the home of Mr. J. E. Chamberlin and his family, was my home. I remember with deepest gratitude the kindness of these dear friends and the happy days I spent with them. The sweet companionship of their children meant much to me. I joined in all their sports and rambles through the woods and frolics in the water. The **_prattle_** of the little ones and their pleasure in the stories I told them of elf and gnome, of hero and wily bear, are pleasant things to remember. Mr. Chamberlin initiated me into the mysteries of tree and wild-flower, until with the little ear of love I heard the flow of sap in the oak, and saw the sun glint from leaf to leaf. Thus it is that

prattle vi. 闲聊；胡说 n. 无聊话

> Even as the roots, shut in the darksome earth,
> Share in the tree-top's joyance, and conceive
> Of sunshine and wide air and wingèd things,
> By sympathy of nature, so do I

gave evidence of things unseen.

It seems to me that there is in each of us a capacity to comprehend the impressions and emotions which have been experienced by mankind from the beginning. Each individual has a subconscious memory of the green earth and murmuring waters, and blindness and deafness cannot rob him of this gift from past generations. This inherited capacity is a sort of sixth sense—a soul-sense which sees, hears, feels, all in one.

I have many tree friends in Wrentham. One of them, a splendid oak, is the special pride of my heart. I take all my other friends to see this king-tree. It stands on a bluff overlooking King Philip's Pond, and those who are wise in tree lore say it must have stood there eight hundred or a thou sand years. There is a tradition that under this tree King Philip, the heroic Indian chief, gazed his last on earth and sky.

I had another tree friend, gentle and more approachable than the great oak—a linden that grew in the dooryard at Red Farm. One afternoon, during a terrible thunderstorm, I felt a tremendous crash against the side of the house and knew, even before they told me, that the linden had fallen. We went out to see the hero that had withstood so many tempests, and it wrung my heart to see him prostrate who had mightily striven and was now mightily fallen.

But I must not forget that I was going to write about last summer in particular. As soon as my examinations were over, Miss Sullivan and I hastened to this green nook, where we have a little cottage on one of the three lakes for which Wrentham is famous. Here the long, sunny days were mine, and all thoughts of work and college and the noisy city were thrust into the background. In Wrentham we caught echoes of what was happening in the world—war, alliance, social conflict. We heard of the cruel, unnecessary fighting ill the far-away Pacific, and learned of the struggles going on between capital and labor. We knew that beyond the border of our Eden men were making history by the sweat of their brows when they might better make a holiday. But we little heeded these things. These things would pass away; here were lakes and woods and broad daisy-starred fields and sweet-breathed meadows, and they shall endure forever.

People who think that all sensations reach us through the eye and the ear have expressed surprise that I should notice any difference, except possibly the absence of pavements, between walking in city streets and in country roads. They forget that my whole body is alive to the conditions about me. The rumble and roar of the city smite the nerves of my face, and I feel the ceaseless tramp of an unseen multitude, and the dissonant tumult frets my spirit. The grinding of heavy wagons on hard pavements and the **_monotonous_** clangor of machinery are all the more torturing to the nerves if one's attention is not diverted by the **_panorama_** that is always present in the noisy streets to people who can see.

In the country one sees only Nature's fair works, and one's soul is not saddened by the cruel struggle for mere existence that goes on in the crowded city. Several times I have visited the narrow, dirty streets where the poor live, and I grow hot and indignant to think that good people should be content to live in fine houses and become strong and beautiful, while others are condemned to live in hideous, sunless tenements and grow ugly, withered and cringing. The children who crowd these grimy alleys, half-clad and underfed, shrink away from your outstretched hand as if from a blow. Dear little creatures, they crouch in my heart and

monotonous adj. 单调的；无抑扬顿挫的；无变化的
panorama   n. 全景；全貌

haunt me with a constant sense of pain. There are men and women, too, all gnarled and bent out of shape. I have felt their hard, rough hands and realized what an endless struggle their existence must be—no more than a series of scrimmages, thwarted attempts to do something. Their life seems all immense disparity between effort and opportunity. The sun and the air are God's free gifts to all, we say; but are they so? In yonder city's clingy alleys the sun shines not, and the air is foul. Oh, man, how dost thou forget and obstruct thy brother man, and say, "Give us this day our daily bread," when he has none! Oh, would that men would leave the city, its splendor and its tumult and its gold, and return to wood and field and simple, honest living! Then would their children grow stately as noble trees, and their thoughts sweet and pure as wayside flowers. It is impossible not to think of all this when I return to the country after a year of work in town.

What a joy it is to feel the soft, springy earth under my feet once more, to follow grassy roads that lead to ferny brooks where I can bathe my fingers in a cataract of rippling notes, or to clamber over a stone wall into green fields that tumble and roll and climb in riotous gladness!

Next to a leisurely walk I enjoy a "spin" on my tandem bicycle. It is splendid to feel the wind blowing in my face and the springy motion of my iron steed. The rapid rush through the air gives me a delicious sense of strength and buoyancy, and the exercise makes my pulses dance and my heart sing.

Whenever it is possible, my dog accompanies me on a walk or ride or sail. I have had many dog friends—huge mastiffs, soft-eyed spaniels, wood-wise setters and honest, homely bull terriers. At present the lord of my affections is one of these bull terriers. He has a long pedigree, a crooked tail arid the drollest "phiz" in dogdom. My dog friends seem to understand my limitations, and always keep close beside me when I am

eloquent adj. 动人的

alone. I love their affectionate ways and the **_eloquent_** wag of their tails.

When a rainy clay keeps me indoors, I amuse myself after the manner of other girls. I like to knit and **_crochet_**;I read in the happy-go-lucky way I love, here and there a line; or perhaps I play a game or two of checkers or chess with a friend. I have a special board on which I play these games. The squares are cut out, so that the men stand in them firmly. The black checkers are flat and the white ones curved on top. Each checker has a hote in the middle in which a brass knob can be placed to distinguish the king from the commons. The chessmen are of two sizes, the white larger than the black, so that I have no trouble in following my opponent's maneuvers by moving my hands lightly over the board after a play. The jar made by shifting the men from one hole to another tells me when it is my turn.

If I happen to be all alone and in an idle mood, I play a game of solitaire, of which I am very fond. I use playing cards marked in the upper right-hand corner with braille symbols which indicate the value of the card.

If there are children around, nothing pleases me so much as to frolic with them. I find even the smallest child excellent company, and I am glad to say that children usually like me. They lead me about and show me the things they are interested in. Of course the little ones cannot spell on their fingers; but I manage to read their lips. If I do not succeed they resort to dumb show. Sometimes I make a mistake and do the wrong thing. A burst of childish laughter greets my blunder, and the **_pantomime_** begins all over again. I often tell them stories or teach them a game, and the winged hours depart and leave us good and happy.

Museums and art stores are also sources of pleasure and inspiration. Doubtless it will seem strange to many that the hand unaided by sight can feel action, sentiment, beauty in the cold **_marble_**; and yet it is true

---

crochet　vi. 用钩针编织　　pantomime　n. 哑剧

marble　n. 大理石；大理石制品

that I derive genuine pleasure from touching great works of art. As my finger tips trace line and curve, they discover the thought and emotion which the artist has portrayed. I call feel in the faces of gods and heroes hate, courage and love, just as I can detect them in living faces I am permitted to touch. I feel in Diana's posture the grace and freedom of the forest and the spirit that tames the mountain lion and subdues the fiercest passions. My soul delights in the repose and gracious curves of the Venus; and in Barré's bronzes the secrets of the jungle are revealed to me.

A medallion of Homer hangs on the wall of my study, conveniently low, so that I call easily reach it and touch the beautiful, sad face with loving reverence. How well I know each line in that majestic brow—tracks of life and bitter evidence of struggle and sorrow; those sightless eyes seeking, even in the cold plaster, for the light and the blue skies of his beloved Hellas, but seeking in vain; that beautiful mouth, firm and true and tender. It is the face of a poet, and of a man acquainted with sorrow. Ah, how well I understand his deprivation—the perpetual night in which he dwelt—

O dark, dark, amid the blaze of noon,
Irrecoverably dark, total eclipse
Without all hope of day!

In imagination I can hear Homer singing, as with unsteady, hesitating steps he gropes his way from camp to camp—singing of life, of love, of war, of the splendid achievements of a noble race. It was a wonderful, glorious song, and it won the blind poet an immortal crown, the admiration of all ages.

I sometimes wonder if the hand is not more sensitive to the beauties of sculpture than the eye. I should think the wonderful rhythmical flow of lines and curves could be more subtly felt than seen. Be this as it may, I know that I can feel the heartthrobs of the ancient Greeks in their marble gods and goddesses.

Another pleasure, which comes more rarely than the others, is going to the theater. I enjoy having a play described to me while it is being acted on the stage far more than reading it, because then it seems as if I were living in the midst of stirring events. It has been my **_privilege_** to meet a few great actors and actresses who have the power of so bewitching you that you forget time mid place and live again in the romantic past. I have been permitted to touch the face and costume of Miss Ellen Terry as she impersonated our ideal of a queen; and there was about her that divinity that hedges sublimest woe. Beside her stood Sir Henry Irving, wearing the symbols of kingship; and there was majesty of intellect in his every gesture and attitude and the royalty that subdues and overcomes in every line of his sensitive face. In the king's face, which he wore as a mask there was a **_remoteness_** and inaccessibility of grief which I shall never forget.

I also know Mr. Jefferson. I am proud to count him among my friends. I go to see him whenever I happen to be where he is acting. The first time I saw him act was while at school in New York. He played "Rip Van Winkle." I had often read the story, but I had never felt the charm of Rip's slow, quaint, kind ways as I did in the play. Mr. Jefferson's beautiful, pathetic representation quite carried me away with delight. I have a picture of old Rip in my fingers which they will never lose. After the play Miss Sullivan took me to see him behind the scenes, and I felt of his curious garb and his flowing hair and beard. Mr. Jefferson let me touch his face so that I could imagine how he looked on waking from that strange sleep of twenty years, and he showed me how poor old Rip staggered to his feet.

I have also seen him in "The Rivals." Once while I was calling on him

privilege n. 特权；优待   remoteness n. 遥远

in Boston he acted the most striking parts of "The Rivals" for me. The reception-room where we sat served for a stage. He and his son seated themselves at the big table, and Bob Acres wrote his challenge. I followed all his movements with my hands, and caught the drollery of his blunders and gestures in a way that would have been impossible had it all been spelled to me. Then they rose to fight the **_duel_**, and I followed the swift thrusts and parries of the swords and the waverings of poor Bob as his courage oozed out at his finger ends. Then the great actor gave his coat a hitch and his mouth a twitch, and in an instance I was in the village of Falling Water and felt Schneider's shaggy head against my knee. Mr. Jefferson recited the best dialogues of "Rip Van Winkle," in which the tear came close upon the smile. He asked me to indicate as far as I could the gestures and action that should go with the lines. Of course, I have no sense whatever of dramatic action, and could make only random guesses; but with masterful art he suited the action to the word. The sigh of Rip as he murmurs, "Is a man so soon forgotten when he is gone?" the dismay with which he searches for dog and gun after his long sleep, and his comical irresolution over signing the contract with Derrick—all these seem to be right out of life itself; that is, the ideal life, where things happen as we think they should.

  I remember well the first time I went to the theater. It was twelve years ago. Elsie Leslie, the little actress, was in Boston, and Miss Sullivan took me to see het in "The Prince and the Pauper." I shall never forget the ripple of alternating joy and woe that ran through that beautiful little play, or the wonderful child who acted it. After the play I was permitted to go behind the scenes and meet her in her royal costume. It would have been hard to find a lovelier or more lovable child than Elsie, as she stood with a cloud of golden hair floating over her shoulders, smiling brightly, showing no signs of shyness or **_fatigue_**, though she had

duel n. 决斗；斗争；抗争 fatigue n. 疲劳；疲乏

been playing to an immense audience. I was only just learning to speak, and had previously repeated her name until I could say it perfectly. Imagine my delight when she understood the few words I spoke to her and without hesitation stretched her hand to greet me.

Is it not true, then, that my life with all its limitations touches at many points the life of the World Beautiful? Everything has its wonders, even darkness and silence, and I learn, whatever state I may be in, therein to be content.

Sometimes, it is true, a sense of isolation enfolds me like a cold mist as I sit alone and wait at life's shut gate. Beyond there is light, and music, and sweet companionship; but I may not enter. Fate, silent, pitiless, bars the way. Fain would I question his imperious decree; for my heart is still ***undisciplined*** and passionate; but my tongue will not utter the bitter, futile words that rise to my lips, and they fall back into my heart like unshed tears. Silence sits immense upon my soul. Then comes hope with a smile and whispers, "There is joy in self-forgetfulness." So I try to make the light in others' eyes my sun, the music in others' ears my symphony, the smile on others' lips my happiness.

undisciplined adj. 无训练的；混乱无纪律的

Chapter 23

WOULD THAT I could enrich this sketch with the names of all those who have ministered to my happiness! Some of them would be found written in our literature and dear to the hearts of many, while others would be wholly unknown to most of my readers. But their influence, though it escapes fame, shall live immortal in the lives that have been sweetened and ennobled by it. Those are red-letter days in our lives when we meet people who thrill us like a fine poem, people whose handshake is brimful of unspoken sympathy, mid whose sweet, rich natures impart to our eager, impatient spirits a wonderful restfulness which, in its essence, is divine. The perplexities, irritations and worries that have absorbed us pass like unpleasant dreams, mid we wake to see with new eyes and hear with new ears the beauty and harmony of God's real world. The solemn nothings that fill our everyday life blossom suddenly into bright possibilities. In a word, while such friends are near us we feel that all is well. Perhaps we never saw them before, and they may never cross our life's path again; but the influence of their calm, mellow natures is a libation poured upon our discontent, and we feel its healing touch, as the ocean feels the mountain stream freshening its brine.

I have often been asked, "Do not people bore you?" I do not understand quite what that means. I suppose the calls of the stupid and curious, especially of newspaper reporters, are always inopportune. I also dislike people who try to talk clown to my understanding. They are like people who when walking with you try to shorten their steps to suit yours; the hypocrisy in both eases is equally exasperating.

The hands of those I meet are dumbly eloquent to me. The touch of some hands is an impertinence. I have met people so empty of joy; that when I clasped their frosty finger tips, it seemed as if I were shaking hands with a northeast storm. Others there are whose hands have sunbeams in them, so that their grasp warms my heart. It may be only the clinging touch of a child's hand; but there is as much potential sunshine in it for me as there is in a loving glance for others. A hearty handshake or a friendly letter gives me genuine pleasure.

I have many far-off friends whom I have never seen. Indeed they are so many that I have often been unable to reply to their letters; but I wish to say here that I am always grateful for their kind words, however insufficiently I acknowledge them.

I count it one of the sweetest privileges of my life to have known and conversed with many men of genius. Only those who knew Bishop Brooks can appreciate the joy his friendship was to those who possessed it. As a child I loved to sit on his knee and clasp his great hand with one of mine, while Miss Sullivan spelled into the other his beautiful words about God and the ***spiritual*** world. I heard him with a child's wonder and delight. My spirit could not reach up to his, but he gave me a real sense of joy in life, and I never left him without carrying away a fine thought that grew in beauty and depth of meaning as I grew. Once, when I was puzzled to know why there were so many religions, he said: "There is one universal religion, Helen—the religion of love. Love your Heavenly Father with

spiritual adj. 精神的；心灵的

your whole heart and soul, love every child of God as much as ever you can, and remember that the possibilities of good are greater than the possibilities of evil; and you have the key to Heaven." And his life was a happy illustration of his great truth. In his noble soul love and widest knowledge were blended with faith that had become insight. He saw

God in all that liberates and lifts,
In all that humbles, sweetens and consoles.

  Bishop Brooks taught me no special creed or **_dogma_**; but he impressed upon my mind two great ideas—the fatherhood of God and the brotherhood of man, and made me feel that these truths underlie all creeds and forms of worship. God is love, God is our Father, and we are His children; therefore the darkest clouds will break, and though right be worsted, wrong shall not triumph.

  I am too happy in this world to think much about the future, except to remember that I have cherished friends awaiting me there in God's beautiful Somewhere. In spite of the lapse of years, they seem so close to me that I should not think it strange if at any moment they should clasp my hand and speak words of endearment as they used to before they went away.

  Since Bishop Brooks died I have read the Bible through; also some philosophical works on religion, among them Swedenborg's "Heaven and Hell" and Drummond's "Ascent of Man," and I have found no creed or system more soul-satisfying than Bishop Brooks's creed of love. I knew Mr. Henry Drummond, and the memory of his strong, warm hand-clasp is like a **_benediction_**. He was the most sympathetic of companions. He knew so much and was so genial that it was impossible to feel dull in his

dogma n. 教条；教理
benediction n. 祝福；赐福；恩赐；祈求上帝赐福的仪式

presence.

I remember well the first time I saw Dr. Oliver Wendell Holmes. He had invited Miss Sullivan and me to call on him one Sunday afternoon. It was early in the spring, just after I had learned to speak. We were shown at once to his library where we found him seated ill a big armchair by an open fire which glowed and crackled on the hearth, thinking, he said, of other days.

"And listening to the murmur of the River Charles," I suggested.

"Yes," he replied, "the Charles has many dear associations for me." There was an odor of print and leather in the room which told me that it was full of books, and I stretched out my hand instinctively to find them. My fingers lighted upon a beautiful volume of Tennyson's poems, and when Miss Sullivan told me what it was I began to recite:

Break, break, break
On thy cold gray stones, O sea!

But I stopped suddenly. I felt tears on my hand. I had made my beloved poet weep, and I was greatly distressed. He made me sit in his armchair, while he brought different interesting things for me to examine, and at his request I recited "The Chambered Nautilus," which was then my favorite poem. After that I saw Dr. Holmes many times and learned to love the man as well as the poet.

One beautiful summer day, not long after my meeting with Dr. Holmes, Miss Sullivan and I visited Whittier in his quiet home on the Merrimac. His gentle **_courtesy_** and quaint speech won my heart. He had a book of his poems in raised print from which I read "In School Days." He was delighted that I could pronounce the words so well, and said that

courtesy n. 礼貌；好意；恩惠

he had no difficulty in understanding me. Then I asked many questions about the poem, and read his answers by placing my fingers on his lips. He said he was the little boy in the poem, and that the girl's name was Sally, and more which I have forgotten. I also recited "Laus Deo," and as I spoke the concluding verses, he placed in my hands a statue of a slave from whose crouching figure the fetters were falling, even as they fell from Peter's limbs when the angel led him forth out of prison. Afterward we went into his study, and he wrote his autograph for my teacher and expressed his admiration of her work, saying to me, "She is thy spiritual liberator." Then he led me to the gate and kissed me tenderly on my forehead. I promised to visit him again the following summer; but he died before the promise was fulfilled.

Dr. Edward Everett Hale is one of my very oldest friends. I have known him since I was eight, and my love for him has increased with my years. His wise, tender sympathy has been the support of Miss Sullivan and me in times of trial and sorrow, and his strong hand has helped us over many rough places; and what he has done for us he has done for thousands of those who have difficult tasks to accomplish. He has filled the old skins of dogma with the new wine of love, and shown men what it is to believe, live and be free. What he has taught we have seen beautifully expressed in his own life—love of country, kindness to the least of his brethren, and a sincere desire to live upward and onward. He has been a prophet and an inspirer of men, and a mighty doer of the Word, the friend of all his race—God bless him!

I have already written of my first meeting with Dr. Alexander Graham Bell. Since then I have spent many happy days with him at Washington and at his beautiful home in the heart of Cape Breton Island, near Baddeck, the village made famous by Charles Dudley Warner's book. Here in Dr. Bell's laboratory, or in the fields on the shore

proficient adj. 熟练的；精通的

of the great Bras d'Or, I have spent many delightful hours listening to what he had to tell me about his experiments, and helping him fly kites by means of which he expects to discover the laws that shall govern the future airship. Dr. Bell is **_proficient_** in many fields of science, and has the art of making every subject he touches interesting, even the most abstruse theories. He makes you feel that if yon only had a little more time, you, too, might be an inventor. He has a humorous and poetic side, too. His dominating passion is his love for children. He is never quite so happy as when he has a little deaf child in his arms. His labors in behalf of the deaf will live on and bless generations of children yet to come; and we love him alike for what he himself has achieved and for what he has evoked from others.

During the two years I spent in New York I had many opportunities to talk with distinguished people whose names I had often heard, but whom I had never expected to meet. Most of them I met first in the house of my good friend, Mr. Laurence Hutton. It was a great privilege to visit him and dear Mrs. Hutton in their lovely home, and see their library and read the beautiful sentiments and bright thoughts gifted friends had written for them. It has been truly said that Mr. Hutton has the faculty of bringing out in every one the best thoughts and kindest sentiments. One does not need to read "A Boy I Knew" to understand him—the most generous, sweet-natured boy I ever knew, a good friend in all sorts of weather, who traces the footprints of love in the life of dogs as well as in that of his fellow-men.

Mrs. Hutton is a true and tried friend. Much that I hold sweetest, much that I hold most precious, I owe to her. She has oftenest advised and helped me in my progress through college. When I find my work particularly difficult and discouraging, she writes me letters that make me feel glad and brave; for she is one of those from whom we learn that one painful duty fulfilled makes the next plainer and easier.

Mr. Hutton introduced me to many of his literary friends, greatest of whom are Mr. William Dean Howells and Mark Twain. I also met Mr. Richard Watson Gilder and Mr. Edmund Clarence Stedman. I also knew Mr. Charles Dudley Warner, the most delightful of story-tellers and the most beloved friend, whose sympathy was so broad that it may be truly said of him, he loved all living things and his neighbor as himself. Once Mr. Warner brought to see me the clear poet of the woodlands—Mr. John Burroughs. They were all gentle and sympathetic and I felt the charm of their manner as much as I had felt the brilliancy of their essays and poems. I could not keep pace with all these literary folk as they glanced from subject to subject and entered into deep dispute, or made conversation sparkle with epigrams and happy witticisms. I was like little Ascanius, who followed with unequal steps the heroic strides of Eneas on his march toward mighty destinies. But they spoke many gracious words to me. Mr. Gilder told me about his moonlight journeys across the vast desert to the Pyramids, and in a letter he wrote me he made his mark under his signature deep in the paper so that I could feel it. This reminds me that Dr. Hale used to give a personal touch to his letters to me by pricking his signature in braille. I read from Mark Twain's lips one or two of his good stories. He has his own way of thinking, saying and doing everything. I feel the twinkle of his eye in his handshake. Even while he utters his **cynical** wisdom in an indescribably droll voice, he makes you feel that his heart is a tender Iliad of human sympathy.

There are a host of other interesting people I met in New York: Mrs. Mary Mapes Dodge, the beloved editor of *St. Nicholas*, and Mrs. Riggs (Kate Douglas Wiggin), the sweet author of "Patsy." I received from them gifts that have the gentle concurrence of the heart, books containing their own thoughts, soul-illumined letters, and photographs that I love to have described again and again. But there is not space to mention all my friends, and indeed there are things about them hidden behind the

cynical adj. 愤世嫉俗的；冷嘲的

wings of cherubim, things too sacred to set forth in cold print. It is with hesitancy that I have spoken even of Mrs. Laurence Hutton.

I shall mention only two other friends. One is Mrs. William Thaw, of Pittsburgh, whom I have often visited in her home, Lyndhurst. She is always doing something to make some one happy, and her generosity and wise counsel have never failed my teacher and me in all the years we have known her.

To the other friend I am also deeply indebted. He is well known for the powerful hand with which he guides vast enterprises, and his wonderful abilities have gained for him the respect of all. Kind to every one, he goes about doing good, silent and unseen. Again I touch upon the circle of honored names I must not mention; but I would fain acknowledge his generosity and ***affectionate*** interest which make it possible for me to go to college.

Thus it is that my friends have made the story of my life. In a thousand ways they have turned my limitations into beautiful privileges, and enabled me to walk serene and happy in the shadow cast by my deprivation.

affectionate adj. 深情的；充满深情的

译后记

　　李月华编辑嘱咐我写篇译后记,我感谢她为出版此书付出的智慧和汗水。感谢江西人民出版社的支持,也感谢余晖老师一直以来对我的翻译工作所给予的指导和鼓励。

　　翻译本书的这半年多时光,是一次学习提高的历练,也是一段苦乐参半的日子。从小,海伦·凯勒就是我无比景仰的英雄,能有机会翻译她的作品,我甚感荣幸。于是,白天工作,夜深人静时,我就坐在电脑旁,噼啪敲打键盘,聚精会神地琢磨,游弋沉浸于原文和译文之中,感受着创造的愉悦和乐趣。

　　为了译好本书,我重读了《圣经故事》、相关的英美诗歌和外国文学名著。对于原文中自己感觉似是而非的地方,总是查阅背景资料,字斟句酌,绞尽脑汁,力求把海伦的精彩文字和欢喜悲伤投射到译文之中。有时,对一些简单的词汇,也没有望文生义,而是认真查询。如 mountain lion 应译作"美洲狮"而不是"山狮";世界博览会上的 this white city of the West,最后译为"西部的白城建筑群"。总之,翻译于我而言,是工作之外的闲情雅趣，我无惧其孤独枯燥，而怡然自得。就像李宗盛在《致匠心》中所言："一辈子总是还得让一些善意执念推着往前，我们因此能愿意去听从内心的安排，专注做点东西，至少，对得起光阴岁月……"

在翻译过程中，我一次又一次地被海伦·凯勒的乐观坚毅所感动；也被她和沙利文老师之间的关爱和友谊所震撼。沙利文老师寓教于乐、循循善诱的教学方法，在今天也很值得我们学习和借鉴。她把大自然当作课堂，让海伦从万事万物中发现美，激发孩子的学习兴趣。在启迪智慧的同时，还用细腻的情感和善良的心性对海伦进行道德教育，让海伦走出了蒙昧和乖戾，成长为一名博学多才、仁爱幸福的杰出女性。

我希望本书的出版能促使更多的人去关注盲聋人的教育权和生存权。1899 年，海伦·凯勒曾用盲文试卷答题，并通过了哈佛大学拉德克利夫学院的入学考试。而 2014 年 6 月，欣闻中国也有一位盲人首次使用盲文试卷参加了高考。相信海伦·凯勒的事迹定能点亮盲聋人群体的心灵之灯，引领他们走向更加坚强而积极的人生。

感谢大学同窗马洛红女士对本书的翻译工作所给予的大力帮助！感谢云南文史馆汪宁女士多年来对我的勉励和鞭策！伴着亲朋好友们的高谊暖语，我愿意在翻译之路上，继续执着而快乐地前行。

查文宏

2014 年 10 月于昆明

海伦·凯勒
名著珍藏系列